THE
LIBERATED
GOSPEL

THE LIBERATED GOSPEL

A Comparison of the Gospel of Mark and Greek Tragedy

Gilbert G. Bilezikian

WIPF & STOCK · Eugene, Oregon

Wipf and Stock Publishers
199 W 8th Ave, Suite 3
Eugene, OR 97401

The Liberated Gospel
A Comparison of the Gospel of Mark and Greek Tragedy
By Bilezikian, Gilbert
Copyright©1977 by Bilezikian, Gilbert
ISBN 13: 978-1-60899-617-9
Publication date 4/13/2010
Previously published by Baker Books, 1977

In memory of
Professor George E. Ladd
giant among teachers

Contents

Preface

The concept of a literary rapprochement between the Gospel of Mark and Greek tragedy was first outlined in embryonic form in my doctoral dissertation, presented at Boston University School of Theology in 1953. The idea lay dormant for some twenty years until a scholarship grant from the Institute for Advanced Christian Studies provided the opportunity to pursue the research into its present form.

This is to acknowledge a debt of sincere gratitude to the directors of IFACS and its supporting friends, to Dr. E. Beatrice Batson for reading the manuscript in reference to Greek tragedy, to Dr. I. Howard Marshall for checking it in reference to the New Testament, to Ms. Terri Williams and Mrs. Gerrie Carlson for their longanimous assistance in getting the manuscript into its final form.

Chapter 1

The Genre Approach
and the Gospel

I

The Gospel of Mark has not always occupied the privileged position it currently holds in the critical investigation of New Testament backgrounds. Augustine properly disposed of whatever regard it may have enjoyed in the early Christian centuries, due to its antiquity and probable Roman origin, by declaring it an abridgment of Matthew's Gospel and by describing Mark as Matthew's servant.[1] Until recent times the Gospel was relegated to the shadows in the preoccupations of scholars and in the life of the church.[2] Since most of its content was regarded as a crude duplication of the comparatively more glamorous Gospels surrounding it, Mark was almost ignored as a naive and vaguely superfluous account of the life of Jesus.

The Gospel owes its Cinderella story of rescue from near oblivion to relatively recent developments in New Testament research. When scholars began to concentrate their inquiries on the problem posed by resemblances and differences between the first three Gospels, Mark was suddenly catapulted to a position of preeminence. Although theories abound for the resolution of the synoptic problem and although no single proposal has received the universal consensus of scholars, it was suggested from the early stages of this quest that the Gospel of Mark had played a pivotal role in the formation of the synoptic complex. One of the widely accepted, although still contested, theories for the making of the Gospels accords to Mark chronological primacy and dependence upon it of the other synoptists.[3]

Shortly after the turn of the century, the attention of scholars turned to another avenue of investigation by focusing on source analysis rather than literary interdependence. As efforts were made to separate the

1. *Harmony of the Gospels* 1.2. Note that except for the superscription, the second Gospel is an anonymous work. Throughout this study the author will be designated as "Mark," and unless otherwise indicated his work will be designated as "the Gospel" or "Mark."

2. Stephen Neill pointed to the fact that of the more than seventy Gospel lections for Sundays and saints' days in the Book of Common Prayer, only three are drawn from Mark. He made a similar observation about John Donne's sermons, 160 of which have survived: sixteen are based on texts from Matthew, ten on texts from John, nine on texts from Luke, and only two on texts from Mark. *The Interpretation of the New Testament*, p. 107.

3. B. H. Streeter, *The Four Gospels: A Study of Origins.*

preeditorial layers of tradition fused together in the synoptic matrix, the Gospel of Mark was again brought to the forefront of critical concern. Although this discipline (form criticism) found broad acceptance and contributed many valuable insights, it failed to resolve the questions left unanswered by the literary-critical approach. In fact it raised problems of its own, not the least of them in the area of basic methodology, in determining the extent to which early Christian communities created and transformed Gospel materials, and in evaluating the latter as reports of historical events.

Since the mid-fifties a sort of revolution has been shaking the world of New Testament scholarship, thus opening a new front of investigation. Realizing the limitations of the dissective methods of source criticism, a number of scholars began to regard the Gospels as integral documents reflecting both the theological identity of their authors (called redactors) and the needs, interests, and beliefs of ambient Christian communities for which the Gospels were written.[4] Again, the Gospel of Mark played a preponderant role as it became the basis for determining Matthean and Lucan tendencies reflected in their respective adaptations of the same materials borrowed from Mark. Although significant breakthroughs are considered to have been achieved in the analysis of Matthew and Luke,[5] the redaction-critical approach has not yielded spectacular results with Mark, due to the fact that sources more primitive than the Gospel itself are not available to serve as a basis for comparison.[6] Considerable efforts are being expended to formulate a methodology suitable for redactorial investigation of the Gospel. The multiplicity and diversity of theories that keep appearing, however, give evidence of the continued dissatisfaction of scholars with proposed explanations.[7]

Thus the Gospel of Mark remains tantalizingly at the center of critical pursuits. The discovery of the deceptiveness of its simplicity has res-

4. A classic definition has been offered by Dan O. Via, Jr., in his foreword to W. A. Beardslee, *Literary Criticism of the New Testament*, p. iv.

5. Günther Bornkamm, Gerhard Barth, and H. J. Held, *Tradition and Interpretation in Matthew;* Hans Conzelmann, *The Theology of St. Luke.*

6. Heinz-Dieter Knigge recognized this difficulty: "Sources of the oldest Gospel are not accessible to us, so the changes which Mark made in his tradition can be detected only with the help of literary and form-critical analysis, a task which involves a factor of considerable uncertainty." "The Meaning of Mark," p. 56.

7. See, e.g., Quentin Quesnell, *The Mind of Mark: Interpretation and Method Through the Exegesis of Mark 6:52.* The author surveyed the positions of some seventy scholars who, before 1966, had worked on Mark 6:52 in relation to the feeding-of-the-multitude pericopes. The names of an additional fifteen scholars could be added who have made various contributions to those sections of the Gospel during the intervening years. Suggested interpretations are almost as numerous as their authors. Surveys of recent redaction criticism of Mark are found in: Frank J. Matera, "Interpreting Mark: Some Recent Theories of Redaction Criticism"; Paul E. Dinter, "Redaction Criticism of the Gospel of Mark: A Survey"; Ralph P. Martin, *Mark: Evangelist and Theologian.*

cued it from wallflower status. But, like a plain-looking maiden who suddenly appears mysterious and beautiful, the Gospel seems reluctant to yield its secret. Like Cinderella, the Gospel has at last been discovered but not yet explained.

Of all those who attempt to elucidate the riddle of the Gospel of Mark, the promise of reward may well belong to scholars who respect its integrity as a literary document rather than to those who dismember it into fragments and thus lose sight of the Gospel as an entity. The present study is conducted on the premise that an important clue to the question of the purpose of Mark may be found in its literary form. Obviously this approach is not original. The structure of the Gospel has already received considerable attention. For some reason this type of research seems to elicit a sort of lyrical fervor that expresses itself in a variety of images, some poetic, some less felicitous. Thus the elements of tradition collected in the Gospel have been compared to fragments of rocks thrown together in the bed of a mountain torrent (Wrede). In the same bucolic mood, the outline of the Gospel is said to be partial and broken like the course of a river that intermittently disappears underground but that eventually reaches the sea (Taylor). Turning to domestic life, the Gospel has been likened to an oriental rug in which patterns cross one another, not drawn in mathematical exactitude but developed spontaneously (Johnson). The creation of a Gospel out of isolated stories and sayings has evoked the image of a child at play arranging beads on a string (Schweizer). Its elements are said to be like the stones of a mosaic, polished and arranged with the care of an expert craftsman (Beach). And more prosaically, caution is made against considering the Gospel a haphazard collection of sayings and stories used by missionaries and jumbled together like groceries in a shopping basket (Neill).

The outline of the Gospel also seems to have provoked misgivings as early as the second century. Eusebius cited Papias as recalling a declaration of the Elder according to which Mark wrote accurately what he received from Peter, "but not, however, in order."[8] It is difficult to determine whether the Elder was excepting the Marcan order per se or Mark's sequence compared to the other Gospels.[9] Modern scholarship has not fared much better in its search for an outline to the Gospel. It is usually agreed that the passion story (chaps. 14—16) forms a consistent unit. But the rest of the Gospel has been divided to fit an incredible number of schemes. During the nineteenth century when lives of Jesus were in vogue, the Gospel, because its assumed simplicity was interpreted as relative antiquity and therefore greater historical accuracy, was thought to provide a biographical outline of the ministry of Jesus. In the heyday of form criticism, the Gospel was commonly regarded as a mass of heterogeneous elements gathered pell-mell without any discernible outline. Sometimes, when order and progression were recognized, they were posited as a fabrication of the

8. *Historia Ecclesiastica* 3.39.15.
9. Vincent Taylor observed that according to Moffatt and Streeter, the Elder was thinking of John; according to Grant, of Matthew; and according to Bacon, of the oral teaching. *The Gospel According to Mark*, p. 2.

author (Schmidt). When a rapprochement was made between the kerygmatic pattern of Jesus' ministry in the speeches of the Book of Acts and the drift of the Gospel narration, a standard outline was thought to be reflected in both (Dodd). Geography has been said to provide structural significance to the Gospel because of the alleged theological significance of designated locations (Lohmeyer, Grant). Didactic or topical motifs have also been presented as the key to Mark's outline (Schweizer). Surprisingly original proposals for the Marcan structure have resulted from the application of varying combinations of erudition, ingenuity, and persistence to the problem. According to one theory the Gospel was built with minute precision according to complex patterns of cyclic and alternate numerical recurrences based on Old Testament typology (Farrer). More plausibly, the Gospel has also been viewed as a succession of liturgical readings comparable to synagogue lectionaries and patterned on the order of the Jewish calendar (Carrington).

Despite the mystifying proliferation of theories in regard to something as basic as the outline of a literary composition, it must be observed that whether topical, geographical, biographical, or theological, the interpretation of Mark's outline most commonly found in commentaries follows a five- or sixfold division. The caesuras of the composition and the designation of the sections may vary from author to author,[10] but a consensus has emerged according to which the author of the Gospel intended to write a sequential and progressive narration. The examination of redactorial features such as summaries, links (or seams), consecution, and groupings indicate that the author was not just copying stories but that he was writing a story. Opinions to the contrary notwithstanding,[11] the Gospel appears as something more than a random collection of materials held together artificially like interchangeable sheets in a loose-leaf binder. The parts of the Gospel cannot be separated, shaken, scattered, and bundled again helter-skelter without losing a sense of the progressive action and coherence that constitute a part of its message and produce much of its impact.[12]

Although the labors of redaction-history research have resulted in the recognition of the Gospel as a purposeful story, attention has been

10. A standard outline would result in approximately the following divisions: 1:1–15; 1:16–8:26; 8:27–10:52; 11:1–13:37; 14:1–16:8.

11. Wilfred L. Knox wrote that the Gospel is composed of "a number of tracts containing accounts of the ministry of the Lord on earth, either written or committed to memory." *The Sources of the Synoptic Gospels,* p. 4. According to Harold A. Guy, the Gospel is made of unconnected papyrus pages that were gathered into a book. *The Origin of the Gospel of Mark.*

12. "Mark is a collection of self-contained narratives, many of which are grouped topically and others chronologically; but it is not a heap of unstrung pearls." Taylor, *The Gospel According to Mark,* p. 47. Taylor also quoted C. H. Dodd—"There is good reason to believe that in broad lines the Marcan order does represent a genuine succession of events, within which movement and progression can be traced"—and F. C. Burkitt—"In Mark there is movement and progression." Ibid., p. 148.

concentrated more on the purpose than on the story. Inquiries regarding the form of the narrative, its possible affinity with established literary types, and the relationship between form and content have not been pursued with sufficient persistency. Yet they could furnish clues that would not only elucidate the mystery of the form of the Gospel but also provide an answer to the conundrum of its purpose. In fact it would seem that questions pertaining to the origin and nature of the Gospel's framework should be settled prior to the quest for Mark's intentions in selecting that particular framework.[13] The search for the origin of Mark's framework can follow four lines of inquiry.

First, it can be supposed that the Gospel is an original literary creation. Neither was there a precedent for it in ancient literature nor did the elements of the Gospel reach the author in a form that would lend itself to a particular mode of presentation. At best they were episodic, independent fragments of tradition devoid of consistent historical or biographical indications. According to this view, generally held by form-critical scholars, Mark created the *Gattung* Gospel,[14] the pattern of which represents the creative achievement of the evangelist.[15] Thus Mark was the first organizer of the Jesus story since he caused a coherent literary work to emerge from the magma of tradition.[16] He was the pioneer writer, allegedly an unlearned, creative genius, who unwittingly devised a new literary form destined to assure the survival and expansion of Christianity.

This ex-nihilo production of a Gospel out of the magic hat of diffuse traditions is not universally accepted. It leaves obvious questions unanswered. If the emergence of a new literary type as enduring and as influential as the Gospel is attributable to the organizing, cohesive force of an overriding practical purpose or theological perspective, why is there intense disagreement on a question as basic as the nature of Mark's Gospel-writing enterprise? To revert to metaphors mentioned above, the conjuring

13. David Blatherwick wrote, "The clearest indication we can have of what Mark intended lies in the final form of his work." "The Markan Silhouette," p. 186. Eduard Schweizer wrote, "The particular message which Mark is endeavoring to express will be found, for the most part, in this very 'framework' and in the special arrangement of his Gospel." *The Good News According to Mark*, p. 13.

14. "The literary *Gattung* 'gospel' is the unique literary creation of early Christianity. This is a statement which I would make with confidence because for all that we may learn from Hellenistic or Jewish texts, none of them is adequate to provide the model for the Christian 'gospel.' " "The Literary *Gattung* Gospel," p. 4.

15. Mark's structure is often considered completely artificial. Martin Kähler, for instance, explained that the Gospel was developed "backwards," the sequence of events in the first part being determined by pre-established themes contained in the passion narrative. *The So-Called Historical Jesus and the Historical, Biblical Christ*.

16. Of Matthew and Luke, Etienne Trocmé said, "*L'auteur de Marc devait leur apparaître avant tout comme l'organisateur qui avait fait émerger du magma de la tradition une oeuvre littéraire cohérente.*" *La formation de l'Evangile selon Marc*, p. 58.

of indefinable motivations for a work as forceful as the Gospel makes no more sense than patterns on an oriental rug without supporting fabric, necklace beads without connecting thread, mosaics without mortar, and a basketful of groceries without a basket.

It can also be asked if the ready acceptance of Mark's outline by the other synoptists and its integration into their own Gospels does not point to widespread familiarity with a schema of the ministry of Jesus in early Christian communities.[17] Mark could count more on the security of recognition than on the shock of innovation for his contemporaries' acceptance of the Gospel. It has often been argued, not unconvincingly, that early Christians would not have been indifferent to biographical information relative to the Christ whom they worshiped and for whom they sometimes endured persecution, dispossession, and even death. It is difficult to imagine that tradition failed to furnish Mark with some sort of comprehensive, preliterary overview of the career of Jesus along with form-units and larger groupings of materials assembled in the Gospel.

Against this view, it has been objected that the experience of the risen Christ rather than factual information about the earthly Jesus was necessary to secure the life-allegiance of Christians during the early stages of the development of the Jesus traditions. A concern for biographical data is said to have arisen later as a recourse to history to defend particular viewpoints.[18]

However, in support of this second line of inquiry, according to which Mark inherited a schema from tradition, it has been observed that the vital, ebullient, aggressive, to-the-death commitment to Christ reflected in accounts of the life of first-generation Christians holds nothing in common with wide-eyed romantic notions of ethereal wonderment about an otherworldly, disembodied savior. Consequently it has been argued that Mark followed, however freely, an outline for the ministry of Jesus that had been known since the first stages of preliterary transmission. Some consider the pattern of apostolic preaching to have been the vehicle for such a summary outline.[19] Others trace the preservation of a biographical outline back to apostolic reminiscence. Still others, finding a correlation between christological summaries in the New Testament and the outline of the Gospel, affirm the existence of a standard catechetical summary of the

17. Trocmé remarked that although Matthew and Luke were aware of the inadequacies of Mark's Gospel to the point of completing and qualifying its teachings and correcting some of its literary shortcomings while writing their own Gospels, they nevertheless felt impelled to rely on it. He conceded that the main reason for their dependence on Mark is their respect for the Marcan order, which each followed in his own way. Ibid., p. 58.

18. Trocmé claimed that Mark's Gospel is *"un appel à l'histoire contre l'institution gardienne de la tradition, qui avait, a son sens, devié du droit chemin."* Ibid., p. 68.

19. C. H. Dodd proposed that an outline of the life of Christ was part and parcel of the kerygma as reflected in samples of apostolic preaching preserved in the Book of Acts. *New Testament Studies.*

life of Christ in early Christian circles.[20] In order to substantiate the corollary of historical plausibility that often accompanies the theory of a transmitted outline, it has been claimed that the invention of the Gospel's outline by a writer of limited ability such as Mark would constitute a miracle more remarkable than the occurrences it describes.[21] Thus, against the view that the framework of the Gospel is a Marcan innovation, there stands the claim that an outline of the ministry of Jesus was available to Mark and that this outline is reflected in the general structure of the Gospel. As valuable as this insight may be, however, this second line of argumentation does not suffice to explain the form of the Gospel whose inner dynamic is the result, as will be shown below, of much more than simple adherence to biographical indications.

A third avenue of inquiry should be surveyed. If it is supposed that Mark neither invented nor received the pattern of his story, it is conceivable that, to give it shape, he imitated a compatible model available in contemporary forms of literature. He lived in a sophisticated, polycultural, multilingual, erudition-conscious age, when the works of the masters of Greece and Rome along with the sacred texts of Judaism were available to scholar and layman alike. The treasures of Greek literature were cherished, studied, memorized, translated, and imitated wherever Hellenistic culture had penetrated. All forms of Roman literature originated in or were influenced by the literary genius of the Greeks. These genres included dramatic, epic, lyric, and satiric poetry. Prose forms consisted of history, biography, essay, oratory, and philosophic literature. The degree of dependence of Latin literature upon its Greek progenitor can be measured by the fact that the former had its beginnings in the translations of Homer's *Odyssey* and of the tragedies of Aeschylus, Sophocles, and Euripides by Livius Andronicus in the third century B.C.

The Golden Age of Roman literature, which politically covers the period of the Republic and the Augustan Empire, is traditionally considered to span the careers of Cicero, Sallust, Julius Caesar, and Livy in prose and, in poetry, of Lucretius, Virgil, Horace, and Ovid, to mention only a few of the outstanding authors of this epoch rich in literary productions. By comparison, the following period, the beginning of which coincides with the start of the reign of Tiberius in A.D. 14, has been called the Silver Age of Roman literature. The books of the New Testament were written during this time. Due to constraints imposed by autocratic rulers, letters did not flourish on the same scale as previously. But even if the literary accomplishments of this period do not possess the classic brilliance of the preceding era, they nevertheless bear witness to an intense traffic of ideas, old and new, and to the intermingling of currents of cultural influence. It was no age of decadence or stagnation. "Tradition and inheritance,

---

20. Gottfried Schille, *"Bemerkungen zur Formgeschichte des Evangeliums,"* 4:1—24.

21. Frederick C. Grant wrote, "The general outline of the ministry, as given by Mark, is not only the earliest outline we have, but commends itself upon grounds of probability." *The Earliest Gospel*, p. 50.

both Greek and Roman, operated side by side with fresh problems and interests."[22] The literary production of this period is often considered to have been dominated by an obsession for rhetorical and stylistic refinements. But this literature also gives evidence of effervescent creativity. Notably, the Stoic philosopher Seneca wrote several works on ethics and nine tragedies. His nephew Lucan, who like him died in A.D. 65, wrote the *Pharsalia*, an epic poem describing the struggle between Caesar and Pompey. The *Satyricon* of Petronius, who died one year later, represents the first realistic novel in Western literature.

Thus the authors of New Testament books lived in an age fond of literary arts and conscious of the greatness of its inheritance. Consequently the question of whether they took into account classical precedents as they set themselves to convey their message in writing cannot be avoided. Predictably, modern scholarship raised the question and engaged in comparative studies, searching for correspondences between New Testament documents and contemporary genres. Such studies have led to the conclusion that "all the literary forms of the New Testament, even those that may seem to have a pagan background, fall definitely outside the categories of formal literature as practiced in the world of culture of that time."[23]

The reasons for such a categorical statement are obvious. The New Testament documents appear as spontaneous writings created out of situations of urgency in response to specific needs and contingencies. Their intent was not literary but functional. They give no evidence of elaborate efforts to achieve conformity to existing literary canons. They are popular writings, forged in the heat of action, at the convergence of surging faith and down-to-earth expediency. As such, they do not correspond to any of the categories of classical literature. More specifically as regards Mark, some see, at best, the historical books of the Old Testament and perhaps the Book of Jonah as the only parallels.[24] Others have found some points of likeness between the Gospel and the ancient biography form,[25] but the notion of a conscious correlation has been strongly contested.[26] Comparisons have been made between the Gospel and Greek tragedy, but they

22. John Wright Duff, *A Literary History of Rome*, p. 17.

23. Amos Wilder, *The Language of the Gospel*, p. 36. Wilder based this opinion on the work of classicists like Eduard Norden; of authorities on Hellenistic literature like Paul Wendland; and of New Testament scholars like Martin Dibelius, Carl L. Schmidt, and Rudolf Bultmann.

24. See Schweizer, *The Good News*, p. 24.

25. C. W. Votaw, "The Gospels and Contemporary Biographies."

26. Henry J. Cadbury wrote: "The differentiating factor in the gospels that separates them from biographies is their popular character. They are not popular in the sense that they are written for uneducated people, by experts for the inexpert, by specialists catering to a general interest; but rather in the sense that they are natural growths, self-made, not artificial or artistic productions." *The Making of Luke-Acts*, p. 130.

have met with swift dismissal.[27] An interesting variant of this approach appears as the theory according to which the Gospel is patterned on the threefold dramatic scheme of enthronement rites in ancient Egypt: adoption by the ruling god, corresponding to Christ's baptism; presentation to the Egyptian gods, paralleled in the transfiguration; and proclamation as ruler of the world, likened to the crucifixion.[28] It has been objected, however, that this theory connects only a few elements of the Gospel to each other and leaves important motifs out of consideration.

The conclusion that the Gospel was not written with the intent of imitating a contemporary literary model seems inevitable. Like other New Testament writings, Mark's Gospel is described as a subliterary creation belonging to the class of *Kleinliteratur* rather than the sophisticated and self-consciously artistic works that fall in the category of *Hochliteratur*.[29] Nowhere in the Gospel does the author give evidence of being motivated by a deliberate concern to adorn his work aesthetically or to embellish it artistically in order to imitate a classic model. His writing belongs to the tradition of the Koine and bears the marks of a common man's labors. Although his story reaches heights of divine grandeur, most of the narrative takes place at the level of ordinary men and women. In antique terms this would be permissible only in farce or comedy. Such easy access into the vulgarities of common life was incompatible with the sublime style and vision of classic literature.[30] Moreover, the tendency of a cultured writer composing a literary work in ancient times would have been to omit names, numbers, and repeated mention of geographic locations. But out of ignorance or indifference to such conventions, Mark used profusely names of persons and places, and numerical indications.[31] It can be determined from Horace's *Ars Poetica* ("On the Art of Poetry"), the major work of literary criticism published around the time when Mark was born, that the norms regulating formal types of written art were precisely delineated in those days. Obviously the Gospel falls outside such definitions. Its author nowhere betrayed any yearning for literary status, neither did he flaunt any knowledge of the techniques of professional literati. His Gospel can-

27. "Neither do we think that the format of, say, Mark was shaped on the precedent of a Greek tragedy." Wilder, *The Language of the Gospel*, p. 30.

28. Philip Vielhauer, *"Erwägungen zur Christologie des Markus Evangeliums."*

29. ". . . Mark is unquestionably folk-literature and lower-middle-class religious propaganda; it has no indirection whatever and its composition is slipshod." Morton Smith, "Comments on Taylor's Commentary on Mark," *The Harvard Theological Review* 48 (1955): 38 (n. 23).

30. Erich Auerbach illustrated this point with reference to Peter's denial: "A scene like Peter's denial fits no antique genre. It is too serious for comedy, too contemporary and everyday for tragedy, politically too insignificant for history—and the form which was given it is one of such immediacy that its like does not exist in the literature of antiquity." *Mimesis*, p. 45.

31. C. H. Turner, "Marcan Usage: Notes, Critical and Exegetical, on the Second Gospel," 26:338.

not even be considered a bad piece of literature since it makes no pretension to being literature at all. This method of investigation into the mystery of the origin of the Gospel's format also leads to an impasse.

If the pattern of the Gospel seems to be neither a new creation nor the result of imitation of an existing model, and if an outline of the life of Jesus handed down through tradition does not account for the form of the Gospel, a fourth channel of inquiry remains to be pursued. It is conceivable that the Gospel form could be the product of the skillful combination of elements as disparate as the evangelical narrative on one hand, and on the other, compatible literary devices borrowed piecemeal from an established classical paradigm—specifically that of Greek tragedy.

A positive response to this possibility has come from a few students of Mark's Gospel. The suggestion that elements of correspondence might exist between the two seems to have been first propounded by Ernest W. Burch in a paper entitled "Tragic Action in the Second Gospel," which he read before the Chicago Society of Biblical Research in 1920. A few years later his thesis was cited approvingly by Donald W. Riddle in an article on "The Martyr Motif in the Gospel According to Mark." In 1931 Burch published his paper in which he compared the treatment of the plot and of the hero in both Gospel and tragedy, concluding that "the Second Gospel comes under the classification of Greek tragedy."[32] In his book *The Gospels: Their Origin and Growth*, published in 1939, Riddle devoted three pages to the observation that Mark's story accords generally with the well-known canons of the Greek tragic drama.[33] Frederick C. Grant seems to have been aware of Riddle's contribution to the thesis. But in his book entitled *The Earliest Gospel*, he simply noted that some scholars have recognized in Mark the pattern of a Greek tragedy and added his brief appreciation, ". . . indeed with some probability."[34] In his *The Gospel of Mark: Its Making and Meaning*, published in 1959, Curtis Beach included a three-page section entitled "Similarity to Greek Tragedy." Since no reference is made to other works in this connection, it is assumed that his remarks represent the result of his own independent observations. As far as can be determined, only one other author touches upon this thesis. Theodore J. Weeden stated in *Mark: Traditions in Conflict* that the Gospel "approximates the style of the Greek drama." However, leaving aside literary and structural implications, he claimed that Mark had recourse to dramatic characterization to resolve, in support of his own views, conflicting christological tendencies within his community.[35]

32. "Tragic Action in the Second Gospel: A Study of the Narrative of Mark," p. 346.

33. Pp. 142–44.

34. P. 133. Grant referred his readers to Burch's article and to two other articles that focus on the dramatic structure of the Gospel of Mark without reference to Greek tragedy: Walter E. Bundy, "Dogma and Drama in the Gospel of Mark"; and Henry Beach Carré, "The Literary Structure of the Gospel of Mark," in *Studies in Early Christianity*, ed. S. J. Case (New York: Century, 1928), pp. 105–26.

35. P. 17. Howard Clark Kee, in a just-published book, cited two un-

The interesting feature in these studies lies in the fact that in each case (except Weeden's) the similarity between the framework of the Gospel and the formal design of tragedy provides the starting point for the comparison. Since this thesis will be closely examined below, all that needs to be said at this point is that when compared to Greek tragedy, the framework of the Gospel seems to yield a clue regarding the mystery surrounding its formation. The concentration of recent Gospel research on the Marcan framework seems to be vindicated.

As a matter of fact, such efforts might have yielded richer results had they been directed toward a search for definite precedents in the cultural milieu of the Gospel's author. As bold as the thesis advanced by Riddle and Beach may appear, their treatment of it stops short of a full investigation of the possibilities it suggests. Such restraint may have been inspired by their reluctance to impute direct knowledge of the Greek classics to Mark. Both Riddle and Beach rejected the supposition that Mark might have been familiar with classical Greek tragedy. They attributed the similarity between Gospel and tragedy to "a real, but quite unconscious, instance of adaptation to environment." Evidently it is the gap in literary artistry separating the Gospel from Greek tragedy that constitutes the main obstacle to recognizing Mark's dependence on tragedy. As Riddle put it, echoing a majority of commentators, "There is no evidence that the writer of Mark was an educated man or a cultured man. There are no marks of literary style in his work."[36] Hence the nebulous theory according to which the similarity between the two forms is due to a process of cultural osmosis from tragedy to Gospel. But when it is admitted that Mark wrote the Gospel without any literary pretensions, that he had no intention of producing a Christian version of Greek drama, and that his principal concern remained that of an evangelist rather than that of a playwright, his contribution becomes clearer. He obviously did not set about to write something that is to Greek drama what *Jesus Christ Superstar* is to grand opera. His work is dominated by evangelical passion, not by concern for literary effect. But if Mark was acquainted with Greek tragedy, especially in its Roman form as "closet drama," what was to prevent him from plundering the rich traditions of this noble art for elements uniquely suitable for the attainment of his objectives? The temptation inherent in such an endeavor would have been to let tragedy, the established form, dominate his composition. This would have inevitably occurred had he attempted to imitate Greek tragedy. By letting the

published dissertations in which the Gospel of Mark is examined from the perspective of tragedy: Vernon Robbins, "The Christological Structure of Mark" (Ph.D. diss., University of Chicago, 1973); David L. Barr, "Toward a Definition of the Gospel Genre" (Ph.D. diss., Florida State University, 1974). (The author has had no opportunity to consult these dissertations.) Kee summarily dismissed the possibility that Mark had used the tragic genre. He viewed the Gospel as an apocalyptic narrative reflecting the concerns of a primitive, sectarian Christian community in southern Syria. *Community of the New Age: Studies in Mark's Gospel*, esp. pp. 18, 64–65.

36. *The Gospels*, p. 144.

integrity of his story determine the choice of usable elements from the classical model, however, he avoided writing a cheap, low-grade pastiche of tragedy with a Greek Jesus as its hero. Instead he animated the presentation of his themes with the discreet utilization of resources available in the most powerful dramatic artifice ever achieved in literary history.

II

As useful as they have proven to be, the methods of New Testament criticism through dissection are limited in their scope. Minute analysis of the parts represents but one thrust in the various approaches now available. Recent research has made evident the need for identifying literary forms and examining the relationship between form and content as a means of more fully understanding literary compositions. In order to discover the creative forces undergirding a document and to assess the fullness of its message, it is necessary to extend the concerns of literary criticism beyond questions of authorship, sources, stratification, redaction, and transmission to the examination of form.[37] Such a procedure is not a concession to the "new hermeneutic."[38] It finds support in New Testament concepts reflected in such Koine terminology as *form* ($\mu o \rho \varphi \acute{\eta}$), *likeness* ($\sigma \chi \hat{\eta} \mu a$), and *image* ($\epsilon \grave{\iota} \kappa \acute{\omega} \nu$), which usually refer not to the external appearance but to the total reality of the person or thing in question. The value of this kind of holistic thinking is recognized in many disciplines, as evidenced in its application in philosophy, aesthetics, psychology, and other fields. Amos Wilder emphasized this point: "In all genuine artifacts, including language-forms, shape and substance are inseparable and mutually determinative."[39]

The application to the Gospel of this approach—the definition of form and content and the study of their interrelation—should be productive. Of course it is possible to regard the form of the Gospel as purely fortuitous and incidental to the development of its content. According to this position the Gospel form would convey no meaning beyond the recog-

37. "The literary criticism of the New Testament has begun to reflect an interest in questions such as the relationship of content to form, the significance of structure or form for meaning, and the capacity of language to direct thought and to mold existence itself." Via, in Beardslee, *Literary Criticism*, p. iii.

38. According to Beardslee the "new hermeneutic" "seeks to listen to and interpret the whole vision of reality expressed in a type of faith and does not just focus on the human stance of response toward that reality. It moves toward a thorough statement of what the text 'means' and what the 'point being scored' is. Such thorough restatement is required to make the thrust of the New Testament meaningful, but, as it is practiced, contemporary interpretation, or hermeneutic, does not always grapple seriously with the relation between formal structure and the 'thrust' or 'point' of a book." Ibid., pp. 12—13.

39. *The Language of the Gospel*, p. 33. In making these points Wilder acknowledged indebtedness to Rudolf Bultmann, *Theology of the New Testament*, vol. 1 (New York: Scribner, 1951), pp. 192—93.

nition of its insignificance, since it would be the inadvertent result of the random assemblage of originally disconnected units. This position is untenable, however, since order and progression, and therefore structure and form, are discernible in the Gospel. Moreover, not only its content, but the drift of the Gospel story has been recognized as conveying a message. Readers of the Gospel have reported that fresh exposure to it, preferably at one sitting, has resulted in a strange experience involving emotion and intellect, in a cycle of oppressive tension and cathartic release. While maintaining a thorough-going form-critical approach to the composition of the Gospel, Henry J. Cadbury observed that it possesses "an indefinable weirdness, a sense of mystery and tragedy which, though not characteristic of conscious art of intention, produces an individual coloration and editorial effect upon the *disjecta membra* of a miscellaneous and polychrome tradition."[40] This captivating power has sometimes been attributed to editorial naiveté and to the primitive artistry reflected in the rugged simplicity of the narrative. But close scrutiny reveals that sustaining the entire story is a current of pathos and dramatic intensity that can only be the product of careful editorial application. As a result, frequent references have been made to the artistry of Mark, although thorough efforts to analyze it are singularly lacking.[41] The present study will suggest a solution to the enigma of the form of the Gospel by showing its resemblance to that of antique tragedy, and it will reveal, through appropriate inferences, something of Mark's purpose.

In order to proceed with the comparison, one might be tempted to reduce a subject as vast and varied as ancient tragedy to a few easy formulas. To avoid such oversimplifications, an analysis of the elements of tragedy will be conducted later in the areas in which they seem to relate to the Gospel. At this point some general observations about the origin and the subject matter, the mood and the ideological drift of tragedy will suffice.

A comparative study of the Gospel and of tragedy finds a natural starting point in basic definitions. The story of the rejected Messiah marching unflinchingly to a redemptive death at the hands of those He has come

40. *The Making of Luke-Acts,* p. 80. Neill made a similar observation: "It is a book of extraordinary dramatic intensity. For many years it has been my custom, at the beginning of Holy Week, to read Mark 10—15 straight through at a sitting. I cannot imagine any reader doing this without becoming aware of the mounting tension in the mind of Jesus himself and of those who followed him, tension which reaches the point of agony." *Interpretation,* p. 275. A Jewish scholar, Samuel Sandmel, concurred: "Mark is short enough to read at one sitting. The reader, in identifying himself with Jesus, goes through exciting and triumphant incidents. When he has read through the Gospel he has experienced a great emotional release." *A Jewish Understanding of the New Testament* (Cincinnati: Hebrew Union College, 1956), p. 134.

41. Sherman E. Johnson wrote about "the combination of art and apparent artlessness, of simple verisimilitude and theological reflection, which tends to make the Gospel difficult to analyse." *A Commentary on the Gospel According to St. Mark,* p. 19.

to save is often considered the quintessential tragic situation. Numerous playwrights in medieval times and since have used its dramatic potential for stage and pageant presentations. On the other hand, it is sometimes claimed that a strict definition of tragedy excludes ipso facto the Gospel as "good news," and that nothing in literature can be both Christian and tragic at the same time. Thus Laurence Michel: "Christianity is intransigent to tragedy; tragedy bucks and balks under Christianity."[42]

In order to properly define the essence of tragedy, it is necessary to divorce the concept of tragedy as a dramatic literary work from the popular connotations of hopeless and unrelenting disaster attached to the substantive *tragedy*. Should literary tragedy be the description of a series of adverse happenings leading inevitably to a horrible end from which no rescue exists, and should the Gospel be a description of a series of potentially disastrous events culminating in the cross but with a benevolent God hiding behind the scenes to make everything right in the end, then tragedy and the Gospel hold very little in common. However, this is far from being the case. A number of Greek tragedies have a happy or conciliatory ending, and none of them is simply designed with the superficial intent of harping on what is morbid and macabre in life. In times when *"panem et circenses"* sufficed to pacify the restive populace, Seneca could write unstageable melodramas—cast in stilted school-rhetoric, gravid with Stoic ennui, capped with *Grand-Guignol* finales—and christen the result "tragedy." Not so with Attic tragedy. "The tone of this drama is essentially meditative and religious. Whatever the subjects or issues it treats, a view of profound and earnest thoughtfulness runs through every part of the composition. Beneath all the movement and turmoil of the action there is present continually the same pervading sense of the dark mystery of existence, and the same wistful craving for knowledge concerning the ways of providence and the destiny of mankind."[43]

In its origins, ancient tragedy was essentially religious. It grew out of the dithyramb, a wild, impetuous Dorian lyric performed in honor of Dionysius, the god of wine and fertile crops. The etymology of the word *tragedy*, which identified very early such performances, remains obscure. It is generally believed that tragedy (meaning "goat-song") was so designated because the sacrifice of a goat or the gift of a goat as a prize accompanied the performances.[44] As tragedy evolved to serve more sophisticated aesthetic needs, its religious vision also acquired increased depth and perception. The presentation of tragedies remained a public

42. Quoted in Richard B. Sewall, *The Vision of Tragedy*, p. 156.

43. Arthur E. Haigh, *The Tragic Drama of the Greeks*, p. 323.

44. It has also been suggested that the designation derives from the fact that the original choric dancers were dressed in goatskins—or acted like goats. Frank L. Lucas reported that, according to Dante, the actors' voices evoked the bleating of goats. Da Buti's more ingenious suggestion is that, like tragedy, a he-goat majestically bearded and adorned in front appears miserably bare and squalid behind. *Tragedy: Serious Drama in Relation to Aristotle's "Poetics."*

function supported by city or state. In Greece as well as Rome, the theater never became a private commercial enterprise.

With very rare exceptions the themes of the great tragedies were borrowed from ancient mythology.[45] As such, the function of tragedy was etiological and kerygmatic. It was a reenactment, for the benefit of believers, of the aition, the mythico-historical event that had generated their faith and rituals. The drama titled *Eumenides* explained the worship of the furies at the Areopagus; the tragedy of *Hippolytus*, the worship of its hero by Greek maidens; the *Iphigenia in Tauris*, the ritual of Artemis at Brauron; and the Promethean trilogy, the Prometheia.

This aition, the belief or ritual to be explained by reenactment, was often attached to the veneration of a tomb or to the memory of a deified hero who had died in unusual circumstances. Dramatic conventions required that the hero be a person above ordinary humanity. Usually of noble or divine descent, his or her destiny would entail suffering and death, often sacrificial death as the pharmakos, a substitute bearing vicariously some pollution for the sake of others. It was not rare for such tragedies to be presented in the spring since they contained some type of resurrection-ritual celebrating the resurgence of life after the winter months. In rare cases, when the plays took place at the turn of the year, a ritual of animal sacrifices was performed concurrently. The nature of the connection between such religious themes and tragedy was recognized by George G. Murray: "Most influential of all the ritual types is the pharmakos, the old polluted year, the sin-bearer, who has to be stoned or cast out, to suffer for his people. Oedipus and Orestes are typical; but almost every tragic hero has the traces of the pharmakos in him—he bears some pollution and he dies for the sins of others."[46]

The myths and beliefs of the Greeks were neither the naive fantasies of simple-minded primitives nor the supreme attainment of mankind in religious perception.[47] They depict man's quest for an explanation of a baffling and merciless universe, a reason for his own constricted existence, a resolution of the cruel contradictions of life, and a yearning for ultimate reality. Since such gropings were popularly expressed in grossly anthropomorphic allegories and legends, and since the fifth-century dramatists drew their subjects from the storehouse of mythology, it would seem that their inspiration could not have risen higher than their sources. One of the marks of their genius, however, was their ability to use and transcend ancient and sometimes vulgar motifs. In some measure the Attic tragedians were also theologians. They participated in the strivings of the human

45. "The rule which restricted Greek tragedy to mythological subjects was seldom disregarded at any period of its history." Haigh, *Tragic Drama*, p. 328. Aeschylus's contemporary *Persians* was a notable exception.

46. "Greek Drama," in *Encyclopaedia Britannica* (Chicago: Benton, 1953), 7:582.

47. Philip W. Harsh seemed to reflect the latter position when he stated, "A colorful and glorious past was blended with productive imagination to form a result far superior to Hebrew or Germanic myth and legend." *A Handbook of Classical Drama*, p. 8.

mind for answers to the dilemmas of destiny, and they explored for their contemporaries the mysterious twilight world of the spirit. But they also returned from their search with penetrating insights which they pro-, claimed with the passion of new convictions on the stormy stage of tragic drama, that microcosm of the upheavals of life which they transformed into a portal to the temple of truth. In this perspective it has been rightly said that tragedy was "preoccupied with fundamental religious problems— the nature of God or the gods, the relationship of the human and the divine, or the nature of God's ways to man."[48]

The capricious and vindictive Zeus, who takes pleasure in tormenting Prometheus while he is chained to his rock, is indeed the bungling god to whom the ancients ascribed their sorrows. But Aeschylus's *Prometheus Bound*, which depicts a Zeus of such despicable character, emphasizes the radical difference between this popular conception of the gods and the lofty, serene, sovereign divinity in the *Suppliants* or the *Agamemnon*. There, Aeschylus, by ascribing almost monotheistic attributes to Zeus, elevated him to the role of an all-knowing, wise, omnipotent dispenser of justice and ruler of destiny. With such a god in charge of the universe, the tragedians could posit a moral order within which heaven wreaks retribution upon crime and oppression and brings reward to the righteous. A character like Agamemnon is destroyed because of his responsibility in the death of his daughter Iphigenia. The sins of the fathers can also be visited upon the sons for several generations, as in the downfall of the house of Laius resulting from the curse of Oedipus in the *Seven Against Thebes*. The exercise of freedom and responsibility is implied in the concept of retribution. And, indeed, Greek tragedies celebrate the dignity of man as a free moral agent. In the *Antigone* of Sophocles, the heroine chooses to obey the gods rather than men in full knowledge of the hopelessness of her cause and of the violent end awaiting her. In the *Medea* of Euripides, punishment is meted out to unfaithful Jason by his wife Medea as she kills their sons with her own hands. She does not commit her crime in blind fury. She realizes the monstrous character of her plan but chooses to proceed with it because of its vindictive efficiency. As John Gassner put it, "Always, somewhere in the course of the tragedy, comes the stage direction (actual or implicit) 'Enter the gods.' "[49]

The universal scope and depth of the tragic quest is illustrated by the diversity of descriptions of the religious soul of tragedy: affirmation of moral order (Kitto), assertion of transcendence (de Romilly), reflection on the problem of evil (Oates), faith in overruling justice (Wilder), revelation of mystery (Hathorn), and mimesis of sacrifice (Frye).[50] Dorothea Krook

48. Whitney J. Oates, *The Complete Greek Drama*, 1:xxiii.

49. "Tragedy," in *Dictionary of World Literary Terms*, ed. Joseph T. Shipley, p. 340.

50. H. D. F. Kitto, *Form and Meaning in Drama*, pp. 237–38; Jacqueline de Romilly, *Time in Greek Tragedy*, p. 31; Whitney J. Oates, *The Complete Greek Drama*, 1:xxvii; Amos Wilder, *The Language of the Gospel*, p. 84; Richmond Y. Hathorn, *Tragedy, Myth, and Mystery*, p. 223; Northrop Frye, *Anatomy of Criticism*. Kitto provided a one-sentence sum-

saw "an objective moral order which at once incorporates the human and transcends it" as the foundational *raison d'être* of tragedy. She added: "This, I am suggesting, is what is finally affirmed in great tragedy. That this is true of classical Greek tragedy can hardly be contested."[51] Albin Lesky cited Goethe's definition: "All tragedy depends on an insoluble conflict. As soon as harmony is obtained or becomes possible, tragedy vanishes." Lesky contested this definition, however, arguing that a totally tragic conflict does not necessitate the destruction of the whole world. In fact "the stormy heavens may break to shed the light of salvation."[52]

Northrop Frye, whose work on the theory of myths stands as a classic statement, also has drawn an incisive definition of *tragedy*—it is an affirmation of the inviolability of moral law. The gods exist merely to ratify the order of nature. They have veto power over the binding character of law, but they exercise it only in contradiction to their nature. He observed, possibly with the prayer "Not my will but Thine" in mind, that "in Christianity much the same is true of the personality of Christ in relation to the inscrutable decrees of the Father." Viewed in this perspective, tragedy and the Gospel meet in the realm of absolutes—"Whether the context is Greek, Christian, or undefined, tragedy seems to lead up to an epiphany of law, of that which is and must be." This immutable order is a "something beyond" about which the hero holds exclusive knowledge. In a definition applicable to the Jesus of the Gospel, Frye stated, ". . . tragic heroes are wrapped in the mystery of their communion with that something beyond which we can see only through them, and which is the source of their strength and their fate alike."[53]

If genuinely religious elements comparable to Biblical themes can be recognized in tragedy, it is conversely true that the Gospel possesses an authentically tragic dimension, in the classic sense of the word *tragic*. In the Gospel the human condition is fraught with tragedy because it is caught in the gigantic conflict between good and evil. It is true that the immutable decrees of a just and omnipotent God make the end secure and determine favorably the outcome of the struggle. But eschatological deliverance belongs to the realm of transcendence whence it issues. In the meantime, man labors under the tormenting suspense of uncertainty. He strains after "the substance of things hoped for, the evidence of things not seen," which the New Testament calls faith. Caught in the ambiguity of the reality of evil and the hope of deliverance, he can only cry out: "I

---

mary when he stated that tragedy was "religious—not necessarily in the sense of being pious, but of trying to see the worlds of gods and men as one, and of expressing in the traditional Greek way all that is permanent in its Θεοί, gods." Ibid., p. 313.

51. *Elements of Tragedy*, p. 15.

52. *Greek Tragedy*, p. 14. In fact it should be noted that a number of tragedies have a happy ending—the *Eumenides* of Aeschylus, the *Philoctetes* of Sophocles, and the *Alcestis* of Euripides.

53. *Anatomy of Criticism*, p. 208.

believe; help my unbelief!" Just as the suspense in the life of Jesus is maintained till the very end, the escape from the grip of evil is revealed only after the abyss of desolation has been fathomed, so even the disciple knows that in this world he must suffer tribulations and that his allegiance, far from lessening the tragic tension of life, has rendered him more vulnerable to the cruelties that are the common lot of mankind. He knows that the last act of his earthly life may be played in the Roman arena where he will be dismembered alive for having refused to escape his tragic end.

Lesky, noting that for some, tragedy is the very stigma of the paganism that the Christ has left far behind, asked whether tragedy is conceivable within the scope of a Christian view of the world. He also gave the obvious answer. A tragic situation is conceivable within the Christian world as it is anywhere else. In fact, since the Christian world has acquired an added dimension, the occurrence of tragedy is even more likely.[54]

The foregoing development is not an attempt to perform a magic permutation of Greek tragedy into Gospel, and of Gospel into tragedy. From the viewpoints of literary character, religious content, inherent world view, and intended function, they remain distinct. But they coincide at crucial points. They both manifest a preoccupation with the serious and profound questions of life, and they propose answers that take for granted the relevance of a moral order issuing from transcendence. The fact that the deeper significance of both tragedy and Gospel arises out of a plot revolving around a central figure, points to affinities in substance that, in turn, justly warrant investigation of possible correspondence in formal features.

In Mark's day, when Hellenism was still the dominant cultural force in the ancient world so that Greek tragedies were commonly performed and studied, there arose out of the religious life of an obscure believing community, a story recounting events that had given birth to its faith—a faith fixed upon the commanding figure of a supernatural being who had suffered undeservedly and died for the sake of others. This story was tragic not only in the sense that the unjust rejection and execution of a good person elicits indignation and sympathetic response. It was also tragic in a technical sense since it resembled the revered dramatic rituals devised by ancient seers to describe their search for meaning and to express their yearning for transcendence.

With materials in hand as varied as miracle and pronouncement stories, sayings of and stories about Jesus, and in all probability an outline linking some of those elements together, the task of a would-be Gospel-writer was considerable. Assuming that his was the first written Gospel, Mark undertook to create a composition for which there existed no precedent. His future Gospel was in search of an appropriate mold. It is therefore not inconceivable that, faced with a challenge calling for literary skills beyond his own, Mark was attracted to the dominant literary model of his day. As many have done since who have been further removed

54. *Greek Tragedy*, p. 15.

chronologically from both the sources of the Gospel and Greek tragedy,[55] Mark may have noticed and exploited the dramatic potential of the alliance between the tragic thrust of the Gospel and the stylized power of drama. Under the pressure of necessity, Mark probably required little imagination to pass from resemblance in content to resemblance in form. By borrowing and adapting some of the formal features of tragedy to meet the exigencies of his own story, Mark found the form of the Gospel. The classical model, hallowed from birth, consecrated by four centuries of noble use, and exceptionally conformable to the Gospel he wished to write, enabled Mark to create a form that endowed its very structure with a significance arising from its profound mystery. This may well constitute one of the distinctive features of the second Gospel: its form came into being as a reflection on its content. That the form of the Gospel was also chosen to provide an interpretation of its intent will be shown in the conclusion of this study.

The one author who has been described as the supreme authority on literary art in the Gospels—Wilder—has flatly denied Mark's dependency on Greek tragedy.[56] Yet he engaged in startling lucubrations that perhaps betray an unconscious attraction to the idea. For example: "A Gospel like that of Mark is a book of epiphanies, a tragedy yet not a tragedy, a sacred drama which culminates not in the death of a hero or a martyr—and as such appealing to our sense of pathos or admiration—but in a final austere transaction between God and men."[57] Ambivalence seems to characterize other statements: "The new movement of the Gospel was not to be identified with a new teaching or a new experience but with an action and therefore a history. The revelation was in an historical drama." Wilder continued: "The narrative mode inevitably imposed itself as the believers rehearsed the saving action, including particular scenes of it that played themselves out in the market-place or the temple-court, at a dinner with guests or in a synagogue."[58] Similar perplexity is expressed by other critics. Gassner stated that although the theater was far from the mind of the authors of the Gospels, these Gospels, "which are rich in dialogue and characterization, possess a supremely dramatic conclusion. . . . If structurally the Gospels are narratives, their pattern and effect are unmistakably dramatic."[59]

The seemingly ambiguous attitude of such eminent classicists is understandable. As a hybrid literary form—if it is literature at all—the Gospel does not readily fit in any of the categories delineated in manuals of literary criticism. Hence Wilder's apparent bafflement when he stated that the Gospel of Mark is "a tragedy yet not a tragedy." The explanation of this problem may reside in the fact that interwoven into the body of a

55. Medieval mysteries, nativity and passion plays constitute colorful instances.

56. See note 27 above.

57. *The Language of the Gospel*, p. 128.

58. Ibid., p. 77.

59. *Masters of the Drama*, p. 113.

non-literary piece of writing like the Gospel, are subtly concealed literary features borrowed from Greek drama. And yet the Gospel manages to remain a narration, not a play for theatrical performance. It follows a pattern of reenactment but cannot be acted out. Like the aition, the original myth that tragedy was devised to recall, the Gospel evokes the Christian faith-events at their point of origin. But whereas tragedy acted out the myth in live portrayal, the Gospel describes its beginnings through verbal evocation, thus magnifying the awesomeness of its mystery through the simplicity of its presentation. Willi Marxsen pointed to this trait of the Gospel when he observed that the word εὐαγγέλιον in 1:1 referred, in Mark's mind, to traditions that "are not meant simply to preserve the memory of Jesus' ministry, but are intended to be an address, a proclamation that 're-presents' Jesus. In other words, in writing his Gospel Mark created a literary type that is unique."[60] Wilder also recognized that the Gospel stands in lieu of a representation: "Mark represents a divine transaction whose import involves heaven and earth. . . . The Gospel action is not history so much as a ritual re-enactment or mimesis."[61] That a re-enactment can occur with no other medium than the written (and therefore read) word constitutes the very genius of Mark. His secret may well reside in the blending of variegated elements of episodic narrative into a harmoniously connected whole by means of the judicious incorporation of the most effective dramatic devices ever discovered by man to penetrate the mysteries of the gods.

With the demands of worship and rites pressing upon the early church, the concept of reenactment had not been left waiting to be discovered by the first Gospel writer. Large sections of the Gospel, such as the passion story, were probably used regularly in the worship and instruction of Christian communities long before Mark incorporated them in his Gospel. The observance of the Lord's Supper was itself an acted-out gospel, a reenactment of the Christian aition through recall (in its memorial aspect) and through actual presence (in its celebration aspect). But having recourse to Greek tragedy in order to portray this reenactment was a boldly original venture that points to the surging revolutionary temper of the author and of the community for which he was writing.

The explosive impact of the first Easter and Pentecost, and the irresistible advance which it fostered—especially in Gentile territory—convinced the early Christians that a new age had dawned upon them and that they had become the "new Israel," the invincible people of destiny. The motto "Everything is possible with God" echoes as a leitmotif throughout the New Testament. It receives a threefold proclamation in Mark (9:23; 10:27; 14:36), and the apostle Paul emphatically declared to the Corinthian Christians that everything in heaven and on earth belongs to them (I Cor. 3:22). The ends of the earth were the limits of their conquering passion. Amid the exuberance of newly received power and release, the apostle Peter approved the shattering of cultural, social, and

60. *Introduction to the New Testament*, p. 138.

61. *The Language of the Gospel*, p. 60.

racial dividers as expressed in the language-explosion at Pentecost and in his prediction on the same occasion of the Gentile mission (Acts 2:39). His reservation was that his euphoric companions be not found inebriated at nine in the morning. Most of the struggles and torments of the early church (as reflected in Acts and the Epistles) illustrate a tenacious determination to protect Christian freedom from the encroachments of integrative Judaism and against the dissolution of ambient paganism.

It was inevitable that the liberation consciousness ostensibly reflected in the substance of the documents of the apostolic church should also permeate the form of their writings. This fact has not escaped the notice of classical scholars such as Erich Auerbach, who pointed to the capacity for reinterpretation and innovation in the early Christian community: "The first effect of the Judaeo-Christian manner of dealing with the events in the world of reality led to anything but rigidity and narrowness. The hiddenness of God and finally his *parousia*, his incarnation in the common form of an ordinary life, these concepts brought about a dynamic movement in the basic conception of life, a swing of the pendulum in the realm of morals and sociology, which went far beyond the classic-antique norm for the imitation of real life and living growth."[62] In the same vein Wilder referred to "the new speech-freedom of Jesus and his followers,"[63] which he attributed to the fact that "the coming of the Christian Gospel was in one aspect a renewal and a liberation of language. It was a 'speech-event,' the occasion of a new utterance and new forms of utterance, and eventually new kinds of writing."[64] He added, "These early Christian styles, these voices, oracles and texts, all bear the marks of the forge of the new fellowship and of the Spirit, whether in the dynamic privacy of their meetings or in the external activities of the mission."[65]

And W. A. Beardslee explained the capacity of the Gospel to seek new forms of expression without breaking down into absurdity: "Though the Gospels are strongly coherent narratives, and though they function as religious narratives to re-enact the point of origin, the Gospels have in them a strong eschatological-revolutionary component that rebels against order imposed from the past. This element is most visible in Mark."[66]

Although these authors have not acknowledged the contribution of ancient tragedy to the Gospel of Mark, they have recognized that audacious initiatives were needed to find new wineskins for new wine. Liberated from the restraints and prejudices of the past into a faith that encompasses heaven and earth, Christians like Mark were set free to speak the tongues of men and angels. For Mark the supreme act of Christian liberation may well have been to proclaim the universal relevance of a very Jewish story by telling it in the manner of a Greek tragedy.

62. *Mimesis*, p. 119.

63. *The Language of the Gospel*, p. 97.

64. Ibid., p. 26.

65. Ibid., p. 34.

66. *Literary Criticism*, p. 28.

Chapter 2

Tragic Drama
in Mark's Day

Before undertaking an analysis of lines of convergence between the Gospel and tragedy, it would be appropriate to survey briefly the origins, development, and influence of tragedy in order to determine the degree of probability that an individual like Mark had access to it. Inductive evidence should be sufficient to establish whether or not Mark was dependent on the tragic form. But the argument would be stronger if it can be shown that tragedy was alive and well in Mark's day, that it was accessible to a person like him, and that the particular forms of development it had attained during Mark's lifetime rendered it especially suitable for his use.

It is generally agreed that tragedy was born in Athens and that it evolved from choral performances traditionally connected with the worship of Dionysius.[1] Although precise information on early forms of tragedy is lacking, there is no doubt regarding its association from the very beginning with some kind of religious ritual.[2] One of the earliest references indicates that tragedies were performed as an official part of the festivities at the great Dionysia in 534 B.C.

Thespis, an author of the second half of the sixth century about whom very little is known, seems to be the one who gave tragedy its first impulsion as a performance involving dialogue. To the chorus he added one actor—generally himself—who played the part of diverse personae by raising questions and answering them himself.

This innovation led to the invention of tragedy proper by Aeschylus (525–456), whose addition of a second actor gave more semblance to dialogue and action. He wrote some ninety plays, only seven of which have been preserved.[3] In all of his plays except the *Persians* (*Persae*)—the only extant historical drama in Greek literature—Aeschylus drew all of his plots from mythology. They are embued with deep religious conviction and a

1. "Greek dramatic performances took place on the special occasion of an annual spring festival for Dionysius, a god of wine and fertility who was symbolically present at the annual performances in the form of a statue which stood beside the stage. His altar was a permanent part of the theater precinct." Albert Cook, *"Oedipus Rex": A Mirror for Greek Drama*, p. 1.

2. Herbert J. Rose, *A Handbook of Greek Literature*. Rose discussed several theories of the origin of Greek tragedy: it arose from the dithyramb (Aristotle); it arose from performances of a mimetic character at the graves (Ridgeway); and it arose from a ritual contest between the gods of fertility and death (Farrell).

3. They are *Suppliants, Persians (Persae), Prometheus Bound, Seven Against Thebes*, and the Oresteia trilogy—*Agamemnon, Choephoroe* ("Libation-Bearers"), and *Eumenides*.

33

high conception of divinity. "He was one of those poets who are also prophets."[4]

Sophocles (496–406) introduced the third actor, and with this playwright "Greek tragedy reached its culmination."[5] Although he authored more than 125 plays, only seven have survived.[6] In them, form has evolved in near-perfect conformity to content. Their theme, without neglecting fate and the supernatural, deals more with man, his moral and spiritual life, so that Sophocles has been regarded as one of the great humanists among the poets of Western civilization.

The third and last of the great classical tragedians, Euripides (485–406) produced ninety-two plays, eighteen of which are extant as complete tragedies.[7] Although generally faithful to the form created by the other masters, Euripides directed tragedy along more secular lines and infused it with a preoccupation for human character and psychological subtleties.

"It so happened that in the fifth century there existed in Athens a little group of first-rate poets, whereof two must be reckoned among the very foremost of the whole world, while the other, if a little less great than they, would alone be sufficient to make any literature famous."[8] Thus was invented and perfected in Athens the most influential and enduring aesthetic form designed by men to portray the great dilemmas of existence, the universal imperatives of justice and retribution, and the torments brought upon mortals by their mysterious passions.

The creative genius of this epoch was not confined to the towering figures of these three tragic poets. A multitude of lesser writers—their imitators and their sometimes successful competitors at Dionysiac festivals—wrote tragedies. Although their plays were generally eagerly received, the judgment of their contemporaries as well as the verdict of history (not a single specimen of their tragedies has been preserved) agreed in recognizing the definitive superiority to them of the three poets of the fifth century. "The three great masters of tragic poetry soon began to be separated, in the minds of the people, from the general mass of writers for the stage, and to be regarded with peculiar and almost religious veneration, as models of dramatic excellence, and inspired teachers of virtue and knowledge."[9]

In the fourth century, Athens remained the privileged center for the creation of new tragedies, an enterprise that became most fashionable

4. Rose, *Greek Literature*, p. 159.

5. Ibid., p. 177.

6. They are *Ajax, Antigone, Trachiniae* ("Trachinian Women"), *Oedipus the King, Electra, Philoctetes,* and *Oedipus at Colonus.*

7. Some of them are *Alcestis, Medea, Hippolytus, Trojan Women (Troades), Iphigenia in Tauris, Electra,* and *Bacchae.*

8. Rose, *Greek Literature*, p. 147.

9. Arthur E. Haigh, *The Tragic Drama of the Greeks*, p. 403. Haigh also cited the names of the minor dramatists of the fifth and fourth centuries, and the titles of some of their work.

judged by the extraordinary proliferation of productions. There was no lack of emulation among established professional dramaturges. But toward the end of the century, a new source of competition appeared as amateur writers of tragedy, many of them living outside Athens, began to write and to enter their works in the program of official festivals.[10] The tone, subject, and form of such productions usually followed the pattern established by the original inventors of the genre. Their inglorious extinction may be interpreted as a lack of distinction. As a result of their disappearance, the older plays continued to be performed and came to be regarded as unsurpassable objects of quasi-veneration. Such was the degree of respect they inspired that a law was adopted in Athens to protect them from the slightest change during performances. A city official would be present with an approved copy from the public archives in order to follow the presentation word by word and prevent actors from taking liberties with the text for the sake of theatrical convenience.

It was also during the fourth century that a systematic treatise on literary criticism of Greek tragedy appeared, defining its nature and function and delineating the conventions regulating the genre. Although Aristotle's (384–322) *Poetics* ("On the Art of Poetry") originally dealt with epic, tragedy, and comedy, the part dealing with epic has been mutilated and that dealing with comedy has completely disappeared. The essay on tragedy, however, constitutes an invaluable document. It bears testimony to the vitality of dramatic production and interest in Aristotle's times. It also enunciates a formal theory of tragedy and provides substantial information on contemporary requirements for the composition and presentation of tragic drama.

Critical and interpretative problems arising from aspects of Aristotle's work have resulted in controversies that at times have tended to discredit the *Poetics*. In particular the charge has been made that Aristotle's theory of tragedy does not accord with the surviving plays of the fifth century. Several explanations have been offered to explain this alleged discrepancy. The developments that affected the conception and techniques of tragedy during the interval of time which separated Aristotle from the writers of the fifth century have been adduced by some classicists. *Ad misericordiam* explanations have also been offered. The competence of Aristotle as a literary critic and theorist has been questioned. It has also been claimed that his key concepts have been misunderstood and mistranslated by successive generations of classical scholars.[11] However, a

10. History reports that Dionysius, the "tyrant" of Syracuse who reigned from 405 to 367, wrote his plays on a desk that had been used by Aeschylus, and with pen and tablets that had belonged to Euripides. Obviously the genius of his noble models was not as readily accessible to him. Success persistently eluded his efforts—except the one time he won first prize at the Lenaea in Athens. If popular tradition is right in ascribing his death to overindulgence while celebrating his achievement, his victory proved to be his undoing. Ibid., p. 432.

11. See, respectively, H. D. F. Kitto, *Form and Meaning in Drama*, p. 241; John Jones, *On Aristotle and Greek Tragedy*, p. 50; and Rose, *Greek*

number of authoritative students of ancient literature insist, sometimes with considerable vehemence, on the normative value of the *Poetics*. Some consider this treatise "the fountainhead of dramatic criticism" and its author "infallible," claiming that "no author, ancient or modern, compares with him for authority."[12]

Obviously any attempt to resolve the controversy regarding the validity of the *Poetics'* norms in reference to extant tragedies of the fifth century falls outside the purview of this study. But it can be safely affirmed that if Aristotle's formulations regarding tragedy are not descriptive of earlier tragedies, in any case they were intended to regulate the works of his own day. Otherwise Aristotle's undertaking would have been quite pointless. Consequently, references will be made to the *Poetics* later in this study with the understanding that in the *Poetics* Aristotle attempted to draw from the diversity of experiments borne out of the surging euphoria of literary invention in the fifth century, prescriptive rather than descriptive formulations, affected by his own preference and by contemporary trends in dramatic theory. Lane Cooper correctly stated: "We may assume that here as elsewhere in the realm of knowledge [Aristotle] is far from being an isolated scholar, but systematizes and completes the work of predecessors, with an eye to the best thought and practice of his own time—and yet—unquestionably, with great independence of judgment."[13]

Although tragedy was born and flourished in Athens, it rapidly spread throughout the entire Hellenistic world. By virtue of its early association with the worship of Dionysius, tragic drama became a regular feature of religious festivals wherever they were held in the Greek-speaking world. "By the time of Alexander it may be said to have become coextensive with the Bacchic worship, and to have penetrated into every region of the world in which the Greek language was spoken."[14] As tragic performances gained popularity on their own merits, they eventually became dissociated from Dionysiac celebrations and were presented during manifestations of a literary, artistic, or musical character. Arthur E. Haigh described the quasi-universal range of the popularity of Greek tragedy as spreading from France and Italy in the west to Syria and Phoenicia in the east. He indicated that an enormous number of Greek theaters was erected in a continuous series from Sicily to Phoenicia. When the Roman general Lucullus fought the king of Armenia and captured Tigranocerta, he found the city full of Greek actors who had been summoned by the king to celebrate the opening of his new theater.

Literature, p. 277. Rose also stated: "Within its self-imposed limits, it [the *Poetics*] is admirable, and has exercised an enormous influence, largely through translations amidst a fog of misunderstanding."

12. Respectively: Charles W. Cooper, *Preface to Drama*, p. 127; Gilbert Norwood, *Greek Tragedy*, pp. 42–43; C. M. Bowra, *Sophoclean Tragedy*, p. 361.

13. In Aristotle, *On the Art of Poetry*, ed. and trans. Lane Cooper, p. xvii.

14. Haigh, *Tragic Drama*, p. 435.

Guilds of actors were organized in almost every part of the ancient world, even in such remote regions as Nismes in France, Messene in Sicily, Naples and Rhegium in Italy, Cyprus, Cythera, Ptolemais, Thyatira in Lydia, and Ressinus in Galatia. The guild of Greek actors was flourishing in Rome as late as the second century A.D. Euodanius, the professor of rhetoric who was appointed head of their guild, is said to have found them "vain and difficult to manage."[15] Such was the fame of Greek tragedy that even nations with only a tinge of Hellenic culture were familiar with it. When Artavasdes, king of Armenia, and the king of Parthia celebrated, soon after the defeat and death of the Roman consul Crassus, the marriage of their children, the program of entertainment called for a recitation from the *Bacchae* of Euripides. Tradition reports that one of the actors, a certain Jason of Tralles, declaimed the verses of Agare with the head of Crassus in his hands. The populace of Hipola in Spain, however, seems to have been less inured to tragic spectacles. When the actor who was to initiate them to tragedy appeared on the stage, they fled out of the theater in panic, taking the lugubrious-looking figure for a ghost.[16]

I

One of the most significant developments for Western literature took place when Greek tragedy reached and implanted itself firmly in Italy. Not only did it thrive and survive in Italian soil long after it became extinct almost everywhere else, but also it gave birth to Latin drama, which in turn made a decisive impact upon the theater of Europe and England up to modern times. During the age of Pericles, a Greek colony was established in southern Italy that soon distinguished itself by its affluence and cultural sophistication. Dramatic representations imported from Greece were eagerly welcomed in cities such as Rhegia, Naples, and Tarentium, which eventually became important theatrical centers. In the early part of the third century, when the conquering Romans drove their legions into the southern part of the Italian peninsula, they found that the highly cultured Greek cities controlling the area (designated as Magna Graecia by the Romans) were no longer warlike. The mercenaries hired by the Greek cities to defend them could not resist the onslaught of the Romans, who soon extended their domination over the whole colony. One might expect that Roman rule would stamp out Greek culture and eradicate Greek tragedy from Italian territory because it exalts Hellenic ideas and Greek mythology, but the opposite happened. In Horace's celebrated words, "Captive Greece took captive her savage captor and brought civilization to barbarous Latium."[17]

The Romans, who were admittedly devoid of literary creativity, "derived their first taste for Hellenic art and literature from their constant intercourse with these Italian Greeks; and the drama was the chief instru-

15. Cited from Plutarch and Philostratus in ibid., p. 456.

16. Ibid., pp. 438–39.

17. *Epistles* 2.1.156.

ment by which that taste was disseminated."[18] The presence of a substantial segment of Greek population in Rome later facilitated the adoption of tragic drama as an essential part of the cultural life of the city. References to the presentation of Greek plays abound in Roman annals, beginning with the record of performances given by the general Fulvius in celebration of his Aetolian campaign and continuing with notices of Greek tragedies as a regular feature of important Italian festivals. They were frequently exhibited by Julius Caesar, Augustus, and Nero. In fact, one of Nero's monomaniac delusions consisted in regarding himself as a tragic actor; he undertook a tour of Greece, inflicting his grotesque performances in the roles of Creon and Oedipus upon bewildered natives. Mention is made in various chronicles of contests in Greek tragedy as a regular institution in Rome as late as the second century A.D., and even of presentations during the fifth century in Constantinople.[19]

Since most of the representations in Rome took place on occasions of official festivities, attendance was open to the general public. Nothing would have prevented an ordinary denizen such as the author of the second Gospel from being present at such performances. His knowledge of the Greek language would, in fact, have made him even more likely to attend Greek plays, much as French-speaking persons in London or Boston are likely to be attracted to presentations of Corneille and Molière in the original language. The fact that admission to theatrical performances was generally free in Rome (which is hardly the case in Boston and London) was an additional inducement. On the basis of the evidence, it can be safely stated that the enduring success of Greek tragedy in the Roman world, including the city of Rome, was such that a person sufficiently conversant with cultural endeavors to undertake a project like writing the Gospel of Mark would have had at least a general acquaintance with it, such as was accessible to the common man, especially if he was literate in Greek—as Mark was.

II

A development of even greater significance for this study than the perpetuation of Greek tragedy through Mark's time, may well be the emergence of its immediate progeny, the Latin drama. If the Romans were not gifted as creators of dramatic art, they could at least imitate. And they imitated abundantly, taking again as their point of departure the showcase of Greek culture on Italian soil, the conquered colonies of Magna Graecia. Roman literature is traditionally considered to have begun around 240 B.C. with the translation of the *Odyssey* into Latin by Livius Andronicus (284–204), a Greek born in Tarentum and taken as a slave-scholar to Rome. He translated into Latin some fourteen Greek tragedies that, although lost, testify to the ready acceptance of dramatic art by the Romans. Before he died, another dramaturge appeared in Rome in the

18. Haigh, *Tragic Drama*, p. 455.

19. Ibid., pp. 456, 458.

person of Gnaeus Naevius (270–200 B.C.). Since he was also born in the southern Greek colony (at Campania), Naevius was well versed in Attic poetry. But he was an Italian and no slave. Consequently when he used Greek models, as he did for several tragedies, he did not simply translate or imitate, but he adapted them to the Latin temper. Departing from traditional recourse to mythological themes, he also wrote historical plays based on contemporary events. The creation of the Roman historical drama (or *fabula praetexta*, a Latin tragedy with a theme drawn from Roman legend, history, or contemporary events, as against *fabula crepidata* or *togata*, tragedies with traditional Greek themes and setting) is therefore to be ascribed to Naevius. He paid dearly for his invention; allusions to political personages of his day resulted in his imprisonment and eventually in his exile from Italy.

The greatest literary figure of this period was Quintus Ennius (239–169), who also came from Tarentum in Magna Graecia. His indebtedness to the Greek heritage is reflected in the fact that of the twenty tragedies he composed, all but one are adaptations of Greek originals. "The fragmentary state of these tragedies makes them hard to evaluate; the extant bits and scraps show a man who had studied Andronicus and Naevius and learned from them how to handle the problem of putting Greek into Latin. The quality of his work with tragedy is attested at least in some degree by the fact that his plays were read and revered as masterpieces for many centuries after his death."[20] Ennius was followed by two great dramatists. His nephew Marcus Pacuvius (ca. 220–ca. 130 B.C.), also born in southern Italy (at Brindisium), is said to have written tragedies, fourteen of which are known to us by their titles only. Pacuvius seems to have followed the models of Sophocles and Euripides in all except one titled *Paulus*, which was a historical drama. The last of the great Roman dramatists and perhaps the most successful was Lucius Accius (170–ca. 86 B.C.). Fragments from some forty of his plays indicate a prolific and versatile writer. Except for two *fabula praetexta—Brutus* and *Decius*, both based on events in Roman history—his plays follow themes of fifth-century Attic tragedies.

Although Roman tragedy, like its Greek model, enjoyed continued popularity through the first century of our era, it is difficult now to define its exact nature. Only fragments quoted in other works have survived, affording meager grounds for evaluation. Except for assigning a subsidiary role to the chorus, the Roman tragedians seem to have adopted the form of the Greek model without much alteration. In substance, the paucity of native subjects and the resulting dependence on themes already treated by Greek tragedians has been attributed to the lack of dramatic invention on the part of Latin writers (Sellar), the scarcity of native legends and the undramatic nature of Roman history (Bailey),[21] and the hazards of depicting aspects of national life in politically tense periods. Through the trans-

20. Frank O. Copley, *Latin Literature*, p. 14.

21. William Y. Sellar, *The Roman Poets of the Augustan Age*, p. 121; Cyril Bailey, *The Mind of Rome*, p. 8.

fer from Greece to Rome, however, the soul of tragedy was inevitably subjected to a transformation. The Roman vision of life, society, and religion were bound to leave their imprint on this form of writing. William Y. Sellar stated that in extant Roman fragments, the themes drawn from Greek tragedy "are expressed not with the subtlety and reflective genius of Greece, but in the plain and straightforward tones of the Roman Republic."[22]

The enduring popularity of Roman tragedy is attested by several factors. The three tragedians, Ennius, Pacuvius, and Accius, were honored during their lifetimes. They received the favor of the leading men of the state, and after their deaths they were venerated by the people.[23] Cicero (106–43 B.C.), more than any other ancient man of letters, showed in his writings a keen interest in Latin drama and dramatists. Numerous references in his works to tragedians, tragedies, and actors give a picture of the vitality of drama during his age. F. Warren Wright stated that Cicero had mentioned some twenty-one Latin playwrights, given the names of many of their plays, and quoted many, many of their fragments.[24] Sellar noted that "Cicero in many places mentions the great applause with which the expression of feeling in different dramas was received, and speaks of the great crowds ('*maximus consessus*' or '*magna frequentia*'), including women and children, attending the representation." The scholar-writer Varro (116–27 B.C.), a contemporary of Cicero, complained that "the heads of families had gradually gathered within the walls of the city, having quitted their ploughs and pruning-hooks, and that they liked to use their hands in the theatres and circuses better than on the crops and vineyards."[25] Although Varro did not refer specifically to tragedies, it is more than likely that they were included in the theatrical performances he did mention. The public calendar of Rome posted some four or five great festivals every year, some lasting as long as two weeks, and dramatic presentations constituted a regular feature of such festivities. There were, in addition, exceptional games—games like those instituted by Caesar to dedicate the temple of Venus Genetrix (26 September 46 B.C.), which included dramatic contests; or the games instituted by Pompey to celebrate the opening of Pompey's theater and temple in October 55, which included performances of Accius's *Clytemnestra* and Naevius's *Equus Trojanus*; or the games instituted by Lentulus in 57 B.C., which included performances of Afranius's *Simulaus* and Accius's *Eurysaces*.[26]

The demand for such performances was apparently sufficient to propel gifted actors to fame and wealth. Cicero and other writers referred frequently to Aesopus and Roscius, regarded as the leading interpreters of Roman tragic roles. They are said to have amassed huge fortunes in the

22. *Roman Poets*, p. 122.

23. Ibid., p. 128.

24. *Cicero and the Theater*, p. 31.

25. *Roman Poets*, p. 128.

26. Wright, *Cicero and the Theater*, p. 2.

exercise of their profession and to have been highly esteemed by their influential contemporaries. Aesopus is known to have played the lead in the games of both Pompey and Lentulus.

One of the strongest indications of the vitality of drama during this time is provided by Horace (65–8 B.C.) in his *Ars Poetica* ("On the Art of Poetry"), where he devoted a considerable amount of space to tragedy. In this document he propounded a doctrine of literary forms that follows traditional lines and lays down rules for the composition of tragedy that would result in closer imitation of the ancient models. In keeping with this antiquarian tendency, Horace elsewhere rebuked audiences of his day for preferring sensuous spectacles to good plays and fine acting, while he praised the emperor's good taste and asked him to give his patronage also to other kinds of poetry than the dramatic.[27]

The necessity for a manual of drama writing like the *Ars Poetica* leads to another discovery that testifies to intense interest in drama during this period. Numerous incidental references in Latin authors indicate that the writing of tragedies had become a hobby for amateurs such as literary personalities, political figures, and other unqualified individuals. Horace, writing to Florus and inquiring about the literary activity of the staff of Tiberius (the *studiosa cohors*, as he called it), asked with some apprehension if his friend Titius was writing a tragedy.[28] It is believed that Horace wrote his *Epistle to the Pisos* principally to discourage young men who, without qualifications, set themselves to write tragedies out of conformity to the fashion of the day. Alfred Bates stated that in the reign of Augustus, the rage for tragedy had developed almost into a mania, and some dramas had been written by the emperor himself.[29] As a matter of fact, it is known that Augustus composed an *Ajax* and that, before him, Julius Caesar had written an *Oedipus* that Augustus considered unfit for publication. Time has not been more charitable to his own work, since nothing remains of it. A friend of Augustus (when he was still Octavian), of Horace, and of Virgil, Asinius Pollio (76 B.C.–A.D. 4) wrote several tragedies of which nothing remains. Cicero's brother, Quintus Tullius Cicero, is said to have composed four tragedies in sixteen days. Even the great Ovid tried his hand at tragedy with a *Medea* that was held in high regard by Tacitus and Quintilian. His friend Varius Rufus wrote a *Thiestes* that Quintilian thought compared favorably with any of the classical Greek plays.[30]

A curious story reported by Asinius Pollio provides another example of this infatuation with drama writing. A minor Roman official by the name of Lucius Cornelius Balbus was sent, in the interest of the state, on a mission to Italy from his residence in Spain. During his travel he went to

---

27. *Epistles* 2.1 (Epistle to Augustus). See T. S. Dorsch, in Horace, *On the Art of Poetry*, p. 20.

28. *Epistles* 1.3. See John F. d'Alton, *Horace and His Age*, p. 287.

29. *Greek and Roman Drama*, 1:100.

30. See Herman Fränkel, *Ovid*, p. 47.

Brindisium (at Formiae) to meet Cicero, and they proceeded across the water to Pompey's camp at Durazzo. His journey so impressed him, despite the fact that it met with failure, that upon his return to Spain, he wrote a tragedy which was presented in Cadiz in the spring of 43. Pollio reported that Balbus had been so moved by the depiction of his deeds on stage that he wept uncontrollably. The play is lost, but this event provides an intriguing instance of a nonprofessional writer composing a *praetexta* based on contemporary events in which he had had a part. That this was not an isolated case will be shown later during an examination of the tragedy titled *Octavia*, which was written at approximately the same time as the Gospel of Mark.

The volume of dramatic works resulting from the aristocratic pastime of writing tragedy was so considerable that the first century B.C. has been called "the golden age of theatre production in Rome."[31] Of the many factors that account for this phenomenon, three will be briefly mentioned. First, tragedy as a concentration of serious deeds and timeless themes suited well the Roman character, with its grim determination and its aspirations for destiny. The citizens of the eternal city found in the ancient dramas echoes of the struggles and convulsions that were shaping their national fortunes. When caught in the grip of momentous historical events, men seek guidance and security in the most profound and eloquent forms of ancient wisdom. Second, tragedy lent itself easily to misuse as a means of satisfying the compulsive proclivity of educated Romans for grandiloquent declamation. For philosophically shallow minds the temptation to exploit serious situations for rhetorical effect is nigh irresistible. Tragedy provided both the substance and the pretext for high-sounding and self-admiring literati to indulge in their favorite pastime. Third, the use of drama as a more or less subtle medium for communicating political opinions was tolerated in Rome. Philip W. Harsh noted that in such cases "extended allegory was not necessary; a single line of an old play was often interpreted in the light of contemporary events and greeted with applause and hissing."[32] Specific references to the use of drama as political criticism abound in the annals of Roman history.[33] Although no work written during this period has survived in its entirety, sufficient evidence exists to indicate that tragedy-writing became a fad because it was a form of reflection on and expression of current issues that was suitable to the ethos of a proud people and to the assumed dignity of their national destiny.

31. J. A. S. Evans, "*Aeneid* 2 and the Art of the Theater," p. 255. John Wright Duff cited Ribbeck's census through ancient writings. Ribbeck found the names of thirty-six tragic poets and the titles of 150 tragedies. *A Literary History of Rome*, p. 169.

32. *A Handbook of Classical Drama*, p. 406.

33. See Wright, *Cicero and the Theater*, pp. 4—9; and Ludwig Friedländer, *Roman Life and Manners*, pp. 93—94. Duff said of the Romans that "they found something congenial to the existing order of things in such political thought as tragedy admitted—for the Greek 'tyrannophobia' was shared by the optimates of Rome." *A Literary History of Rome*, p. 168.

That the extent of this dramatic vision and the recourse of Latin writers to a particular species of dramatic expression cannot be lightly dismissed is further substantiated by the impact made on other forms of literary endeavor by the effervescent vitality of first-century theatrical production in Rome. Students of classical literature have observed that while the popularity of tragic representation was at its height, theatrical production exerted pressure on nondramatic forms of literature. J. A. S. Evans noted that the works of poets were recited with pantomimic accompaniment in theaters where dramas were commonly presented. Virgil's *Eclogues* were said to have been performed in public, and Ovid became very popular with theater-goers. Likewise it is possible to make a dramatic analysis of the structure of Virgil's epic, the *Aeneid*, into two acts made up of separate scenes, carefully framed and balanced, each constituting a dramatic entity. Evans also adduced devices in Virgil that are derived from the workshop of dramatic composition, such as the use of dramatic irony in the Sophoclean manner and the balancing, in the *Aeneid*, of Dido's and Aenas's speeches like those of Euripides.[34] Martin Dibelius also noted the tendency of writers during the period under study to have recourse to "a new, dramatic method of presentation." He cited norms set by Duris and Cicero for literary works, requiring them to be constructed with dramatic clarity and with a view to entertain. And Dibelius showed how, in the two main works of the historian Sallust (86–34 B.C.), the *Bellum Jugurth* and *De Coniatione Catilinae*, the action rises and falls, having a climax in the middle and a catastrophe at the end.[35] Although a case cannot be built upon a few indications of a popular infatuation, it is important to remember not only the pervasiveness of the dramatic style during the time when Mark wrote his Gospel, but also the possible influence of that style upon nondramatic forms of literary expression.

III

But by far the most impressive chain of evidence suggesting a possible link between classical tragedy and the Gospel of Mark is provided by the existence, long before and notably during Mark's time, of a kind of tragedy specifically written not for stage presentation, but simply for reading—as the Gospel was. This form of writing, which Haigh called "the literary drama—a new species of compositions,"[36] was practiced in Greece as early as the age of Aristotle. In the *Rhetoric* Aristotle made clear that such plays were written for individuals who enjoyed reading or reciting them, their merit consisting in beauty of diction and style.[37] He cited Chaeremon, a poet of the fourth century, as an author of such tragedies, of which only fragments have been preserved. Philosophers eventually ex-

34. *Art of the Theater*, pp. 255–58.
35. *Studies in the Acts of the Apostles*, p. 142.
36. *Tragic Drama*, p. 426.
37. 3.12.

ploited this form of writing to popularize their teachings. Haigh cited as examples seven tragedies, worthless from a theatrical point of view but full of expositions of Cynical doctrines, which were handed about in later times as the work of Diogenes; plays of a "lofty and philosophical character published by his disciple Crates"; and sixty tragedies authored by the Greek philosopher Timon the Skeptic at the beginning of the third century B.C.[38] The writing of didactic dramas persisted through New Testament times and beyond. Nicolaus of Damascus, the famous historian and friend of Herod the Great, composed tragic dramas, among them one on the subject of Daniel and Susannah—a literary curiosity that is not likely to have been presented in a Greek theater. Philostratus, an Athenian rhetorician who lived in the time of Nero (not to be confused with his famous grandson who lived under Septimius Severus), wrote forty-three tragedies. Scopelianus, who was teaching rhetoric at Smyrna in the time of Domitian, and Oenomaus the Cynic, who lived in the time of Hadrian, also wrote numerous philosophical tragedies in Greek.[39] In a somewhat different category but worthy of mention in this connection is the work of an obscure Jewish poet of the second century B.C. His name was Ezekiel, and he wrote in Greek a Biblical drama titled *Exodus*, based on the Old Testament story of the deliverance from Egypt, with Moses, Saphira, and God (speaking from the bush) as its chief characters.[40] Like Nicolaus's *Daniel and Susannah* this work was obviously intended for reading rather than staging. That such works could be written on Biblical themes was all the more remarkable in view of the Jews' abhorrence of drama. Because of the association of Greek drama with comedy, which was hardly an appropriate vehicle for conveying religious truth, the Jews seem to have had the same contempt for the Greeks' theater that they had for their gymnasium.

If the Greeks had written philosophical or didactic dramas, so could the Romans. The numerous tragedies composed in Latin by thinkers, poets, and literary dilettanti were generally not intended for stage presentation. Upon learning that his *Medea* was being produced on the stage, the lyrical poet Ovid objected that he had not written for the theater: "You tell me that my poetry is being performed to full houses and winning much applause," he dryly protested. "As far as I am concerned, I never wrote with the theater in mind, as you very well know, and my Muse was always indifferent to applause."[41] This kind of narrated or recited tragedy, usually called "closet-drama," would have remained practically unknown to us but for the strange preservation of nine usually complete works attributed to Seneca. This is the younger Seneca, Lucius Annaeus Seneca (4 B.C.–A.D. 65), son of the famous rhetorician, born in Spain during the reign of Caesar Augustus, brought to Rome at an early age, Stoic philosopher and tutor of young Nero who, when emperor and para-

38. *Tragic Drama*, pp. 426–28, 447.

39. Ibid.

40. See Adolphus W. Ward, *A History of English Dramatic Literature on the Death of Queen Anne*, p. 3.

41. *Tristia* 5.7.27.

noiac, had him commit suicide. His tragedies, based on mythological motifs, follow themes treated in extant tragedies of Aeschylus, Sophocles, and Euripides. The only exception is the *Thyestes*, although Greek tragedies now lost are known to have been written by other authors under that designation.

During the Renaissance, Seneca's tragedies were regarded as the ultimate models of dramatic perfection, surpassing by far the works of the Attic masters. Recent scholarship has generally been less kind to Seneca. He is often portrayed as a verbose pedant, using tragedy to display clever epigrams or to describe gory scenes of sadistic violence. A typically depreciative opinion of his tragedies is this one: "They are beyond all description bombastic and frigid, utterly devoid in character and action, full of the most revolting violations of propriety, and so barren of all theatrical effect that they were probably never intended to leave the schools of the rhetoricians for the stage. . . . All is sacrificed for phrase, even the expressions of the simplest thoughts being forced and stilted. Every common-place of tragedy is pressed into service, and an utter poverty of mind is tricked out with a semblance of wit and acuteness. . . . Their persons are neither ideal nor real, but misshapen giants and puppets, and the wire that sets them a-going is at one time an unnatural heroism, at another a passion alike unnatural, which no atrocity of guilt can appall."[42] Such vehemence is mostly unjustified when Seneca's work is evaluated in relation to contemporary dramatic aspirations and practices. As George E. Duckworth stated, Seneca "was the product of the age in which he lived, and description and declamation were characteristic of the literature of the period."[43]

An essay in literary criticism on Seneca's tragedies would be out of place in this study. Mention should be made, however, of the controversy concerning their purpose. Classicists agree almost unanimously that they were closet-dramas, intended to be read privately or recited to small gatherings, and that they could not have been presented to theater audiences.[44] Duckworth seems to have settled for a compromise, saying that whether or not the plays were actually presented on stage, Seneca's tragedies were so written as to make stage presentation possible.[45] There is no historical evidence, however, indicating that they ever were performed as theater plays. Duckworth's judgment may apply to a few of Seneca's tragedies, but it does not apply to the majority, due to Seneca's habit of including all events, however fantastic, blood-curdling, and unstageable, in his plots. T. S. Eliot compared Seneca's plays to the modern "broadcast drama": "If, as I confidently believe, they are intended for recitation—

42. Bates, *Greek and Roman Drama*, pp. 132–33.

43. *The Complete Roman Drama*, 1:xli.

44. For example: Rose, *A Handbook of Latin Literature*, p. 371; Moses Hadas, *A History of Latin Literature*, p. 248; Harsh, *Classical Drama*, p. 404; Duff, *A Literary History of Rome*, p. 201; and E. F. Watling, in Seneca, *Four Tragedies and "Octavia,"* trans. E. F. Watling, p. 19.

45. *The Complete Roman Drama*, 1:xxxviii.

they are better recited than read. And I have no doubt—though there is no external evidence—that Seneca must have had considerable practice himself in reciting the plays."[46]

If Seneca did not write his tragedies primarily for stage presentation, his motive remains to be defined. Harsh presented the interesting theory that Seneca, like other ancient literati, intended his plays as a medium for political criticism. He noted that at a time when the tyrannies of the emperors made open criticism of political affairs dangerous, all genres of literature were used for covert criticism. He cited the case of a certain Cremutius Cordus who wrote a history in order, perhaps, to praise Brutus and to call Cassius "the last of the Romans"; Cordus was forced to commit suicide. Another contemporary of Seneca, Curiatus Maternus, wrote tragedies with a political purpose and sometimes on Roman historical figures. These were publicly read by the author and were apparently not intended for production in the theater. One of the men under whom Seneca in his youth mastered rhetoric, Mamercus Aemilus Scaurus, is said to have incurred the wrath of the emperor Tiberius with a tragedy titled *Atreus*, in which a commonplace from Euripides was included: "One must bear the follies of his rulers." Harsh claimed that every play of Seneca contains similar lines. He stated, ". . . it is not inconceivable that Seneca, though no extremist, should write a whole play for one well-placed line of this type."[47] This theory, according to which Seneca, the contemporary of the author of the second Gospel, wrote narrative tragedies because of their applicability to the current situation, raises intriguing points of comparison with the Gospel of Mark.

Another interesting theory is propounded by Moses Hadas: Seneca had, in writing his tragedies, a catechetical purpose. He devised his tragedies as a means of propagating his Stoic doctrine. Hadas considered it significant that the best manuscripts contain the tragedies in the same specific order. The complete sequence is an attempt to present a systematic course, each play in its proper place illustrating some Stoic principle. "According to this system, the plays on Hercules (a Stoic hero) are the framework; *Troades* and *Phoenissae* center upon the problems of life, death and destiny; *Medea* and *Phaedra* provide exemplars for a treatise on the passions; and *Agamemnon*, *Oedipus* and *Thyestes* deal with free will, sin and retribution."[48]

And if this hypothesis causes Seneca's intention to appear unduly evangelistic, another author, Harsh, drew attention to even closer similarities between the last play of the series, the *Hercules on Oeta*, and the Gospel. In this drama Hercules, a divine hero who has fulfilled his earthly mission, is to ascend to heaven. However, he becomes the victim of intrigues prompted by jealousy that lead to his death. But he overcomes death in a sort of resurrection and final apotheosis. The structure of the

---

46. In "Introduction," Seneca, *Seneca: His Tenne Tragedies*, ed. and trans. Thomas Newton, 1:xi.

47. *Classical Drama*, pp. 406–7.

48. Hadas, *Latin Literature*, p. 249.

play is rendered implausible by the interminable repetition of lengthy, introspective, Stoic jeremiads. But Harsh affirmed that its moral spirit "looks to the Christian future rather than to the Greek past. The triumph of this laboring Stoic over suffering and death, the feeling that the world should end with his destruction, and his epiphany to his mother—all this breathes a mystical allegory not unlike that of the story of Seneca's contemporary, Jesus of Nazareth."[49] It may well be that if, of all Latin tragedies, only Seneca's collection has survived, it did so because it was preserved and transmitted by later Christians who took his expressions of mysticism and Stoic morality at face value and were ignorant of the corresponding inconsistencies in his manner of living.[50]

The document that comes the closest to providing a precedent of a story cast in dramatic form and based on contemporary events is the anonymous *Octavia*. We probably owe the survival of this tragedy to its inclusion with Seneca's collection. It bears similarity to Seneca's style and methods, but specific references to events posterior to Seneca's death in 65, in particular Nero's death in 68, invalidate the theory of Senecan authorship. The original idea of such a play may have come from Seneca, and he might have had a hand in the early stages of the manuscript's preparation. But the play was at least completed by someone else, a person presumably well acquainted with Seneca's work.

The *Octavia* is the only surviving sample of a Latin historical drama. Since such plays had been written by Greek and Roman authors, the concept of a *fabula praetexta* was as widespread in Seneca's time as the knowledge of tragedy itself. What characterizes this one is the vehemence and zeal with which the author attempts to convince the reader of the monstrous character and deeds of the play's anti-hero. It is a vindictive denunciation of Nero and of the system that enabled him to assume power and to commit brazenly and with impunity atrocious crimes. At the same time it constitutes an amazingly accurate chronicle of well-known historical events that occurred during the author's lifetime and culminated in 62 with Nero's divorce from Octavia and his marriage to his mistress Poppaea.

The action of the play takes place in Rome and spans a two-day period. Nero dispatches his wife Octavia to exile and death in order to replace her with Poppaea. Octavia's life is shown to have been haunted by misfortune at the hand of the malevolent Nero: her mother, the third wife of Claudius, was put to death by him; her father Claudius was in turn killed by his fourth wife, Aggripina, the mother of Nero; her brother, the rightful heir to the throne, was killed by Nero. In order to proceed with his divorce, Nero had his own mother Aggripina killed. But she returns to him in the form of a ghost to pronounce doom on Nero and his new wife. In the course of the play, Seneca, the former mentor of the emperor, appears to advise moderation, but in vain.

49. *Classical Drama*, p. 432.

50. Tertullian and other church fathers held Seneca and his writings in high regard. See Rose, *Latin Literature*, p. 375.

Assessments of its dramatic quality are generally negative. It is said that its effectiveness as drama suffers from its adhering too close to historical fact. The tentative explanation of Harsh is significant: "Perhaps it was the tradition in Roman historical plays to adhere very strictly to the known facts, especially since such plays had often been written on contemporary events."[51] For the purposes of the present study, it is only necessary to note the existence in Mark's time of a form of literature devoted to the narration of contemporary events in dramatic form and designed to convey a message. Furthermore, as with the case in hand, concern for dramatic propriety was subordinated to accuracy in transmitting the story.

The foregoing is not to be interpreted as an attempt to establish a relationship between Mark and Seneca. By no means is it implied that Mark was acquainted with Seneca's tragedies or with the *Octavia*. On the other hand, it would be interesting to conjecture to what extent the common man in Neronian Rome was familiar with the political figures of the Empire, what were the chances of his being touched by their direct influence, and whether the literate Roman had access to their written works. All that needs to be said now in summary of the findings of this chapter is that in Mark's time, tragedies in the classical style were still being written in both Greek and Latin, in the city of Rome as well as in other parts of the Graeco-Roman world. [52] Likewise, tragedies—old and new, Greek and Latin—were performed on the stage in Rome and elsewhere. Moreover, a long-standing tradition was revived in Mark's day of tragedies composed in the classical form, but for reading rather than staging. Of such narrative-tragedies, ten that were probably written during the same decade as Mark's Gospel have been preserved, one of which is a historical drama recounting events that had taken place during the author's lifetime.

IV

Whether Mark was familiar with any of the various forms of tragic drama current in his day depends on the kind of individual he was. The style and language of the Gospel indicate neither an erudite scholar nor a semiliterate rustic. If our author was a Jewish Christian of Palestinian background living in Rome, he at least benefited from broad cosmopolitan cultural and religious exposure. Although the Greeks and later the Romans had built several theaters in Palestine, native Jews were rarely devotees of such institutions. But as C. F. D. Moule pointed out, the average Jew was probably better educated than the average Gentile because of the quality of Jewish life and the conscientiousness of synagogue teachers.[53] And if

51. *Classical Drama*, p. 434. See also Hadas, *Latin Literature*, p. 252.

52. On Quintilian's (A.D. 35—99) evaluation of tragedies written in his own time, see Haigh, *Tragic Drama*, p. 444; and Sellar, *Roman Poets*, p. 131.

53. "It seems fair to assume that, broadly speaking, the average Jew was better educated than the average Gentile, if only because Jewish family life

Jews guarded themselves from deliberate exposure to expressions of a culture that they considered barbaric and idolatrous, they nevertheless were subject to its influence because of the exigencies of life in a pluralistic society. Saul Lieberman asserted that "the Greek language was known to the Jewish masses; certain formulae of Graeco-Roman law were popular among them in the original language; the current motifs of Hellenistic literature may have infiltrated into them, but real Greek culture was probably scarce in Jewish Palestine."[54]

To Diaspora Jews this Greek culture was not only readily available but, most of the time, unavoidable. Whether Mark was a Roman Jew originally from Palestine or a native Diaspora Jew, in all probability his cultural horizon encompassed knowledge of Greek tragedy. In addition to education in homes under private tutors, state-supported communal institutions of primary and secondary education existed throughout the Hellenistic world. They appeared wherever Hellenism took root. They also spread, mostly as bilingual institutions, through the Roman Empire. For instance it is reported that a sophisticated system of secondary education for girls flourished in Asia Minor during the first century B.C. This education was essentially classical; that is, it was concerned not so much with developing logical faculties or imparting technical skills as with transmitting the culture's heritage of great masterpieces.[55] The secondary-school curriculum was dominated by the study of literature. It concentrated on what were considered the four pillars of classical literature: Homer's works, especially the *Iliad*; the tragedies of Aeschylus, Sophocles, and especially Euripides; the plays of the comic poet Menander; and the orations of Demosthenes. Under the guidance of their teachers, students read, analyzed, and memorized these works to recite them competitively at public festivals. Thus, knowledge of the classical masterpieces was broadly disseminated in the first century through the educational process. The fact that the works of Homer, Euripides, and ancient authors were generally known to the common man has been confirmed in the discovery of vast quantities of Greek papyri. Donald W. Riddle stated that sufficient knowledge of the classics "was available in common report. It is no more necessary to suppose that the author of Mark attended Greek plays than to believe that Paul's references to the theater, the gymnasium, and the stadium, imply that he familiarly used these institutions. The writer of Mark had such acquaintance with the Greek drama as was the common posses-

---

was the soundest in the Empire, and also the education which Jewish children received in the synagogue school was, within its limits, probably more conscientious and thorough than the teaching given by Gentile schoolmasters who had not necessarily the intensity of vocation belonging to a devout teacher of the Torah." Moule, *The Birth of the New Testament*, p. 157.

54. *Greek in Jewish Palestine*, p. 2.

55. For a full development of the insights in this paragraph, see H. I. Marrou, *A History of Education in Antiquity*. Marrou defined *classical culture* as "a unified collection of great masterpieces existing as the recognized basis of its scale of values." P. 161.

sion of anyone who was intelligently responsive to the values of Hellenistic civilization."[56] The probability of Mark being familiar with one of the dominant literary forms of the culture in whose language he composed his own work cannot be lightly dismissed.

56. *The Gospels: Their Origin and Growth*, p. 144.

Chapter 3

The Plot:
Complication and Crisis

In comparing the formal features of Greek tragedy with the Gospel of Mark, one specific approach commends itself because of its clarity and aptitude. It is found in Aristotle's celebrated analysis in his *Poetics* ("On the Art of Poetry") of the six essential components of tragedy, which he described in order of importance: plot, character, message, diction, melody, and spectacle.[1] This chapter and the next are devoted to an examination of the first element, the plot. The remaining elements and other dramatic features of tragedy will be surveyed as they apply to the Gospel of Mark in chapter 5.

Aristotle's ascription to the plot of the most prominent role among the constituent parts of tragedy reflects accurately a salient feature of his dramatic theory. For him a play consists primarily of action. He considered the proper construction of the plot "at once the first and the most important thing in tragedy."[2] The etymology of the word *drama* accords with Aristotle's judgment since it can be roughly paraphrased as "something going on."[3] Thus conceived, a play is intended to present a story rather than character. The modern theater's fixation on dramas of character, which probably reflects modern man's loss of identity, may impede full appreciation of Aristotle's emphasis. When he stated that the plot is "the first essential, the life and soul, so to speak, of tragedy,"[4] he affirmed his belief that tragic art is more concerned with happenings than with subjective states of being. Identification with the protagonists of a play is achieved through enacting circumstances that could be anyone's fate rather than through displaying the inner torments of select individuals. His stress on the primacy of action rather than of characterization he developed further: "Tragedy is essentially an imitation not of persons but of action and life, of happiness and misery. All human happiness or misery takes the form of action; the end for which we live is a certain kind of activity, not a quality. Character gives us qualities, but it is in our actions—what we do—that we are happy or the reverse."[5] Therefore the recounting of deeds and events is of highest importance; character depiction follows

---

1. *On the Art of Poetry*, ed. and trans. Ingram Bywater, 6.38 (i.e., chap. 6, p. 38).

2. Ibid., 7.39.

3. H. D. F. Kitto, *Form and Meaning in Drama*, p. 103. See p. 112.

4. *On the Art of Poetry* 6.38.

5. Ibid., 6.37.

ipso facto. In this sense fate becomes the instrument of the action as a test of character, and heroes are at its mercy. They do not shape history; they are its victims. They are afflicted by the blows of destiny; they do not inflict blows upon it. Tragedies display heroes grappling with adversity; however, heroes do not themselves engineer catastrophes. And when their responsibility is involved, their actions generally stem from an insurmountable and predetermined bent or commitment (the hamartia). Thus, in the Aristotelian conception of tragedy, the plot constitutes the primary element. Everything else in the action is subordinated to the interests of what he described as "the proper organization of the incidents into a plot."

Aristotle's preference for plots of action did not result in total rejection of plots of passion, such as those fashioned by Euripides, in which the progress of the play lies in the development of the forces and emotions motivating the characters. But he believed that the ideal tragic plot should be conceived as a sequence of events in which changes are forced upon the hero by circumstances rather than induced by his passions. "In a play," he stated, "they do not act in order to portray the characters; they include the characters for the sake of the action. So that it is the action in it, i.e., its fable or plot, that is the end and purpose of the tragedy, and the end is everywhere the chief thing."[6]

The adoption of Aristotle's definition of tragedy as imitation of an action may appear as an attempt to impose a procrustean oversimplification upon all Greek tragedies, including those that do not readily fall into his neat categories.[7] But as the advice of a guide rather than the dictates of an infallible oracle, his dramatic scheme has the advantage of disclosing the source of dynamic development in tragic art, as conceived by the one literary critic who surveyed not only the tragedies extant today but also those which have not survived and whose number is greater. The fact that his stress on the importance of the plot generally conforms to tragedies typical of the genre, especially if the works of Sophocles can be regarded as models in structure and in harmony between content and form, corroborates his analysis. The pattern of the action in a tragedy required that there be first an exposition of the potentially tragic situation and of the significance of the hero. This is followed by a series of events precipitating a climax in the action, usually a recognition scene. The true nature or identity of the hero is dimly perceived in the play, although it has been clearly revealed to the spectator-reader. Subsequently the protagonists or the forces threatening the hero redouble their efforts to bring disaster. But while the situation changes for the worse, the determination of the hero remains unperturbed. Finally comes the great reversal or the

6. Ibid.

7. In an incisive article entitled "The Criticism of Greek Tragedy," William Arrowsmith claimed that neither traditional nor recent criticism has done justice to the complexity of Greek tragedy because it has failed to realize "turbulence: turbulence of experience, turbulence of morality in the process of being made, and the turbulence of ideas under dramatic test." (This article is partially reprinted in *"Oedipus Rex": A Mirror for Greek Drama*, ed. Albert Cook, pp. 155–69.)

resolution of the action when the forces set against the hero seem to crush him. But tragedy usually ends with the intimation that in spite of appearance, the hero and his cause have triumphed.

This conception of tragedy as an imitation of human beings in action or subjected to stress,[8] emphasizing the action rather than the dispositions of the characters, is not far from the Gospel as "gospel" or good news about a specific person and events related to His presence on the scene of history. Granted, the Gospel concerns essentially a person, Jesus Christ. But apart from sparse references to ephemeral shows of emotion by Jesus—such as compassion, sorrow, anger, and anguish—the Synoptics as well as the rest of the New Testament emphasize the events of Christ's ministry rather than the development of His own consciousness and character. They focus on the passion of Jesus rather than on His passions. They define the gospel as what Jesus did rather than how He felt. What they consider of first importance are deeds—how Christ died, was buried, and raised on the third day according to the Scriptures, and how He appeared to His disciples (I Cor. 15:3–5). Although prevalent in the New Testament, this concentration on action in reference to Jesus Christ is more characteristic of the Gospel of Mark than it is of the other Gospels. In the Pauline writings the deeds of Jesus are generally adduced in summary form for the sake of theological exposition and hortatory address. In the Book of Acts they constitute the framework of the apostles' preaching. But for Mark the action represents the substance of the gospel. The narrative is pared down to an unbroken sequence of breathless activity. The Son of God—Messiah appears among His people. In spite of an accumulation of evidences, He is not recognized but opposed by the very ones who should acclaim Him. As a few followers finally become dimly aware of His identity, His enemies close in on Him. He accepts His execution as the climax of His messianic mission, which is vindicated in extremis by the deus ex machina of the resurrection. The christological argument is cast in the form of an incontrovertible reenactment of the events. The dramatic potential of the story could have hardly escaped the notice of an author in search of an effective method of presentation, even if his knowledge of the plot in Greek tragedy was that of only a layman rather than a professional writer.

Regarding the general course of the action, Aristotle stated that "every tragedy is in part complication and in part denouement."[9] All the events constituting the complication need not be included in the play itself. Some may have taken place prior to the beginning of the tragedy.

8. On Aristotle's definition of tragedy as an imitation of an action, Frank L. Lucas exclaimed: "Few sentences in literature have contained a fiercer hornet's nest of controversies. . . . The sentence disappears beneath a crowd of struggling aestheticians; for how far, and in what sense, should Art 'imitate' life?" *Tragedy: Serious Drama in Relation to Aristotle's "Poetics,"* p. 27. See also Erich Auerbach, *Mimesis.*

9. *On the Art of Poetry* 18.63. Gerald F. Else translated δέσις, "the tying of the knot," and λύσις, "the untying." See *The Origin and Early Form of Greek Tragedy,* p. 517.

"The incidents before the opening scene" and leading to it, are also considered part of the complication.[10] The opening scene, called "the prologue," is usually an exposition of what has taken place before the beginning of the play. Then the complication gathers momentum and rises to a crescendo until the breaking point, a crisis that precipitates a change in the course of the play toward its denouement. "By complication I mean," said Aristotle, "all from the beginning of the story to the point just before the change in the hero's fortunes." Then follows the denouement, which consists of everything "from the beginning of the change to the end."[11]

Thus Aristotle distinguished three movements in the development of a tragedy: the complication, the change, and the denouement. The pivotal event that provides the hinge between complication and denouement is sometimes called "the climax" or "the crisis" by classicists. This event often takes the form of a recognition scene, the discovery of an identity previously concealed. Gerald F. Else described this pattern as a "shift in movement from one direction to the opposite, beginning at a definite moment."[12] This definite moment is the change, the turning point of the action from complication to denouement.

To illustrate this pattern, Aristotle cited the *Lynceus* of Theodoctes, in which "the complication includes, together with the presupposed incidents, the seizure of the child and that in turn of the parents; and the denouement all from the indictment for the murder to the end."[13] Unfortunately the text of the play to which he referred is badly damaged, and attempted restorations have been only conjectural. But the story seems to be that of a father accused by his wicked and irascible father-in-law of murdering his own child. While the father is led to the gallows, the child appears and is identified. The subterfuge of the father-in-law is exposed, and he is hanged in place of the child's father.

The complication-crisis-denouement pattern advocated by Aristotle is also recognizable in such extant tragedies as *Oedipus the King* by Sophocles and the *Iphigenia in Tauris* by Euripides. In the former, the Greek city of Thebes is afflicted with pestilence. Its young King Oedipus learns that the pollution is due to the presence within the city's walls of the murderer of Laius, the former king, and Oedipus relentlessly presses the search for the guilty person, in spite of a series of disclosures pointing each time with more precision to himself as the murderer. In a climactic recognition scene, an old shepherd identifies him not as the prince of Corinthian birth he thought himself to be but as the son of Laius whom he has killed, unaware of his identity, and the husband of his own mother. Thus has been fulfilled the prophecy of the oracle of Delphi. The denouement follows as his mother-wife commits suicide and Oedipus puts out his

10. *On the Art of Poetry* 18.63.

11. Ibid.

12. *Greek Tragedy*, p. 522.

13. *On the Art of Poetry* 18.63.

own eyes in despair, asking to be led away from the city so that it can be free from the curse.

In this play, part of the complication precedes the beginning of the action: the ravages of the scourge, the killing of a father by his son, and the son's marriage to his own mother. The complication progresses as evidence accumulates that Oedipus is the unwitting criminal. He precipitates the crisis himself by forcing the shepherd, under threat of torture, to disclose the circumstances of his rescue from exposure as a child and his subsequent adoption by the king of Corinth. From then on, the plot resolves itself as the mother-wife queen dies and blind Oedipus leaves the city, thus removing the curse. It should be noted that one of Seneca's nine closet-dramas is an *Oedipus* inspired by Sophocles' tragedy. The Latin adaptation places great emphasis on the vicarious aspect of Oedipus's suffering; the Thebans are spared because the guilt for the pollution is placed upon Oedipus, who, having sinned unknowingly, is innocent.

The *Iphigenia in Tauris* is the story of a Greek maiden of noble birth who has been forcibly taken away by the Taurians (in Crimea). She serves there as a priestess in the temple of Artemis, whom the savage natives worship by sacrificing to her all strangers arriving on their shores. Iphigenia has a brother, Orestes, who is unknown to her. Orestes and his friend arrive in Tauris, commissioned by the god Apollo to steal the image of Artemis out of the temple. They are captured, and Iphigenia is charged to immolate them. This is the complication of the plot. Then comes the crisis. In an ingeniously contrived recognition scene commended elsewhere by Aristotle,[14] Iphigenia identifies the one she is about to slay as her brother. The denouement follows. The three friends decide on a plan by which they reach the ship with the statue of Artemis. However, contrary winds drive them back to the coast. They are almost recaptured by the Taurians when suddenly the goddess Athena appears ex machina, stops the pursuit, and orders the Greek fugitives to be sent home on their ship.

In this tragedy Orestes—the real hero in spite of the title—has been entrusted by the gods with a mission that becomes gravely imperiled. The recognition scene reverses the situation and renders fulfillment of the mission possible. The complication-crisis-denouement pattern is discernible. This is the structural formula preferred and recommended by Aristotle for developing the action. Tragedies built on this pattern were extant in greater number in Mark's time than they are today. Whether performed, recited, or read, they were certainly accessible to scholar and profane alike. The cogent simplicity of their pattern must have been obvious to an inquisitive mind, however unlearned in formal letters.

The action in the Gospel of Mark follows a course identical to the one recommended by Aristotle for Greek tragedies. In the language proper to dramatic composition, it can be said that the first half of the Gospel constitutes the complication, the recognition at Caesarea Philippi is the crisis, and the remainder of the Gospel is the denouement. The progress of the action in the Gospel will now be surveyed according to this threefold outline.

14. Ibid., 11.48.

I

The opening sentence of the Gospel is charged with momentous suspense. It evokes the unfolding of awesome and compelling supernatural happenings. When cast in its first-century context, the depth and richness of this deceptively simple statement is still being discovered. Thus the word "beginning" means infinitely more than the first line of a book, or the start of a presentation, or the rising of the curtain. For readers familiar with the Old Testament, the ἀρχή may have been, much like the opening words of the fourth Gospel, an allusion to the Genesis beginning, the dawn of creation prefiguring this new beginning, the day of redemption. For Hellenistic minds, the word connoted an inauguration proclamation of universal significance. Although the word εὐαγγέλιον was eventually taken to designate the Gospel document itself, it was also fraught with messianic and eschatological connotations in Jewish usage, and with panegyrical significance in imperial tradition. The titles of "Christ" and "Son of God," in the richness of their Judaic and Graeco-Roman backgrounds, exalt Jesus at once as a figure of superhuman stature. Whatever solutions may be suggested to the minutiae of the textual and philological problems contained in this introductory sentence, its intended purpose can hardly be disputed. On one hand, the sentence has the ring of a proclamation and a universal summons. It is an invitation to witness a drama of cosmic significance. On the other, the sentence is a secret revelation. From the outset of the story, the reader is taken into the author's confidence. He receives privileged knowledge for which the contemporaries of Jesus are described in the Gospel as groping in vain, until the last page when the resurrection illuminates all things. The sentence provides, for the reader only, the answer to the riddle that constitutes the mainspring of the action: the revelation of the secret, supernatural identity of Jesus ("Son of God") and the accomplishment of his mysterious, messianic mission ("Christ").

If the start of the Gospel's action can be considered to coincide with that of the public ministry of Jesus, the plot does not begin unfolding until the middle of verse 14, where Jesus comes into Galilee, preaching the gospel of God. The first fourteen verses of the Gospel, fittingly called "prologue" by a number of commentators, introduce its action. In this introduction the author sets the tone for the whole Gospel with a few masterful strokes. By alternating elements of supernatural and theophanic manifestation accompanying the appearance of Jesus with antithetical signs of His humanity and contingency, Mark created tension from which there is no relief until the very end of the Gospel.

The theme of the supernatural identity of Jesus, announced in the first sentence, is further reinforced by the introduction of John the Baptist. According to Mark the ministry of John had been predicted by the ancient prophets,[15] while John in turn predicts the imminent ("after me comes") appearance of the ultimate fulfiller. Thus Mark showed that a

15. Mark combined Malachi 3:1 with Isaiah 40:3 and ascribed both to Isaiah, using *Isaiah* antonomastically as a synecdoche since Isaiah was regarded, even outside Judaism, as the archetypal Jewish prophet. Both

prophetic chain of prediction and preparation, therefore of supernatural activity, links the ministry of Jesus to the Old Testament through John the Baptist.

John is also presented as a genuine prophet living in the wilderness, nourishing and dressing himself in the same austere manner as the most prestigious of the prophets of old. The genuineness of his divine calling is also demonstrated by the effectiveness of his ministry; *all* the people of Judea and *all* the people of Jerusalem seek from him symbolic purification of their sins by baptism.[16]

And yet, almost abjectly, John declares himself inferior and subservient to the one who will fulfill the καιρός by releasing the fullness of (baptizing with) the Spirit of God, the element of the end-time signifying the immediate presence of God. With this description of John and his ministry, the stage is set for the grandiose appearance of his successor. But having thus created a mood of dramatic expectancy, Mark described the entrance of Jesus in the most shockingly anticlimactic fashion conceivable: "In those days Jesus came from Nazareth of Galilee and was baptized by John in the Jordan." The unadorned abruptness of the sentence, the vagueness of the chronological indication, the absence of any title for Jesus, the full disclosure of His rural background, and His baffling and unexplained subjection to the baptism for confession of sins, cannot be fortuitous.[17] They are intended to rob the entrance of the Son of God upon the scene of history, of the majesty and grandeur befitting the inauguration of the Jewish Messiah, or of the Θεῖος ἀνήρ, the "divine man" of Hellenistic religions. Mark's obvious intention is to warn against false expectations regarding spectacular manifestations of Jesus' messianic identity.

The disappointment caused by the casual and unprepossessing appearance of Jesus, and especially the scandal of His baptism, are partly relieved by a positive reversal in the form of a theophany; the baptism becomes the occasion for transcendence to break upon Jesus and confirm His supernatural uniqueness. Although the revelation is clear to the reader, there is no evidence that John and his entourage are aware of it. Jesus is the one who sees the heavens open and the Spirit descend as a dove. The heavenly voice addresses Him in the second person. In contrast

---

Old Testament texts pertain to the practice of sending heralds to prepare the king's highway prior to a royal voyage.

16. The double emphasis and the specification of Jerusalem apart from Judea may have been intended as an indication of the approval of John's ministry by the Judaic establishment. In Mark, Jerusalem stands for the stronghold of official Judaism. Mention of the city is avoided in the first half of the Gospel except in connection with people coming to Jesus from Jerusalem (3:8), including the sinister emissaries of His remote enemies (3:22 and 7:1). Whereas Jerusalem is mentioned three times during the first part of Jesus' ministry, it is referred to seven times in the second part, each mention being made in connection with Jesus and His disciples intending to go to, going to, and entering the city for the passion.

17. "Nazareth of Galilee" (1:9) stands in sharp contrast with the fashionable "Judea" and "Jerusalem" of verse 5.

to Matthew and Luke, Mark described the experience from a christocentric perspective. The reader, with Jesus, knows what took place, but His contemporaries were presumably left in the dark.[18]

Thus identified and empowered, Jesus will surely manifest Himself gloriously to the multitudes. Again a negative reversal occurs. The Spirit drives Him not into the great metropolis, as would be expected, but "out into the wilderness"; not into a triumphant venture, but into one that places Him at the mercy of Satan and among wild beasts during the traditionally inauspicious period of forty days. Once more a positive reversal releases the tension as a supernatural intervention takes place in the form of angels who appear to serve Him, thus confirming anew heaven's recognition of Jesus' uniqueness. But as Mark was about to move into the main part of the Gospel, he concluded his kaleidoscopic prologue on an ominous note, informing the reader that John was arrested, and that after his arrest Jesus began preaching precisely as John had been preaching prior to his imprisonment.

This paradoxical alternation between evidences of transcendence and reminders of the tyranny of the contingent sets the tone for the first eight chapters of the Gospel. The oscillation between signs of the divine identity of Jesus and instances of subjection to earthly conditions—as illustrated by the impressive forecast of His arrival followed by His unobtrusive appearance, the divine recognition at baptism followed by the harrowing sojourn in the desert—leads to the very core of the complication of the action. In the first few verses of the Gospel, Mark had already adduced massive evidence to establish the supernatural identity of Jesus that is announced in the Gospel's first line. The prophets of ancient Israel predicted the arrival of "the Lord" (1:3); the Baptist presents Him to the multitudes as the fulfiller of history (1:8); the heavens open and the Holy Spirit descends upon Him in physical form (1:10); the divine voice thunders approval (1:11); Satan attacks Him in the desert but angels come to His rescue (1:13); and demons will cringe in terror before Him (1:24). The voice of God, the Holy Spirit, Satan, angels, demons—all supernatural beings or their manifestations—recognize Jesus as belonging to their world. Obviously the Messiah is now among His people. Will the people recognize and accept Him, or will they be blinded by their own conceptions of Messiah and reject Him? If they reject Him, will He be able to accomplish that mysterious messianic task that sets Him at odds with His contemporaries?

Mark answered the first question in the complication phase of the Gospel (1:1–8:26). The complication results from the exposure of Jesus' transcendence through His words, deeds, and destiny to those around Him who do not perceive His otherworldly nature. He is made seemingly vulnerable to constant contingencies created by the misunderstanding and opposition He unintentionally elicits from those surrounding Him. Mark

18. The duality seems to be maintained in the very content of the message from heaven. The first part is a triumphant affirmation drawn from the militantly messianic Psalm 2. The second comes from the introduction to the suffering-servant passage in Isaiah 42.

answered the second question in the denouement phase (8:31–16:8), in which Jesus accepts the consequences of the complication in order to fulfill the peculiar demands of His redemptive mission, which, in contrast to popular, triumphalist messianic expectations, requires vicarious suffering as a means to victory.[19]

The pattern of complication receives full development early in the Gospel as Jesus begins to move, work, and teach among people left mystified by His obvious uniqueness and yet unable to draw appropriate conclusions.

On a few occasions, the secret identity of Jesus is recognized at first sight and noisily proclaimed, but more out of fear than out of reverence. The *demons*, those tenacious emissaries of their prince, Beelzebub (3:22), are no match for Him who overcame forty days' temptation in Satan's very domain. Lesser supernatural beings themselves, they recoil in panic in the presence of Him whose power is greater than theirs. On the first visit of Jesus to a synagogue with His early disciples, an unclean spirit exclaims, ". . . Jesus of Nazareth. . . . I know who you are, the Holy One of God." Perceiving correctly the full extent of Jesus' mission as the destruction of Satan's power, the spirit asks, "Have you come to destroy us?" Jesus grants him the experience of a positive answer by promptly dispatching him (1:23–26). On that very day, "at sundown," Jesus heals the sick and casts out many demons who know Him (1:34). In fact, whenever unclean spirits behold Him, they fall down before Him and cry out, "You are the Son of God" (3:11). These spiritual beings possess a distant acquaintanceship with Jesus, as it were, from a former existence in a different world, much as obscure slaves know the names and titles of the members of a royal family inimical to their own master. Legion, the spirit that dwelt in the Gerasene demoniac, "saw Jesus from afar" and "ran and worshiped him," calling Him "Jesus, Son of the Most High God," and adjuring Him by God not to torment him (5:7). But this spontaneous recognition from demons angered Jesus, and in every case, after imposing silence, He cast them out. Jesus obviously did not appreciate being proclaimed Son of God by the evil spirits. His open display of power over them, however, should have suggested to onlookers the presence of God's agent in their midst. But the evangelist aptly described the anguishing progress of the complica-

19. This thematic division of the Gospel is adopted by T. A. Burkhill: "The evangelist's treatment of his subject—essentially a religious one, the Messiahship of Jesus, the content of the apostolic gospel—resolves itself into the exposition of two central themes, namely, the secret fact of the messianic status of Jesus and the mysterious meaning of that fact. Broadly, the first of these two themes dominates the earlier part of the gospel and the second dominates the later part. For, prior to his account of Peter's confession, the evangelist is mainly concerned to represent the words and deeds of Jesus as esoteric manifestations of the secret fact of the Messiahship; and, after his account of the confession, the evangelist is mainly concerned to show how the fact of the Messiahship mysteriously meant that Jesus had to endure the shame of the crucifixion in the fulfillment of his redemptive mission in the world." *Mysterious Revelation*, p. 5.

tion. The people are capable only of dumb amazement as they question among themselves but fail to draw appropriate conclusions: "What is this? A new teaching! With authority he commands even the unclean spirits, and they obey him" (1:27). The delegation of scribes from Jerusalem ascribes His power over demons to His being in league with Satan. Jesus retorts that Satan is unlikely to destroy himself, but that it takes one stronger than Satan to decimate his cohorts (3:22–27). The complication reaches a frightful point when Jesus pronounces a sentence of unforgivable blasphemy upon the spiritual leaders of the people, "for they had said, 'He has an unclean spirit' " (3:30). As for the compatriots of the exorcised Gerasene, "they were afraid. . . . And they began to beg Jesus to depart from their neighborhood" (5:15–17).

In regard to the demonic world, the paradox of unrecognized transcendence is dramatized by the fact that the very presence of Jesus threatens the forces of evil. Terrified demons openly acknowledge His ascendancy over them. In the sight of all, Jesus displays absolute mastery over them. The spirit world attributes to Jesus the supreme titles of divine sonship. And yet the crowds never go past gaping stupor; the leaders reject the evidence and declare open opposition; and others, uncomprehending and therefore fearful, insist politely but firmly that Jesus leave their premises.

If demons, the archenemies of God, recognize the secret identity of Jesus, one would expect His *relatives and close friends*, who of all humans know Him best, to rally to Him and promote His cause. But the element of complication enters also in this dimension of Jesus' relationships, so that, early in the Gospel, Jesus is challenged and rejected by His own family. As Jesus returns home from His initial preaching and healing tour, such a large crowd is attracted that He and His disciples cannot even eat. When His friends hear of it, they purpose to seize Him, charging Him with insanity (3:19–21). After their attempt to restrain Him fails, His mother and brothers arrive on the scene. Disapprovingly staying outside of the house, they send word for Him to join them. But Jesus refuses, stating that there is a greater kinship between Himself and His followers than between Himself and His relatives, because His followers act according to God's will (3:31–35). Finally Jesus comes once more "to his own country." As He teaches in the synagogue of His childhood, His compatriots stand confounded and ask each other, "What is the wisdom given to him? What mighty works are wrought by his hands!" But they cannot answer appropriately their questions. They marvel at the wisdom and the mighty works. But they cannot rise to comprehend the spiritual meaning of the wisdom and the supernatural implications of the mighty works. Probably inspired by neighborly jealousy, they deny His higher claims by emphasizing His identity with themselves: "Where did this man get all this? . . . Is not this the carpenter, the son of Mary and brother of James and Joses and Judas and Simon, and are not his sisters here with us?"[20] The evangelist care-

20. Attention has often been called to the fact that the designation of a man by his mother's name was intended to cast aspersions on the legitimacy of his birth.

fully noted their rejection by observing that they were outraged on account of Him. Upon this, Jesus remarks that those who recognize a prophet are not the people "in his own country, and among his own kin, and in his own house." But even He wonders "because of their unbelief" (6:1–6). The finality of the break between Jesus and His relatives underscores once more the portentous ramifications of the complication of the Gospel's action.

In regard to the *disciples*, their individual selection by Jesus would seemingly guarantee their ability to rise to His expectations. At first their receptivity and cooperation justify all hopes. When Jesus calls them to His service, they respond without hesitancy, leaving behind nets, boats, fathers, hired servants, and tax office to follow Him (1:16–20; 2:14). Early in His ministry Jesus appointed them privately but formally to be with Him as a group of twelve, to preach and to cast out demons (3:13–19). Within the scope of these specifications, they perform satisfactorily. They remain constantly by Jesus' side, except when He sends them two by two on a preaching and healing mission that they fulfill to the letter (6:7–13). The twelve disciples are also assiduous students. After Jesus teaches the crowds with parables, He takes the disciples aside and privately explains everything (4:34), because to them has been given the secret of the kingdom of God (4:11).

It would therefore seem that conditions are ideal for perfect rapport between Jesus and His disciples. Here again, however, the evangelist described a near total obstruction in the disciples' comprehension of Jesus. In their case the complication derives from the fact that in spite of their privileged proximity to Jesus, they are blind to His supernatural identity. Mark carefully noted that on the very day when Jesus explains privately everything to His own disciples, they lose confidence and fear for their lives on the stormy sea. When Jesus asks them, "Why are you afraid? Have you no faith?", He unwittingly elicits an affirmative response as the awed but undiscerning disciples question each other, "Who then is this, that even wind and sea obey him?" No answer (4:35–41). The tragic complication lies in the fact that despite all they know about Jesus, even the disciples cannot draw the logical conclusions and recognize Him as a supernatural being.

When Peter, James, and John witness the raising of Jairus's daughter, they are "overcome with amazement" (5:42). When after feeding the five thousand Jesus approaches the disciples rowing on a threatening sea and enters the boat, the wind ceases. Mark described the disciples as being "utterly astounded," and he commented revealingly that they were astonished because "they did not understand about the loaves, but their hearts were hardened" (6:48–52). The implication of this editorial comment is that if the disciples had been normally perceptive, they would have understood the supernatural magnitude of Jesus' powers and would have accepted His control over the elements as a matter of fact.

Some time later the occasion presents itself for Jesus to test the disciples' understanding of the feeding of the multitude. Again a hungry crowd has gathered around Jesus. The previous time, the disciples had come to Jesus on their own initiative. This time, after three days, Jesus calls the disciples to Him and presents the situation to them without suggesting a solution. The disciples fall in the trap, so to speak. They fail the test. They see no way out. The previous feeding of the five thousand has not revealed to them the supernatural power of the Son of God. Their naive answer is, "How can one feed these men with bread here in the desert?" It does not occur to them that the miracle Jesus had performed previously in similar circumstances He could now repeat. They have not realized yet that He who is with them is greater than Moses and that He can indeed feed men with bread in the desert (8:1–9).

To dramatize fully this phase of the complication, Mark described Jesus grieving over the disciples' blindness to the nature of His messiahship. Jesus exploits a mention of bread to rebuke the disciples: "Do you not yet perceive or understand? Are your hearts hardened? Having eyes do you not see, and having ears do you not hear?" Jesus presses them to recognize a deeper truth regarding their relationship with Him. He brings to their minds some significant displays of divine power, stressing the supernatural dimension of these displays by the numbers involved: "Do you not remember? When I broke the five loaves for the five thousand, how many baskets full of broken pieces did you take up?"

"Twelve," comes the answer.

Jesus insists again, "And the seven for the four thousand, how many baskets full of broken pieces did you take up?"

"Seven," is their laconic answer.

Jesus repeats, "Do you not yet understand?"

No answer (8:14–21).

The blindness of the disciples certainly constitutes the most pathetic aspect of the complication in the plot of the Gospel. Let His relatives reject Him, let the religious leaders rage at Him, let the sensation-seeking crowd betray Him, but for the twelve disciples who share in the Messiah's ministry not to recognize His essential nature pertains to the very essence of tragedy.

The situation is not entirely without hope, however. Immediately after Jesus rebukes the disciples for their blindness, the evangelist described the healing of the blind man of Beth-saida, perhaps as an answer to His question, "Do you not yet understand?" Jesus is begged to touch the blind man. Instead He takes him by the hand, leads him outside the village (presumably to a private place), produces a personal, intimate contact with the blind eyes through His saliva, and lays His hands upon the man's eyes. The man receives his sight gradually, and after having looked intently, he sees everything clearly (8:22–26). Could a similar illumination be taking place within the disciples? The confession of Peter, which follows immediately, warrants an affirmative answer.

The relationship of Jesus with the *common people* seems to augur more favorably. In this first part of the Gospel, much of Jesus' ministry is devoted to them, and they respond in waves of intense fervor. Very swiftly they give Jesus a fame that spreads everywhere. Multitudes rush to Him from Galilee (1:28) and "also from Judea and Jerusalem and Idumea and from beyond the Jordan and from about Tyre and Sidon" (3:7–8). The ubiquitous crowd is always at the heels of Jesus, pursuing Him and even preceding Him wherever He goes. When He avoids the towns for fear of being recognized, the crowd rushes to Him in the country (1:45). When He retires on a mountain to a lonely place, everyone starts searching for Him (1:35–38). He leaves the countryside for the seashore, and the crowds run to the shore (3:7). Leaving the shore to seek privacy on the other side, He finds the crowd awaiting Him there (6:45, 54). In the first eight chapters there are about twenty descriptions of crowds thronging Jesus. Houses where He is present are beseiged by the population of whole cities (1:33; 2:2; 3:32; 7:24). Crowds gather about Him and almost crush Him (3:9; 5:24). He and the disciples are unable to eat because of the multitude (3:20; 6:31). The crowd, wishing to hear Him teach, becomes so dense that He has to speak from a boat offshore (2:13; 3:9; 4:1; 5:21). Twice the crowd is numbered: the first time there are five thousand men; the second time, four thousand people.

It would seem that this surge of popularity among the common people would compensate for the rejection of Jesus by His kinsfolk and the obtuseness of the disciples. Not so. Actually the populace possesses no more spiritual discernment than the others. They respond to the works and deeds of Jesus in wonderment rather than belief. They are "astonished" at His teaching (1:22), "amazed" when a demon is cast out. Missing the obvious deduction, they merely question among themselves: "What is this? A new teaching!" (1:27). When the former paralytic gathers his couch and walks away, they are "all amazed," they glorify God, and they say, "We never saw anything like this!" without ever discerning the deeper purpose of the healing—"that you may know that the Son of man has authority on earth to forgive sins" (2:10–12). Learning of the Gerasene's deliverance from Legion, "all men marveled" (5:20), and at the healing of the deaf mute in the Decapolis, "they were astonished beyond measure, saying, 'He has done all things well; he even makes the deaf hear and the dumb speak' " (7:37). But they never raise the question at issue: What is the real identity of Jesus? They follow Him and acclaim Him for His deeds without seeing in those deeds their supernatural, messianic character. Mark mentioned that Jesus, confronted with "a great throng," has compassion on them because they are "like sheep without a shepherd" (6:34). And yet they never recognize Him as the Shepherd. About Him some say, "John the baptizer has been raised from the dead; that is why these powers are at work in him." But others say, "It is Elijah." And others, "It is a prophet, like one of the prophets of old" (6:14–15; 8:28). They are willing to identify Him as John the Baptist, Elijah, or one of the prophets redivivus. But no one recognizes Him as the Son of God or as the Messiah. For the crowds as for the relatives and disciples of Jesus, divine transcendence is subject to the limitations of circumstances and of benighted spiritual perception. The superficial acclaim given Jesus only intensifies the drama of the unrecognized Messiah, and it contributes powerfully to the complication of the action.

The spiritual blindness of the relatives of Jesus, His disciples, and the crowds is frustrating but relatively harmless. Not so for the blindness of the *religious leaders* of the Jews, in particular the scribes and Pharisees. It stirs them to bitter antagonism and eventually to a decision to kill. Their opposition contributes the main element in the progress of the complication of the Gospel's action. As self-styled guardians of the spiritual welfare of the people, they should rally behind Jesus and promote His cause. Instead they challenge Him at every turn and, unable to confute Him, seek to destroy Him.

The scribes appear early in the story. As Jesus announces that the sins of the airborne paralytic are forgiven, the scribes are "sitting there," muttering something about blasphemy. They rightly question in their hearts, "Who can forgive sins but God alone?" By performing a sovereign act of healing, Jesus confirms before their eyes His dominion over evil and, therefore, His authority to forgive sins (2:1–12). The scribes and Pharisees regard themselves as the supreme authority in religious matters; they sit on Moses' seat and present themselves as the ultimate interpreters of the Law and the Prophets. But here is this carpenter from Galilee who has never gone to Jerusalem to be approved by the religious establishment. And yet He is gaining preeminence to the point of threatening their supremacy because He ministers in a way that, by their own admission, lies beyond their competence. In the first place, as the evangelist wrote—probably with a tinge of sarcasm—on the very first page of the Gospel, Jesus teaches as one who has authority and "not as the scribes" (1:22). He can also heal— in this case a man so paralyzed that he has to be carried by no less than four attendants—and this they cannot do. Because He can heal, He can also take upon Himself the authority to forgive sins—which they would never do since they consider it a divine prerogative.[21] With Jesus on the scene, they suddenly find themselves completely outclassed at the point of their unchallenged competence and superseded in their hitherto exclusive supremacy. Jesus ignores them by carefully staying away from Jerusalem, but they cannot afford to ignore Him. So they set themselves on His trail. Subsequent dealings between Jesus and them suggest a shadowy retinue of spies watching His every move intently and listening to every word in the hope of finding reason to discredit Him. On the other hand, Jesus draws them into the open to expose the shallowness of their religion and to denounce their evil motives. In authentic tragic fashion, the resulting conflict ultimately causes the entrenched leaders to obtain the execution of their own Messiah as a false pretender.

Following the initial clash at Capernaum, "the scribes of the Pharisees" catch Jesus at Levi's table. They turn to the disciples and charge Jesus with guilt by association: "Why does he eat with tax collectors and sinners?" Hearing the charge, Jesus identifies Himself as the physician available to those who recognize their need (2:15–17). The leaders can hardly make such a claim for themselves. Although they initiated the

21. Eduard Schweizer pointed out that Judaism has never expected the Messiah to forgive sins. *The Good News According to Mark*, p. 61.

attack, Jesus, instead of retreating into the defensive, vindicates Himself and exposes their inadequacy. So the Pharisees wait until a sabbath journey during which the disciples pluck ears of grain. Triumphantly they appear at Jesus' side and accuse the disciples: "Look, why are they doing what is not lawful on the sabbath?" In His answer Jesus not only accords Himself the same privileges as David, but He also explains His freedom in regard to the sabbath day by declaring the Son of man "lord even of the sabbath" (2:23-27).[22] Made by even the greatest of the Pharisees, such claims would sound extravagant. And yet, no protest is raised against Jesus for His appropriation of exceptional distinctions. Immediately following this incident, the evangelist reported a decisive confrontation in a synagogue. There stands a man with a withered hand. The Pharisees watch intently to see if Jesus will heal him on the sabbath "so that they might accuse him." Jesus, claiming the right "to do good" and "to save life" even on the sabbath, heals the man. But He looks "around at them with anger, grieved at their hardness of heart." The *sous-entendu* is aimed at the Pharisees, whose efforts to prevent the healing are described as "to do harm" and "to kill." Jesus' rebuke for their callousness and their inability once more to implicate Him are apparently more than the Pharisees can absorb. So they go out and immediately counsel with the Herodians concerning "how to destroy him" (3:1-6).[23]

Upon this, a delegation of scribes comes from Jerusalem, obviously to precipitate the demise of Jesus. They accuse Him publicly of sorcery. But Jesus, using simple logic, ridicules their sacrilegious attacks and charges them with blaspheming the Holy Spirit (3:22-27). Again, after having initiated the attack, the official religionists come out of the fray battered. The same delegation, regrouped with reinforcements from the Pharisees, takes Jesus to task for His disciples' laxity in regard to the tradition of the elders. Quoting from Isaiah, Jesus denounces them again as usurpers, putting in question the whole scribal institution and accusing them of rejecting God's law to follow human traditions (7:1-13).

The last confrontation in Galilee between Jesus and the religious leaders is again prompted by the latter (8:11-13). It differs from the previous encounters in that this time the scribes and Pharisees come not with an objection but with a proposal. They argue with Him in order to obtain from Him a spectacular sign that would confirm His messiahship. The manner of Jesus' refusal provides an eloquent commentary on their motives. He sighs deeply in His spirit and asks, "Why does this generation seek a sign?" The impatience of Jesus with the leaders points to their tireless cunning. Their request is calculated to force Jesus to recognize their authority and to make Himself subject to their approval. They are, in

22. When Jesus asserted publicly His power to heal, His authority to forgive sins (2:10), and His sovereignty over the sabbath (2:28), He used the cryptic designation "Son of man" in reference to Himself. The choice of the title was deemed felicitous because of its ambiguity. It did not readily lend itself to a triumphalist interpretation of the messianic role.

23. Thus Mark showed the alliance against Jesus of the otherwise bitterly antagonistic religious and political establishments.

fact, presenting themselves as an interview-committee authorized to evaluate the credentials of would-be messiahs. They are saying: "We are ready. Show us what you can do." They shrewdly anticipate that by performing a miracle at their bidding, Jesus would tacitly recognize their self-assumed right to validate His messiahship. On the other hand, a refusal from Him could be misrepresented as a denial of His own claims. They will either control Jesus or discredit Him. But Jesus, perceiving their guile, allows them to do neither. He exposes their dubious motives by asking for the reasons that prompted the request for a sign. Then He places the issue in historical perspective with a solemn prophetic utterance: "Truly, I say to you, no sign shall be given to this generation." The immediate confrontation between Himself and the Pharisees He interprets as symptomatic of the fallacious aspirations of the times. The issue is not the performance of another miracle by Jesus, but the performance of a miracle on command, as proof to the leaders of His messianic qualifications. By extending His refusal to their request, from them to their age as a whole ("this generation"), Jesus emphasizes the futility of their expectations. The kind of messiah they want will never come. They are determined to find a compliant superman who is endowed with heavenly powers and will fulfill their own earthly program. The messiah of their dreams would declare his candidacy for the imperial throne, challenge and defeat Caesar, and rule the world with Israel wielding supremacy over it. But God's program is to send a Messiah who will preach (1:38), forgive sins (2:10), call sinners (2:17), do good and save life (3:4), serve and give His own life as a ransom for many (10:45). This Messiah is present and active, fulfilling God's program in their midst, though He is unrecognized. *Their* messiah is an empty dream from which no sign will ever come forth. Having foiled the leaders' attempt to subjugate Him, Jesus abandons them to their discomfiture. Then, Mark dryly stated, ". . . he left them, and getting into the boat again he departed to the other side." Having proclaimed His independence from the Jewish establishment, He goes his own way. This departure dramatizes the break between Jesus and the ethnarchs and brings the complication of the action to its climax.

The theme of the unrecognized supernatural identity of the Messiah is prominent in the first part of the Gospel. But the development of the second motif of the Gospel, that of the fulfillment of the messianic mission, contributes also to the progress of the action in its complication phase. Although it remains in the background in the first part of the Gospel, this element receives sufficient attention there to prepare for its full treatment in the second part.

The theme of the fulfillment of the messianic task is dominated throughout the Gospel by the prospect of the passion and resurrection.[24]

24. Martin Kähler (in *The So-Called Historical Jesus and the Historical, Biblical Christ*) defined Mark as a passion story with an introduction, whereas Willi Marxsen (in *Introduction to the New Testament*) regarded it as written backwards from the passion story. Although seemingly contradictory as to Mark's methodology, these positions stress the fact that the theme of the passion pervades the whole Gospel.

Explicit predictions of the passion occur only after Peter's confession in the denouement part of the Gospel, but a number of clues in the first eight chapters indicate that humiliation and death constitute the distinctive reality of Jesus' messiahship.

Early in the story John, the herald of Jesus, is arrested (1:14). The absence at this point of any explanation for his arrest and the juxtaposed statement that Jesus then began to preach—which is essentially what John had been doing prior to his arrest—create, at the outset of the Gospel, an ominous conjuncture for the one about whom John had said, "After me comes he who is mightier than I."[25] If they thus seize the servant, what might they do to the master?

The question from the people regarding the fasting of the disciples of John and the disciples of the Pharisees is probably to be understood in the light of the incarceration of John. Like the Pharisees, the followers of John presumably practice ritual fasting. But after John's arrest their fasting may be taking the aspect of mourning because of the threat to the life of their leader. In His answer Jesus likens the time when He is present with His own disciples to a wedding celebration. But He predicts days of gloom and therefore of fasting when He will be "taken away" (2:18–20). The suggestion is that, like John's disciples, the disciples of Jesus will mourn because violence will have been committed against their Master.

The juxtaposition of the sabbath controversies between Jesus and the Pharisees (2:23–3:6) with Jesus' prediction of His disciples' mourning seems intended to illustrate the vicious reality of the forces threatening His life. During this confrontation with those who consider themselves the jealous guardians of the sabbath, Jesus places the sabbath under His own authority ("The Son of man is lord even of the sabbath"). Then Jesus proceeds to manifest in action the meaning of this authority by healing the man with a withered hand on the sabbath in one of their synagogues and in the presence of recriminating Pharisees, but not without having first challenged them to refute His claims on the sabbath. As a result, "the Pharisees went out, and immediately held counsel with the Herodians against him, how to destroy him." This alliance of normally antagonistic factions in the religious and political superstructure of Israel for the purpose of destroying a lone teacher gives occasion for Mark to refer to the supporters of Herod, a reference that will have to be understood in the light of John's martyrdom. Of the two powerful groups plotting the death of Jesus, one serves the ruler responsible for executing John the prophet, and the other relentlessly increases the pressure on Jesus by sending successive delegations from Jerusalem to find fault with and trap Him (3:22; 7:1–13; 8:11–13). Thus, after reporting the murderous decision of the Pharisees and Herodians, the evangelist kept reminding the reader of their threatening presence.

25. Both John and Jesus are introduced into the narration with the same formula, καὶ ἐγένετο (1:4, 9). They both suddenly appear on the scene according to prophecy (1:2), with identical messages and similar ministries. John, however, designates himself as the lesser one and as the herald of the other. His precursory ministry and death foreshadow Jesus' passion.

In fact, except for the intercalation of an editorial summary showing the extensiveness and effectiveness of Jesus' ministry (3:7—12), the account of the appointment of the twelve disciples immediately follows the statement about the alliance of the Pharisees and Herodians. Mark closed the enumeration of the disciples with "Judas Iscariot who betrayed him" (3:13—19). The contiguity of the reference to the Pharisees-Herodians with the mention of Judas's role suggests an answer to the question of the former concerning "how to destroy him." The evangelist revealed that Jesus would be betrayed.

Consequently, time is short. In order to give the good news of God's initiative a wider audience, Jesus multiplies His ministry by sending the disciples two by two as plenipotentiaries invested with His powers and preaching His message (6:6b—13, 30). Theirs is an urgent mission, as indicated by signs that they are responding to an emergency. They travel without the usual provisions except for the indispensable minimum. And when they encounter unreceptive audiences, they are not to insist but to depart for more promising locations. The nature of the crisis could be interpreted eschatologically as the fulfillment of the καιρός, ushering in the kingdom of God. However, the curious insertion of the account of John the Baptist's death between the mission of the twelve and their return to Jesus (6:14—29) indicates that Mark wished the mission to be understood differently.

The narrative of John's martyrdom establishes the following points: (1) John the Baptist is arrested because of his denunciation of Herod, a political ruler. Jesus, at this point of the Gospel, is vulnerable to the same hazard because of His denunciation of religious leaders. It is interesting that Mark postponed the explanation for John's arrest from the very first lines of the Gospel to this point where decisive confrontations have taken place between Jesus and His opponents. (2) Like Pilate with Jesus later, Herod holds John in high respect and is reluctant to order his execution. He is coerced into putting John to death. (3) When the disciples of John hear of his death, they take his body and lay it in a tomb, thus enacting a drama that will be repeated for Jesus. (4) Hearing about Jesus' activity, Herod thinks John the Baptist has been raised from the dead. The circumstances surrounding the death of John suggest a foreshadowing of the passion of Jesus, complete with an allusion to the resurrection. A similar connection between John's martyrdom and the predicted passion of Jesus occurs after the transfiguration. The disciples question Jesus concerning the scribes' insistence on the necessity of Elijah's return prior to eschatological fulfillment. Jesus confirms the doctrine, but instead of treating it in terms of the expected spectacular manifestion, He links it with the messianic ministry of the Son of man, which entails suffering "many things" and being treated "with contempt." Of the second Elijah, Jesus adds that he "has come, and they did to him whatever they pleased," thus identifying Elijah with John the Baptist (9:11—13). By inserting the narrative of John's death into the account of the mission of the twelve, the evangelist gives the impression that what has happened to John may soon happen to Jesus. The time now left for Jesus to make Himself known, so as to produce a full understanding of His messiahship after the resurrection, may be short. Hence the necessity for an all-out preaching mission.

The report of John's death and of its portentous significance for Jesus is again given bold emphasis just prior to Peter's confession (8:15). After consummating the final break with the Pharisees by denying their request for a sign, Jesus, fully aware of the Machiavellian implications of their designs,[26] warns the disciples about such craftiness. Linking together the underhanded practices of Pharisees and Herodians in a saying reminiscent of the joint counsel to destroy Him (3:6), Jesus cautions the disciples, "Take heed, beware of the leaven of the Pharisees and the leaven of Herod" (8:15). In light of the Pharisees' declared opposition, Herod's criminal conduct toward John the Baptist, and the plot of the Pharisees-Herodians to destroy Him, Jesus' linking together the two groups in this saying constitutes a dark foreboding. Jesus intends to forewarn the disciples of the malevolent conspiracies of the Pharisees and Herodians. At the same time, by showing that Jesus is fully aware of what is happening behind the scenes, Mark made it clear that suffering is integral to the messianic destiny.

In the first half of the Gospel, the complication in regard to the accomplishment of the messianic mission arises from the fact that this concept of the suffering Messiah remains hidden from everyone except Jesus Himself. The insertion of the "leaven" saying in the narrative of the disciples' lack of bread stresses their incomprehension of Jesus' mission. While He reveals to them the dangers ahead, they discuss lack of bread. Jesus rebukes them on both counts: first, because they discuss menial matters among themselves when He is trying to reveal to them the mystery of His destiny; second, because their concern for bread betrays blindness to His supernatural identity (8:14–21). The crowds show no more perspicacity. Almost at the end of this first part of the Gospel, when Jesus heals the deaf mute, the people are again astonished and say, "He has done all things well" (7:37). In other words, "He qualifies as a wonder-working messiah. He measures up to our expectations of a superhuman messiah." This sort of acclaim falls in the same category as the Pharisees' request for a sign from heaven. They both make power and miracles the validating trademarks of messiahship, whereas Jesus knows that His messianic destiny is characterized by humiliation and suffering.

This complication pattern is intensified by Jesus' efforts to minimize the repercussion of miracles, which people might interpret as the equivalent of "signs from heaven" and thus miss the deeper meaning (humiliation and suffering) of Jesus' messiahship. When demons, seized by terror at His sight, identify Him publicly as the Son of God, He quickly imposes silence prior to chasing them out (1:25, 34; 3:11–12). He refuses to be cast by demons in the role of a healer-exorcist messiah, which would cause onlookers to adopt a triumphalist view of His mission rather than one that requires suffering. As the three predictions of the passion in the second

26. See pp. 65–66.

half of the Gospel make clear, Jesus will fight the messianic battle not at the level of individual exorcisms but by grappling with death itself, crowned with the all-encompassing victory of the resurrection. This being the case, the vociferous acknowledgments of the demons are a liability. They cause Jesus' acts of exorcism to appear not as truly messianic deeds of mercy, reflecting spiritual supremacy, but as self-conscious, noisy "signs from heaven" *à la* Pharisees. With the demons hushed, the witnesses of exorcisms can draw their own conclusions in regard to Jesus ("understand," in Marcan terminology), especially when such deeds are viewed in retrospect after the passion and resurrection. This particular perspective is clearly spelled out at the beginning of the Gospel's second half. The transfiguration, another experience involving extraterrestrial beings, can also be misunderstood or exploited as a "sign from heaven." Since the passion and resurrection will eventually bring it into proper messianic focus, Jesus enjoins the disciples not to divulge what they have seen until after the resurrection (9:9).[27]

A similar pattern of dramatic complication exists in the first part of the Gospel in regard to another phase of messianic activity—the miracles of healing. In at least three cases and possibly in four, Jesus requests that the miracles not be publicized.[28] Since the striking results of these particular healings are visible to the people at large, and since the identity of the healer is generally known, there cannot be any element of secrecy involved. Rather, this is the same complication scheme of the suffering Messiah refusing to let spectacular miracles be interpreted as the validating proof or end-purpose of His messianic mission. Wishing to be known as playing down the importance of such miracles, Jesus tries to limit their repercussion by enjoining discretion, not secrecy. The nature of His messiahship requires that it be recognized through spiritual perception, not imposed by spectacular manifestations.[29]

After several miraculous cures in this same section of the Gospel, Jesus does not enjoin silence. What distinguishes these occasions is that, in each case, the situation is such that Jesus has no reason to fear the un-

---

27. Likewise for the baptism of Jesus. Supernatural manifestations such as open heavens, the Spirit-dove, and the voice could be misunderstood, in the Marcan scheme, as a "sign from heaven" of a sensation-seeking, wonder-working messiah. Consequently Mark, unlike the other synoptists, emphasized the subjective aspect of Jesus' baptism experience, describing it in the third person singular, with the voice addressing Jesus directly, while abstraction is made of possible witnesses (1:9—11).

28. The healing of the leper (1:43—44); the raising of the daughter of Jairus (5:43); the healing of the deaf mute (7:36); the healing of the blind man (8:26), where instead of commanding silence, Jesus orders him to avoid returning to Beth-saida on his way home.

29. In *Das Messiasgeheimnis in den Evangelien* (Göttingen, 1901) William Wrede propounded the theory that injunctions to secrecy in the Gospel were Marcan superimpositions attributed to Jesus in order to justify the fact that He is not recognized as Messiah during His ministry. Although discredited in its original form, Wrede's theory of the "messianic secret" is still influential. See J. D. G. Dunn, "The Messiah's Secret in Mark."

savory consequences of misunderstanding and reckless publicity. When, for example, Jesus is under attack, a miracle serves to vindicate Him or establish the point He wishes to make rather than give rise to dubious triumphalist claims. Thus the healing of the paralytic, which proves that Jesus has the authority to forgive sins (2:1–12). Since the forgiveness of sins is a spiritual messianic function as over against a spectacular "sign from heaven," the justifying miracle runs little risk of being exploited for the wrong reasons. Therefore, no restriction is imposed. In fact, in this case Mark mentioned that the people properly "glorified God," which he certainly considered an alternative preferable to unwholesome and excited speculations over "signs from heaven."

The account of Jesus healing the man with a withered hand is also devoid of commands to keep silent (3:1–6). Here again the focus of the occasion is not the miracle itself but the controversy over sabbath observances. The miracle demonstrates that Jesus arrogates the right to do good and save life even on the sabbath, thus proving His spiritual lordship over the sabbath. The miracle cannot be interpreted as a "sign from heaven" since it challenges prevalent doctrinal misconceptions and proclaims that life is more sacred than the sabbath. Consequently no restriction is necessary.

In the case of Legion, the fearful Gerasenes beg Jesus to depart from their shores (5:1–20). Their defensive attitude as well as their presumably Gentile background render messianic miracle-worker lucubrations unlikely. So instead of requesting silence, Jesus asks the healed demoniac to go home to his friends and tell them how much the Lord has done for him, and how He has had mercy on him. Jesus' request sets a model for the proper attitude toward His healing and exorcism miracles: they reveal the Lord's willingness and ability to intervene, out of compassion, on behalf of needy individuals. Such an understanding of the miracles of Jesus is far removed from the morbid preoccupation with a wonder-working messiah's supermagical stunts that the Pharisees call "signs from heaven" and that the less sophisticated populace also craves. Consequently Jesus places no restraint upon the divulgence of miracles where noisy publicity and messianic misunderstanding are unlikely consequences and where part of the recipients understand the miracles correctly.

The woman with the flow of blood understands that Jesus performs miracles not to be sensational but to express compassion in supernatural power, concluding, "If I touch even his garments, I shall be made well" (5:25–34). Her belief that she can discreetly steal the healing miracle from Him indicates that she correctly grasps the nature of His mission. Jesus commends her on that very point and dispenses with injunctions to secrecy. The Syrophoenician woman, knowing that the answer to her plea is an exceptional act of mercy, is hardly disposed to publicize Jesus' healing of her daughter as a display of His powers (7:25–28). Accordingly there is no need to impose silence. In both instances the healing is a private transaction between Jesus and the beneficiary on the basis of the latter's proper understanding of Jesus' role. In the Gospel there is no injunction to silence in any of the miracles in which Jesus is approached on the basis of faith (2:5; 5:34; 7:29; 9:24; 10:52). The only exception might be that of the leper who manifests faith by stating, "If you will, you can make me clean." Jesus does not commend him for his faith, however, and sternly forbids the healed leper to divulge the miracle, sending him to perform the temple rituals prescribed for normal, nonmiraculous healing from leprosy. Because the healed leper disobeys the orders, Jesus can no longer carry out His ministry in towns due to the mobs (1:40–45). The leper's disobedience and the mob's response betray an incorrect apprehension of the role of Jesus and justify His command to keep not the fact but the method of His healing in confidence.

The pattern of the injunctions to silence is obvious. There is no secret since the results of miracles, even those accomplished in private, are visible to all.[30] But discretion is requested in order to minimize the spread of false messianic conceptions relative to Jesus. The complication of the action in regard to Jesus' messianic mission reaches a climax when the Pharisees request a sign from heaven. The request shows not only that such false conceptions are current but also that they are forced upon Jesus. In spite of His efforts, Jesus' role as Messiah is distorted, and this will eventually cause Him to be executed as an impostor.

A study of the complication of the action in the first half of the Gospel would be incomplete without considering a significant aspect of the Marcan concept of the Christ, that of Jesus as a teacher. Although the amount of sermons, parables, and instructional material in Mark is smaller than in any of the Gospels, the emphasis on teaching—on Jesus as a teacher and on the disciples as recipients of the didache—is stronger in Mark than in the other Gospels. It remains to be seen whether this dimension of the ministry of Jesus remains outside the dramatic scheme of the Gospel or harmonized with it, and if the latter, in what manner.

Once the leaders have decided to destroy Jesus (3:6), once the friends of Jesus have made their unsuccessful bid to seize Him (3:21), and once the relatives of Jesus have been denied the right to control Him (3:31–35), Jesus initiates a program to teach the two groups remaining loyal to Him—the crowds and the disciples (4:1–34). The crowd is described as "a very large crowd gathered about him," the size of which requires Him to speak from a boat along the shore. His method of teaching the crowd is to teach "them many things in parables" (4:2). Three parables (the sower, the scattered seed, and the mustard seed) are obviously

---

30. The private miracles are the raising of Jairus's daughter (5:40), the healing of the deaf mute (7:33), and the healing of the blind man (8:23). It is significant that Jesus shows His power over death in the raising of Jairus's daughter only to her parents and three disciples. For the "people weeping and wailing" outside, the explanation given in advance to minimize the miraculous dimension of the girl's restoration is, "The child is not dead but sleeping." Likewise, Jesus' dominion over the elements is manifested to no one but the disciples (4:35–41; 6:45–52). As for the two feedings of the multitude—since, according to Mark, the disciples themselves fail to draw inferences regarding their supernatural connotations—Jesus makes no effort to conceal their miraculous character (6:30–44; 8:1–9; see also 8:19–21).

recounted as samples since the evangelist added that "with many such parables he spoke the word to them" (4:33). The evangelist stressed the fact that Jesus intends the crowds to receive the parables with careful attention. Jesus prefaces the parable of the sower with a charge to "listen" and concludes with a challenge to His hearers to use all their perceptive powers in appropriating the parable: "He who has ears to hear, let him hear" (4:3, 9). Likewise, at the end of the teaching session, the evangelist concluded that Jesus teaches the word to the crowd in parables as they are able to hear it (4:33). This emphasis on not exceeding the crowd's ability to hear indicates that Jesus is imparting to them content in parabolic form that is intelligible and therefore retainable.

A seeming paradox appears, however, as Jesus is shown exercising a private, parallel teaching ministry for the disciples. When He is alone, those who are "about him with the twelve"—that is, the privileged circle of followers who have access to His privacy—question Him concerning the parables. Jesus favors them with an interpretation of the parables on the basis that "the secret of the Kingdom of God" has been entrusted to this select group (4:11, 34). "But for those outside," says Jesus, meaning the crowd and possibly His opponents, everything remains in parables that are purposely left unexplained for the moment. The justification for withholding explanations from the crowd appears strange indeed in view of Jesus' warnings to them "to listen" and "to hear" His teaching. They are supposed to see but not perceive, to hear but not understand (4:12). In other words, those outside the inner circle should appropriate the form of the teaching even though its meaning must remain hidden from them. They must hear and remember the parables, but they must not have access to the interpretation; it must be kept a "secret." Anticipating the inevitable question in response to this almost cruel form of discrimination, Mark quoted Jesus saying that it is necessary "lest they should turn again, and be forgiven" (4:12). With this disturbing phrase, the paradox reaches a paroxysm. Jesus seems to contradict the thrust of His own ministry and to forego the claims He has boldly established of possessing authority to forgive sins (2:10).

On the other hand, the corollary of this enigmatic statement reveals the extent of the power locked in the "secret" of the parables. With a proper comprehension of the parables, the secret can be pierced. As a result people will see and perceive, hear and understand, in order to turn again and be forgiven. In other words, the teaching of Jesus is endowed with soteriological potential. The question remains, Why is this saving message concealed from the masses and revealed only to the disciples?

In the first place it should be noted that Jesus is indeed "teaching" the crowd. He is not playing games with them or giving them insoluble riddles.[31] He is imparting truth applicable to their situation. Commentators often conclude that Jesus tries to screen the essential content of His teaching from the crowd. This seems highly unlikely. If the evangelist had

31. *Parables* has sometimes been translated "riddles." See Vincent Taylor, *The Gospel According to Mark*, p. 258.

intended to describe a Jesus bent on keeping secrets, he would not have depicted Him drawing large crowds, seating Himself in front of them, and engaging in a substantial teaching ministry. Should Christ not want to instruct the crowd, He would completely avoid the situations in which He might be expected to teach. Having boarded the boat to escape the pressure of the crowd, He could abscond by sailing across the lake to the other side. Mark obviously depicted Jesus as wanting to teach the crowd and to convey to them a body of truth. But then why does not Jesus complete the instruction by interpreting the parables for the crowd as He does for the disciples?

The embroglio is resolved with an analysis of the parables. Although each of the three parables illustrates a different facet of the same reality, they all hold some features in common. First, as parables illustrating the kingdom of God (two begin with that specific designation), their frame of reference is surprisingly bucolic. Instead of marching armies, heroic deeds, and valorous exploits, Jesus chooses the homely and irenic gestures of seed planting to symbolize the manifestation of the kingdom. Moreover, the seed falls on the ground (4:4–8), is scattered upon the ground (4:26), and is sown upon the ground (4:31). Instead of striking out, defiant and aggressive, the kingdom of God appears lowly and vulnerable.

Second, the kingdom is subject to adversity, rejection, and delays. In the parable of the sower, the acceptance of the word is far from universal. Satan interferes at will. Tribulation and persecution arise on account of the word, and the result is defections. Worldly concerns can compete with and take precedence over the word. The parable contains no promise of instant and universal triumph. If partial loss is stressed in the first parable, the notion of long delays and slow expansion is conveyed in the others. Nights and days succeed each other after the seed is scattered, and the plant grows and matures only gradually. Likewise for the small mustard seed growing into a large tree. Especially the second parable gives the impression that although the seed has been planted, life goes on as usual until the eschatological end (the harvest in 4:29).

The third element describes a positive trait of the kingdom, that of irresistible growth. In the parable of the sower, seed falls on good soil and, regardless of what happens to other seed, it grows and bears fruit. Likewise in the second parable, by an inexorable process "the earth produces of itself" until "the grain is ripe." The mustard seed "grows up and becomes the greatest of all shrubs." The second parable makes it especially clear that, however imperceptible, growth nevertheless takes place.

Finally, the three parables depict the inevitability of a final success that is disproportionate to the seemingly insignificant and precarious beginnings of the kingdom. The seed that falls on good soil yields fruit thirty-, sixty-, and a hundredfold. The seed scattered upon the ground becomes a harvest. The tiny mustard seed becomes a tree that puts forth branches large enough to accommodate birds and even their nests in its shade. Thus the three parables converge on a motif of success and fulfillment. But such gains are relegated to the future. In the present (during the ministry of Jesus as well as in the life-situation of the Marcan church) the kingdom embodied in Jesus before the resurrection and represented by the church after Easter is often ignored, rejected, or opposed. It is considered a negligible entity. Its fulfillment through the course of history includes humiliation and suffering.

Again, recognition of the centrality of the doctrine of a suffering Messiah in the Gospel of Mark provides the key for understanding yet another of its baffling features, this discriminatory approach of Jesus in teaching the crowd and the disciples. There was no room for humiliation and suffering in the prevalent messianic expectations. Consequently the teaching of Jesus is devoted to preparing minds to receive a new concept of the Messiah whose mission would comprise humiliation and death. Since the peculiar reality of His messiahship can be demonstrated only through the crucifixion and resurrection, no amount of verbal teaching can adequately impart in advance "the secret of the kingdom of God," that is, the unexpected nature of Christ's messiahship. As in the case of the miracles, which, when viewed apart from the fuller realization of Christ's messianic task, were often counterproductive, resulting in superficial acclaim and wonderment; so in His teaching, Jesus is concerned not to reveal His messiahship to the multitudes prematurely, apart from the passion and resurrection that will be the climactic explanation of His mission. Just as He tried to give Himself as much exposure as possible for future reference by healing, casting out demons, and going incessantly from village to village, Jesus seizes every opportunity to teach the crowds and prepare them for eventual understanding of His teaching. The content of His instruction is sufficiently specific that, viewed in retrospect after the passion and resurrection, it will become relevant to the participants in the post-Easter experience. In review, the parables, which Jesus insists should be carefully received even though not yet comprehended, will then be understood as the predictions of difficult beginnings and the promise of a glorious fulfillment. The secrecy is only for a time. The passion and resurrection will make all things plain and self-evident. Then even those outside will see and perceive, hear and understand, so that they can turn again and be forgiven. In the meantime the teaching of Jesus directed to the crowd is a revelation in anticipation, a lesson to retain for future reference, a sort of revelational time bomb set to explode into full illumination immediately after the resurrection. When teaching the crowd, Jesus is training future believers to whom He will return, followed by the Twelve, from Jerusalem to Galilee after the resurrection (16:7).

If Jesus has to resort to teaching the crowd in parables—those revelations with a built-in delayed-action mechanism—to protect His messianic integrity and prevent false assumptions by the multitude, recourse to such devices is not necessary with the disciples. Since they can be trusted to keep private His displays of supernatural power, they can also receive in advance the full import of the parables. As a matter of fact, Mark may have been anxious to show that the Twelve, and by extension his own Gospel, constitute the repository of revealed messianic truth. Therefore Jesus carries out a program of private instruction in which He makes explicit to the disciples what will remain veiled to the crowd until after the resurrection.

In this context Mark grouped a number of seemingly cryptic sayings that acquire fresh significance in the light of the dual teaching ministry of Jesus (4:21–25). A lighted lamp cannot be hid very long; its light will inevitably be made manifest (4:21). Likewise, what is hidden and secret now will eventually be made manifest and come to light (4:22). In these two sayings Jesus seems to point to the ephemeral character of the necessity for the secrecy that accompanies His public teaching. Therefore, what the disciples learn now is to be preciously kept. "If any man has ears to hear, let him hear" (4:23) and "Take heed what you hear" (4:24a). For the disciples will be called upon to give account later for the truth they receive now from Jesus in His private instruction. "The measure you give [later] will be the measure you get [now]" (4:24b). In fact, at that time (after the passion and resurrection) more truth will be revealed to them: ". . . and still more will be given you" (4:24c). He who has believed and received the teaching of Jesus will be counted worthy to receive more: "For to him who has will more be given" (4:25a). But he who does not believe will find himself completely destitute: ". . . from him who has not, even what he has will be taken away" (4:25b).

This last warning acquires an ominous character in the light of the incident that immediately follows the teaching in parables. "On that [very] day," Mark reported with intended effect, the disciples, after Jesus stills the storm, shamelessly inquire of each other, "Who then is this?" (4:41). Having heard the parables as taught to the crowd, having received private explanations, having been cautioned to understand, they still do not grasp the significance of the presence of Jesus. Thus the complication pattern of the action in the first part of the Gospel extends as well to the teaching ministry of Christ—this important revelational function of the messianic ministry. Jesus must reveal the significance of His presence. But He finds Himself limited because of the inability of the crowds and even of His disciples to understand. He has no success story to tell. He can make no promises of spontaneous and universal victory. They will not understand the necessity of the passion until it has taken place. Therefore all He can do is give advance knowledge about the meaning of events that will become clear only after the fact. The tragic situation and therefore the complication result not from the uncomprehension of the crowd and the disciples but from the very nature of the messiahship, which can be neither proclaimed nor understood until the passion and resurrection have taken place. The protagonists are all victims of destiny.

II

In the Aristotelian concept of plot structure, the transition between complication and denouement is called the crisis. At this point a climactic event takes place that results in a shift in the action of the play. This climax often takes the form of a recognition scene, as it does in the illustration cited by Aristotle and the two plays briefly analyzed above. In the Gospel the confession of Peter constitutes a turning point in the action. The dramatic tension created by the complication of the incognito presence of the Messiah is partly relaxed when the disciples recognize, on their own and against seemingly contrary evidence, the real identity of Jesus. As a result of the confession, the ministry of Jesus takes a different turn in the last half of the Gospel and the action swiftly enters the denouement phase.

From the very beginning of the Gospel, while Jesus is devoting Himself to a ministry of preaching, teaching, and healing, Mark made clear that the discerning response Jesus expects from His ever-wondering audiences is that of "faith." Jesus launches His ministry in Galilee with the invitation to "believe in the gospel" (1:15), which is equivalent to having faith in Him since He personifies the gospel. But such faith is found on rare occasions and generally in people of minimal importance. Fishermen and a tax collector respond to His call to follow Him (1:16–20; 2:14). A leper kneels before Him, beseeching, "If you will, you can make me clean" (1:40). A paralytic is brought by four unidentified men. Seeing (sic) their faith, Jesus pronounces the man's sins forgiven and raises him up (2:5). A ruler of the synagogue named Jairus falls at His feet, like the leper, and pleads with Him on behalf of his dying daughter (5:22–23). At that time a woman suffering from a flow of blood comes near Jesus, saying to herself, "If I touch even his garments, I shall be made well." Jesus commends her: "Daughter, your faith has made you well" (5:25–34). In the meantime Jairus's daughter is reported dead. But Jesus says, "Do not fear, only believe" (5:32–36). Finally the persistent confidence and trust of a Syrophoenician woman is rewarded (7:29).

The scarce occurrences of faith emphasize its value. Jesus seems to be searching for it and to prize it whenever found. Faith seems to consist of an understanding of the adequacy of Jesus to meet one's need; an apprehension however dim of the real intent of His presence among men; often a public commitment to Jesus of a private sorrow; a last-resort, play-for-broke submission to Jesus of an extreme if not hopeless situation. It seems to establish a peculiar reciprocal relationship of understanding between Jesus and those who trust Him.[32] For them, Jesus does not remain a man of mystery or an object of contention. He becomes the fulfiller of their individual destinies. Thus, having healed the Gerasene demoniac, Jesus refers to a relationship of mutual understanding regarding God's intervention in his life: ". . . how much the Lord has done for you, and how he has had mercy on you" (5:19).

Although here and there some respond to Him in faith, Jesus cannot commend the disciples for their comprehension of Himself. He constantly presses them for an indication of understanding, but, to this point in the Gospel, in vain. In the storm Jesus, surprised at their panic despite His presence with them, rebukes them and asks, "Have you no faith?" They

---

32. Many of the interventions of Jesus into situations of need result in private encounters with an exchange of semiconfidential conversation or the performance of parabolic actions. Cf. 1:41; 2:5; 5:19, 33, 39; 6:37; 7:27–28, 33–34; 8:2–4, 23–25.

immediately answer in the negative, albeit indirectly, saying to one another, "Who then is this?" (4:40–41). A glimmer of hope is provided by
Jesus Himself, however, when, after the second miraculous feeding and the
dismissal of the request for a sign from heaven, He again presses the
disciples to draw perceptive conclusions from the evidence of the feedings.
Challenging them one last time, He asks, "Do you not yet perceive or
understand?" (8:17–21). The "not yet" is indicative of better things to
come. The disciples are bound to recognize sooner or later the identity of
their Master. What is happening to them in the realm of the spirit is
perhaps portrayed by the blind man at Beth-saida. He gains his sight pro-
gressively after an elaborate ritual that includes Jesus giving him private
attention, laying hands on him twice, and questioning him as he gradually
comes to see "everything clearly" (8:22–25). Could a similar transformation be taking place within the disciples?

The dramatic answer to this question follows immediately after the
pericope of the blind man of Beth-saida. On the way to the village of
Caesarea Philippi, Jesus asks the disciples, "Who do men say that I am?"
Their several answers show that public opinion has not changed since the
death of John (6:14–16). The people are ascribing to Him important
roles—John the Baptist, Elijah, one of the prophets—but only roles of
preparation, not that of ultimate fulfillment. Obviously He does not fit
their preconceived notion of the Messiah. They do not possess the spiritual
discernment necessary to recognize in Him the final consummator of all
things. They know Him after the flesh only. The multiplicity of answers is
in dramatic contrast to the tense but brief exchange that follows. In a
moment of breathless suspense, Jesus asks, "But who do you say that I
am?" The form of His question makes it clear that He requires a different
answer.[33] While several disciples volunteered answers to the first question,
only Peter blurts out, with the abruptness of fresh discovery, "You are the
Christ" (8:27–29). At long last the secret of the kingdom of God has been
discovered. The disciples have begun, in Marcan terminology to "understand" the supernatural identity of Jesus and the ultimate nature of His
mission. In familiar fashion Mark immediately introduced a negative
reversal: "And he charged them to tell no one about him." This injunction
to continued discretion is not merely for dramatic effect, but is again to
remind the disciples (and the reader) of the peculiar nature of Jesus'
messiahship, which still prevents its proclamation. The reason for this
prohibition constitutes the subject of the second part of the Gospel, the
denouement.

33. The *but* has the force of an adversative correlator.

Chapter 4

The Plot:
Denouement

I

Nowhere in the Gospel is its dramatic structure as evident as in the change that occurs from complication (1:1–8:26) to denouement (8:31–16:8), a change that is the result of the recognition scene (8:27–30). In the transition both formal and thematic changes take place from one section to the other.

Although the Gospel is strongly structured thematically in the complication phase, the pattern of the narrative is discontinuous and episodic. For instance, indications of geographic location are sufficiently vague and sporadic to render a drawing of Jesus' itinerary impossible. This changes radically in the denouement section. The thematic structure is again salient, but the flow of the narrative is now continuous. It is possible to follow Jesus and the disciples in unbroken sequence as they move from Caesarea Philippi to the transfiguration mountain, through Galilee to Capernaum, and on to Judea and beyond the Jordan, through Jericho, Bethany, and finally to Jerusalem. One gets the impression that whereas in the first part of the Gospel, the author offered selected vignettes to illustrate the themes of misunderstanding and rejection, in the second half he presented a connected story to describe how it all ended. The difference in format obviously reflects the variety of sources available to Mark.[1] But it also shows a concern for correspondence between form and content. By virtue of its nature, a cumulative arrangement could adequately illustrate the complication of the action. But the account of its resolution required a sequential narrative as step-by-step evidence of the redemptive significance of the Gospel.

During the complication phase, the action was constantly prompted forward along the theme of the identification of Jesus as Messiah. The other element of the plot, the fulfillment of the messianic mission, was given a future frame of reference. The recognition of Jesus as Messiah radically reverses this order. In the denouement, the accomplishment of the messianic task abruptly becomes the main concern. The theme of the universal recognition of Jesus slips to the background, and when alluded to, it is essentially reserved for the postresurrection future.

Mark achieved his purpose in the denouement by concentrating on three main lines of development. The first is the training of the disciples

1. Most of the passion narrative that forms the main part of the denouement section probably came to Mark as a prearranged unit.

and their subsequent debacle. The second is the success of the opposition in obtaining the death of Jesus. The third issues from the reciprocal effect of the first two: as Jesus accomplishes the preparations for universal outreach through the disciples and as He fulfills His messianic mandate at the cross, the kingdom of God, described earlier as being "at hand," finally begins its victorious march through history at the signal of the resurrection.

1. *The training of the disciples.* In the first part of the Gospel (the part prior to the recognition of Jesus as Messiah), the theme of humiliation and suffering that dominates the concept of the messianic task acts as a restraint on the teaching ministry of Jesus.[2] The confession of Peter suddenly removes the hindrance and marks the beginning of an intensive ministry of preparing the disciples. This preparation has a twofold purpose. One is to impart to the disciples the doctrine of the suffering and resurrected Messiah, although Jesus knows that the disciples will neither understand nor accept this doctrine until after the passion and resurrection. The other is to teach them the full implications of being the disciple of a crucified and risen Messiah; they too must suffer before attaining glory.

According to the evangelist, Jesus begins teaching the facts of the passion to His disciples immediately after Peter's confession. What had been hinted at in the first part of the Gospel, is now made explicit, "He said this plainly [or, boldly]" (8:32). As Jesus for the first time ("He *began* to teach them," 8:31) informs the disciples that suffering is necessary for Him to achieve the goals of messiahship ("that the Son of man *must* suffer many things," 8:31), Peter reacts spontaneously with vehement objections. In confessing the messiahship of Jesus, Peter has identified Him as the fulfiller of the age. But in typical human fashion and like his unenlightened contemporaries (he is "not on the side of God, but of men," 8:33), Peter does not understand that Christ's destiny requires suffering and that this suffering will be used redemptively by God. Jesus considers such a prejudice a satanic hindrance to His mission ("Get behind me, Satan!" 8:33). He prohibits the disciples from divulging their new-found conviction (8:30), thereby preventing the proliferation of similar obstacles. The secret of the kingdom of God now revealed to the disciples must remain hidden to those outside in order to foil schemes devised to prevent the passion, which would thus thwart the fulfillment of Christ's peculiar messianic destiny as a suffering Savior.

The first initiation of the disciples to the necessity of the passion results in Peter's interposition, which is denounced by Jesus as a satanic scheme intended to pervert His conception of the suffering role of the Messiah into triumphalist expectations *à la* Zealot (8:33). This fiasco compels Jesus to return to the subject several times. After the transfiguration He charges the three accompanying disciples not to divulge what they have just witnessed until after His resurrection from the dead (9:9),

2. See p. 75.

thus reconciling the stark contradiction of this manifestation of supernatural glory with the predictions of His forthcoming death. Again Mark showed Jesus' efforts as being less than successful; the disciples, unable to reconcile the concept of death with that of messiahship, question among themselves the meaning of "the rising from the dead" (9:10). In order to circumvent the obvious meaning of Jesus' prediction, they interpret the reference to the resurrection in eschatological terms and point to the scribes' teaching regarding the prior return of Elijah (9:11). Jesus shows Himself willing to challenge their recalcitrance on their own ground (scribal teaching) by appealing to the Scriptures in order to stress again the necessity of suffering in the accomplishment of the messianic task: ". . . it is written of the Son of man, that he should suffer many things and be treated with contempt" (9:12). As for Elijah redivivus, far from being a herald of future messianic glory, he already "has come, and they did to him whatever they pleased" (9:13). The forerunner of the kingdom did not appear in power, but he became, as will now the fulfiller of the kingdom, the victim of enemies who treated him without mercy. And in order to stress the parallel with the sorrowful destiny of the Son of man, Mark again appealed to the Scriptures by adding also in reference to Elijah—John the Baptist, "as it is written of him."

Knowing that the concept of a suffering Messiah remains alien to the thinking of the disciples, Jesus enters into a second period of instruction for which He secures privacy (9:31–32) and during which He predicts that the Son of man will be delivered into the hands of men,[3] killed, and raised after three days. Predictably the disciples do not understand the saying, and perhaps from fear of being enlightened, they are "afraid to ask him." Again the attempt to forewarn the disciples ends in failure.

During this time Jesus and His disciples have moved from Caesarea Philippi to Galilee. They pass through Capernaum and leave the shores of the lake to go "to the region of Judea and beyond the Jordan" (10:1). Finally they are "on the road, going up to Jerusalem" (10:32). In the words of Luke, "When the days drew near for him to be received up, he set his face to go to Jerusalem" (Luke 9:51). Mark's description is even more gripping. He portrays a sad and silent procession with Jesus walking alone ahead of the apprehensive disciples. This tragic journey toward the place of the Messiah's destiny becomes the setting for the third teaching session. Emphasizing the significance of the itinerary and predicting specific details of the passion, Jesus tells the disciples that "going up to Jerusalem" means the Son of man will be condemned to death, delivered to the Gentiles, mocked, spat upon, scourged, and killed; and that He will rise on the third day (10:32–34). As if in response, the sons of Zebedee "came forward to him" with the inappropriate request for places of preeminence in His glory. Realizing that His dire predictions have fallen on

3. Both Elijah, to whom they did whatever they pleased (9:13), and the Son of man, who is delivered into the hands of men, are depicted not as being in command, as their positions would seem to require, but as passive, defenseless, and subject to the control of others over them.

deaf ears, Jesus again seizes the opportunity to emphasize the passion, telling them about the cup He has to drink and the baptism He has to go through. He summarizes the significance of His ministry in the sentence: "... the Son of man ... came not to be served but to serve, and to give his life as a ransom for many" (10:45). James and John anticipate positions of honor in a glorious kingdom while Jesus defines His ministry as one of service and His life as a ransom for many. The disciples and Jesus are still worlds apart. During His earthly life they will never understand the true meaning of the secret. But they have received it for a later time when the passion and the teaching concerning the passion will reciprocally illumine each other ex post facto. After the third prediction, and more especially after the interpretation of His coming death as a ransom for many, Jesus knows that the message of the gospel is in good keeping. The disciples will be able to discern and reveal at the right time the explanation of the secret that has been entrusted to them.

This accomplishment marks a high point of the Gospel. Delays and secrecy are no longer necessary. Jesus now openly engages in actions that reveal messiahship and precipitate the outcome of His ministry.[4]

After the arrival of Jesus and the disciples in Jerusalem, a series of precursory events occurs that reveals the imminence of the passion. As a woman awaits Jesus at Bethany, He predicts, "... you will not always have me. ... She has anointed my body beforehand for burying" (14:7-8). During the evening meal, in an intensely dramatic scene, Jesus reveals the identity of the "betrayer" as "one of the twelve, one who is dipping bread in the same dish with me" (14:20). Then, holding the pieces of broken bread, He says, "This is my body." Giving them the cup, He again says, "This is my blood." Thus He points to the soteriological significance of the violent death forecast by the simple symbolism of broken bread and poured wine. And to make certain that the disciples are prepared for the imminent passion, He informs them that this will be their last meal with Him until the eschatological reunion (14:25).

And yet, having so carefully prepared the disciples, Jesus harbors no illusions. He forewarns them of their coming defection and cautions Peter of a denial rendered even more pathetic by the latter's protestations of loyalty till death (14:27-31). Proof of the disciples' inability to cope with the crisis ahead is immediately forthcoming. Jesus pleads with His three intimate disciples for some comfort during His lonely agony of soul in Gethsemane. But they are "sleeping and taking their rest," and when awakened they "do not know what to answer him" (14:32-42). The evangelist mercilessly portrayed the disarray of the disciples during the arrest in Gethsemane. Displaying total uncomprehension of Jesus' teaching, one of the disciples attempts to force Jesus into defending Himself by drawing the sword. His futile effort results in a detached ear and causes Jesus to utter the fateful (in the tragic sense of the word) statement, "Let the scriptures be fulfilled." The submission of Jesus to His tormentors

4. See p. 86.

marks the total collapse of the disciples. They forsake Him and flee, one of them running away naked (14:43–52).

After the threefold denial of Peter in the high-priest's courtyard, the disciples disappear entirely. On the way to Golgotha, it is a stranger "who was coming in from the country" who helps Jesus carry the cross (15:21). The evangelist rendered the disciples' absence tragically conspicuous by enumerating those "looking on from afar" during the crucifixion (15:40–41), those involved in the burial of Jesus (15:42–47; Joseph of Arimathea, although not a follower of Jesus, is said to "have taken courage" prior to requesting from Pilate Jesus' body), and those returning to the tomb on Easter Sunday to complete the burial rites (16:1). Peter, who had "vehemently" protested that he would die with Jesus, and the other disciples, who had "all said the same" (14:31), are nowhere to be found.

Of equal dramatic force in Mark's development of the denouement is Jesus' training of the twelve for the demands of discipleship and their shocking failure to grasp His teaching. In the same manner that Jesus has prepared the disciples to comprehend ex post facto His passion by insisting on suffering as a requirement in His messianic fulfillment, so He has prepared His followers to accept hardship, opposition, suffering, and death as a requirement of genuine discipleship.

Immediately after the first prediction of the passion, Jesus lays down the charter of discipleship. He proclaims the conditions for belonging to His community as denial of self, taking up one's cross, losing one's life—all pointing to an antitriumphalist concept of the kingdom of God. The program He lays down is the very antithesis of messianic proposals current in those days, that of saving one's life in order "to gain the whole world." Fully aware of the unexpected and, for some, unacceptable nature of His demands, Jesus has a warning for pusillanimous and retrograde followers who will be ashamed of Him and His words in "this adulterous and sinful generation," Jews for whom the idea of a crucified Messiah is a stumbling block and Gentiles for whom it is folly: if they are unwilling to side with Him in humiliation and suffering, they will be deprived of His glory in the age to come (8:34–38).

Returning from the transfiguration, Jesus finds a group of disciples who are frustrated exorcists. A demon has resisted their efforts to make him depart from a possessed child. The father puts it plainly: "I asked your disciples to cast it out, and they were not able." Jesus immediately analyzes the problem as lack of faith. He exclaims, "O faithless generation" and "All things are possible to him who believes." To the disciples, who asked for an explanation of their failure, He flatly states, "This kind cannot be driven out by anything but by prayer" (9:14–29). The disciples' problem is obvious. They approached the sick child as professional exorcists instead of disciples of Jesus. There was no exercise of faith, no reliance on prayer, and therefore no manifest dependence on God's power. Their failure was due to self-assertion, the very opposite of the attitude of meekness and dependency Jesus requires for discipleship.

Following the second period of teaching concerning the passion, Jesus enters a house with His disciples and asks them almost conversationally what they have been discussing on the way. They remain silent, "for on the way they had discussed with one another who was the greatest." In Mark's vivid account, Jesus, who has brought the situation out in the open, sits down (out of frustration?) and explains that in order to qualify as disciples, they have to consider themselves last of all and act as servant of all. To illustrate humility, Jesus takes a child in His arms and tells them that only the disciple who thus exalts an insignificant child is worthy of his master and of God Himself (9:33–38).

Upon this, John Zebedee boasts to Jesus of the zeal and orthodoxy he displayed in restraining a stranger practicing exorcisms in Jesus' name. In line with the previous teaching, Jesus enjoins the disciples not to reject such assistance in haughty exclusiveness. If they are to accept even as humble an offering as a cup of water provided in the name of Christ, how much more the cooperation of a well-intentioned stranger in fighting evil spirits! (9:38–41).

Probably prompted by John's boast, Mark reported further teachings of Jesus stressing the necessity of radical, self-imposed sacrifices in order to qualify as a disciple and in order not to become an offense to others (9:42–48). In a summary of this teaching designed to jar the ambition-driven and status-seeking disciples, Jesus makes discipleship conditional upon each one's subjection to a stringent process of suffering and purification ("For every one will be salted with fire," 9:49), which renders peace and harmony possible in the life of the new community ("Have salt in yourselves, and be at peace with one another," 9:50). The same principles of abnegation and purity inspire Jesus' private explanation to the disciples of His answer to the Pharisees' question on divorce (10:2–9). His rigorous standards based on self-sacrifice and service to others proscribe the adulterous divorce practices rationalized out of the law of Moses by the Pharisees (10:10–12).

At this point Mark again illustrated the dismal failure of the disciples to assimilate teaching on the conditions for discipleship. He described Jesus catching the disciples in flagrant violation of His injunction to receive little children in true humility. As small ones are brought to Him for His blessing, the disciples act like bumptious bodyguards and repulse the children. Discovering this state of affairs, Jesus becomes "indignant" and sharply rebukes the swaggering disciples, reminding them that they themselves have no part in the kingdom of God unless they become as unpretentious as children. Then, in a graphic gesture of rebuff to the disciples, He lavishes affection upon the children who had been brought merely to have Him "touch them." He takes the small ones in His arms, blesses them, and lays His hands upon them (10:13–16).

The encounter with the rich young man becomes another occasion for Jesus to prepare the disciples for the life of sacrifice and suffering awaiting them. They are quick to realize that renunciation of values conflicting with discipleship is required of them also. As Peter "begins" to congratulate himself and commend his fellow disciples for having left everything and followed the master, he is interrupted by Jesus, who reminds them that they will receive their reward a hundredfold in the new community, but that they also have to expect "persecutions" now, prior to obtaining eternal life in the age to come. And lest they should become puffed up with pride, Jesus adds a warning about the possibility of the first followers becoming last of all (10:17–31).

With his subtle flair for creating dramatic contrast by alternating antithetical pericopes, the evangelist again showed the obtuseness of the disciples in connection with the third passion teaching. In immediate juxtaposition to the poignant enumeration of the torments awaiting Him in Jerusalem, James and John come to Jesus and ask Him to promise them a favor—nothing less than the best seats in His kingdom. In light of their previous instruction on self-effacement, such an egotistical request is scandalous. Following immediately the final prediction of the passion, it exposes even more the callousness of the disciples and their inability to understand the secret meaning of messiahship and the corresponding requirements of discipleship. They pursue dreams of grandeur while Jesus calls them to the cross. Consequently, looking forward to the new community, Jesus warns against hierarchical distinctions among His disciples and reiterates His previous teaching about servanthood as the appropriate basis of relationship among them (10:35–45).

Later, as one of the disciples expresses his fascination with the magnificence of the temple ("... what wonderful stones and what wonderful buildings!"), Jesus announces the temple's eventual destruction. The incident creates the occasion for instruction about upheavals to come on the scene of world history (chap. 13). The disciples will not be spared in the midst of general turmoil. They are to be on their guard, to "take heed" and "watch" (13:5, 9, 23, 33, 35, 37). In the universal sufferings (3:8) the disciples will be especially vulnerable. They will be delivered up to councils, beaten in synagogues, hated by all for Christ's sake. And only those who endure to the end will be saved (13:9–13). Peter is one of the four to whom Christ is speaking (13:3), but when the test comes during Jesus' trial, he invokes a curse on himself and swears (14:71), oblivious of the Master's recommendation not to be anxious beforehand regarding one's defense in such situations but to rely on the Holy Spirit for guidance in what to say (13:11).

This extraordinary portrayal of the disciples' repeated failures to meet the challenges for which Jesus has specifically prepared them, no doubt carries polemical and didactic significance.[5] But above all it dramatizes in the denouement of the Gospel the utter abandonment of Jesus to His tragic fate because of that one ineluctable, and for His disciples unacceptable, singularity of His messiahship, the necessity of suffering and death.

5. See chap. 6.

2. *Confrontation with the leaders.* The same sense of irresistible disaster pervades the description of the relationship between Jesus and the leaders of the Jews. Whereas the defection of the disciples causes Jesus to suffer and die in loneliness, His suffering and death are directly imputable to the incessant machinations of the leaders. Consequently Mark's development of this theme constitutes the very heart of the denouement. The cross represents the climax of the story of the crucified Messiah. Since the immediate causes for the cross arise out of the conflict between Jesus and the leaders, the progress of the action to its final resolution follows the course of their confrontations. This antagonism is described in two clearly delineated, successive phases: first, the efforts of Jesus to bring the leaders' murderous designs out in the open; second, the response of the leaders, who act under the cover of darkness and falsehood.

Once Jesus has secured the disciples' future comprehension of the reason for His death (as the doctrine of the necessity of suffering and humiliation for the fulfillment of His mission) by repeated predictions leading up to the "ransom" saying (10:45), there is no need for further delay. He swiftly proceeds to Jerusalem by way of Jericho and Bethphage. Prior to this point, discretion in the proclamation of His messiahship was necessary to avoid generating a false view of Himself in line with triumphalist messianic hopes and precipitating the passion prematurely, that is, before completing the disciples' indoctrination into the secret meaning of His suffering.

Now, however, Jesus wants to force the issue of His recognition by denouncing the aberrant character of current messianic expectations. This makes concealment of His own messiahship unnecessary. He is intent on compelling the leaders to take a public stand in regard to His messianic role. Therefore, He need not conceal this messianic role any longer. The veil of semisecrecy that has hitherto surrounded His mission can be lifted. As a result, the element of concealment disappears entirely from the Gospel after the third prediction. Instead, Jesus instigates or permits the occurrence of happenings fraught with obvious messianic significance, and He allows ensuing events to follow their inevitable course. With each case of messianic manifestation, however, the point is made that Jesus acts on His own in full independence from the Judaic establishment and in contradistinction to the categories of earthly, triumphalist messianism.

The first such incident of unhindered, public, messianic identification follows immediately the "ransom" saying.[6] Although blind, the beggar Bartimaeus confers upon Jesus the messianic title "Son of David" while appealing for "mercy." Emphasizing Bartimaeus's obstreperous prolixity, Mark quoted twice the wording of his call, explaining that "he cried all the more." In this instance it is not Jesus but His followers who object to the publicity. Jesus seems willing to give Bartimaeus all the time

6. T. A. Burkhill failed to recognize the meaning of this new phase of the ministry of Jesus. He therefore interpreted the sudden explicitness of Jesus as a contradiction imposed by Mark upon the tradition, and he called this chain of events the "strain on the secret." *Mysterious Revelation*, p. 118.

he needs to make Himself known as "Son of David." And when finally Bartimaeus is healed of his blindness, Jesus attributes the miracle to the blind man's faith, that is, to the blind man's recognition of Jesus' healing power (". . . your faith has made you well"). The miracle takes place in the midst of "a great multitude" and not, as did the healing of the blind man in Beth-saida, in private. No secrecy is enjoined. Quite to the contrary, Jesus tells Bartimaeus, "Go your way." The latter "followed him on the way" unhindered (10:46—52). It is important to note that Jesus receives messianic acclaim and sanctions such recognition by refraining from reproving it (while others do) and by being ostentatiously instrumental in performing the expected miracle. Yet He does not exploit the situation like a messiah anxious to muster a following. He tells the man to go his way.

The "way" takes Jesus and His followers, Bartimaeus included, to the Mount of Olives, "near to Jerusalem." Aware that His popularity has preceded Him in the capital, Jesus deliberately stages an entrance that will both sanction the predictable messianic acclaim and deny its popular conception. He comes down the Mount of Olives as the Messiah is expected to do amid shouts of acclamation that echo Bartimaeus's "Son of David" and hail the coming kingdom of David. But instead of marching into Jerusalem arrayed in the martial splendor of a conquering hero, He arrives astride a little donkey. The careful preparation in procuring the colt, a mount hardly suited for proud and aggressive endeavors, indicates the importance that Jesus attaches to its symbolism (11:1—10). At the crucial moment of His entrance into the religious center of the nation, He deliberately accepts messianic homage while clearly dissociating Himself from triumphalist implications. The excited people will eventually understand His intention and, seeing that Jesus will not submit to their preconceived ideas, they will cry, "Crucify him!" after having shouted hosannas (15:13). Seen in retrospect, the "triumphal entry" may have made the people feel strangely uneasy since they and not Jesus had provided the spectacle.

After the dramatic suspense created through the narrative by Jesus' ostentatious avoidance of Jerusalem,[7] the mention of His visit to the temple and withdrawal to Bethany for the night seems intended to call attention to the fact that He deliberately chooses not to dwell in the city. During the few days prior to His death, Jesus is shown as visiting Jerusalem (and especially the temple precincts) during the day and staying in Bethany at night (11:11, 12, 15, 19, 27; 14:3). By beginning His ministry and exercising the larger part of it away from Jerusalem, Jesus had affirmed His complete independence from the Judaic establishment. In response, Jerusalem had sent a delegation of religious inquisitors to harass Jesus (3:22; 7:1). Now Jesus comes Himself to Jerusalem, and before doing anything else, He surveys the temple. He has already predicted,

7. Prior acquaintanceship with Jerusalem by Jesus is presupposed by 11:2—6 and 14:13—16, which suggests at least one earlier sojourn in the capital. An account of it may have been omitted by the evangelist out of concern for the dramatic structure of the Gospel. See p. 106.

referring namely to Jerusalem, that He would die at the hands of the religious leaders, chief priests, elders, and scribes whose seat is in Jerusalem (8:31; 10:33). In view of this background, the brief description of Jesus going through the temple looking "round at everything," and the mention of Him withdrawing to Bethany because it is "already late," increase the suspense. The question comes to mind, "Late for what?"

The surprising answer is provided the next day as Jesus boldly launches a raid, not against the Roman occupants and their collaborators, but against the sordid protection-racket being operated in the courts of the temple under the cover of religion and the control of the chief priests (11:15–19). Mark explained that Jesus is able to carry out such an enterprise singlehandedly thanks to the tacit support of the multitude who, though uncomprehending, still give Him the benefit of the doubt (the leaders "feared him, because all the multitude was astonished at his teaching," 11:18). As Jesus explains His action, He emphasizes again the spiritual focus of His mission. Quoting a text from Isaiah, He points to God's original intention that the temple serve as a universal center of spiritual reference ("My house shall be called a house of prayer for all the nations," 11:17; Isa. 56:7). Instead, the leaders are dishonestly exploiting it to promote their own interests, having turned it into "a den of robbers." In other words, the misused temple, dominated by its present leadership, symbolizes the apostasy of the Jewish establishment. Jesus obviously intends His action to be interpreted symbolically as a protest, since He hardly expects the physical effects of His incursion to last permanently. By carrying out the demonstration, He once more emphasizes the spiritual frame of reference of His messiahship. He also dramatizes the extent of the leaders' apostasy. That He nurtures no illusions in regard to their reform is indicated by His prediction of the destruction of the temple (13:2). Reciprocally, that the leaders understood exactly the meaning of the temple incident and apply its lessons to themselves, albeit in a spirit of vindictiveness rather than repentance, is shown by their renewed resolve to kill Jesus ("And the chief priests and the scribes heard it and sought a way to destroy him," 11:18), by the subornation of false witnesses accusing Jesus of declaring His intention to destroy the temple and replace it magically with His own in three days (14:58), and by references to Jesus' temple-sayings in the taunts at the cross (15:29–30).

The story of the withering of the fig tree that frames the account of the temple demonstration is evidently to be understood in conjunction with it (11:12–14, 20–25). On His way to the temple, Jesus, hoping to find figs on a tree that because of its luxuriant foliage might be expected to bear fruit out of season, curses it in disappointment. The next day Peter observes that the tree has "withered away to its roots." Jesus explains this phenomenon as an instance of God-given authority ("Have faith in God," 11:22) to dispose of that which does not serve its purpose (the fruitless fig tree) or which constitutes an obstruction ("this mountain," 11:23).[8] Until

8. "This mountain" probably means the mount of the temple viewed from the Mount of Olives.

this point, apart from the casting out of evil spirits, the miracles of Jesus have always been positive achievements. The only miracle with destructive consequences was the healing of the Gerasene demoniac, in Gentile territory, when Legion drove the herd of swine into the lake. But with this parabolic action Jesus seems to claim the right to render judgment as one of His messianic prerogatives, and to trace the implementation of such judgment to divine intervention activated by "faith in God." He also calls the disciples to exercise the same authority through the medium of unwavering prayer (11:23-24) and within the context of the unbroken fellowship of the redeemed (11:25).[9] In this case the intercalation of the temple demonstration in the midst of this object lesson shows that the messianic judgment is not directed at the impious heathen, as the Jewish leaders expect, but at themselves because of their spiritual sterility. The prophecy of the destruction of the temple is undoubtedly an extension of this teaching (13:2). Thus, in order to demonstrate the exact nature of His messiahship, Jesus finds Himself obliged to challenge the practices and positions of the Jewish leaders. In the dramatic structure of the Gospel, this development has the effect of forcing the leaders to take a position publically vis-à-vis Jesus and precipitates the inevitable terminal clash between them, consequently accelerating the denouement.

"The chief priests and the scribes and the elders" come out in the open the very next day when He returns to the temple (11:27-33). Referring to the changes brought about in the temple courts as the result of Jesus' sortie, they ask Him for His credentials: "By what authority are you doing these things, or who gave you this authority to do them?" In formidable array the supreme guardians of the status quo press Jesus to account to them for His actions. He refuses and counterattacks by trying to obtain from the opponents themselves an admission of His divine authority. To recognize the now-deceased John the Baptist as a divinely appointed messenger is, because of John's early endorsement of Jesus, to authenticate Jesus. So Jesus asks the leaders to pronounce themselves on the origin of John's mission: "Was the baptism of John from heaven or from men?" This places them in a dilemma. Since they now oppose the very one John presented as the fulfiller of the kingdom, they cannot say, "From heaven" (If they did, Jesus would ask them, "Why did you not believe him?" 11:31). Neither can they say, "From men," for fear of the multitudes. Thus the learned leaders pitifully answer, "We do not know." In response, Jesus curtly dismisses their own question and, by so doing, denies them the self-assumed right to control Him. He does not deny His

9. The Gospel of Matthew contains also a statement conferring similar authority on the disciples, but in a context and wording entirely different (". . . whatever you bind on earth shall be bound in heaven, and whatever you loose on earth shall be loosed in heaven," Matt. 16:19). This declaration, made in connection with Peter's confession, is therefore linked with the possession of faith. The same text repeated in 18:18 associates such authority with harmony within the Christian community and with prayer. Although different sayings are quoted in each of the two Gospels, the three ideas of faith, community, and prayer are linked together in connection with the exercise of authority.

divine authority. By His allusion to the continuity between John's ministry and His own, He claims for His ministry the same divine origin as John's. But He firmly withholds from the Jewish leaders the prerogative of sitting in judgment over Him ("Neither will I tell you by what authority I do these things"). He does not grant them the authority to question Him about His own authority. He refuses to be held accountable to them. In other words, Jesus uses the confrontation to affirm once more His supreme independence from the Jewish establishment.[10]

But Jesus does not leave it at that. Now that the delegation of priests-scribes-elders has been turned from public accuser to defendant, Jesus presses the issue further with the parable of the vineyard (12:1–12). According to Mark the ethnarchs perceive rightly that the parable is directed against them. Their opposition to Jesus ("the beloved son" in the parable) represents the culmination of a long-standing refusal on the part of Jewish leaders to let God run the kingdom according to His will. Being only tenants, they commit violence and murder in order to become owners. They are usurpers who wish to substitute their program for God's by appropriating the kingdom for themselves (". . . the inheritance will be ours"). In the conclusion of the parable, Jesus combines three themes that receive considerable emphasis in the denouement section of the Gospel. The first is that sonship entails death ("And they took him and killed him, and cast him out of the vineyard"). As a matter of fact, the theme of the death of Christ constitutes the essential part of the denouement. The second is that the depraved tenants are judged by the owner ("He will come and destroy the tenants. . . ."). This theme is amplified to cosmic proportions in chapter 13. The third motif is that the vineyard is transferred "to others." The universal scope of Jesus' ministry has already been given some notice in the Gospel with the accounts of His incursion in Gentile territory as well as His ministrations to non-Jews.[11] But in the denouement, the universal range of the divine concern receives special attention. The temple, within the limits of which this parable is presumably spoken, was originally intended to be "a house of prayer for all the nations" (11:17). After the prediction that the tenants will be destroyed and the vineyard given to others, Jesus announces the eventual ruin of the temple and the preaching of the gospel "to all nations" (13:2, 10). On the day of salvation the elect will be gathered "from the four winds, from the ends of the earth to the ends of heaven" (13:27). Finally, the passion narrative closes with a Gentile's witness to the divine sonship of the crucified Messiah (15:39). Thus, in keeping with the removal of secrecy after Peter's confession, this parable is sufficiently explicit so that its recipients

10. Similar results were achieved previously at the end of the complication phase of the Gospel by the denial of the request for a sign from heaven (8:11–13).

11. Jesus traveled in "the region of Tyre and Sidon" (7:24); in the "region of Tyre . . . through Sidon . . . through the region of the Decapolis" (7:31). He ministered to the demoniac in "the country of the Gerasenes" (5:1); the woman who was "a Greek, a Syrophoenician by birth" (7:26); and crowds that came from Gentile territories (3:8).

understand precisely the application. Since it condemns them, they wish to arrest Jesus on the spot but are prevented from fear of the multitude. So they depart and try to create a more favorable opportunity (12:12).

To this end they engage Jesus in a series of debates designed "to entrap him in his talk" (12:13). In accord with Mark's method of developing the denouement, however, Jesus succeeds in turning each encounter into an exposure of the wicked motives and errors of the leaders, thus accelerating the fall of the action toward its inevitable outcome. The first exchange is initiated by the Pharisees and Herodians who question Jesus about payment of the Roman tax, each group representing antithetical and bitterly disputed positions on this burning issue (12:13–17). Beginning with a compliment exalting the uncompromising attitude and independent spirit of Jesus, probably designed to forestall an evasive answer, they force Him to incriminate Himself in the eyes of the Roman authorities by declaring Himself against the highly unpopular tax. But "knowing their hypocrisy," Jesus makes a frontal counterattack and exposes the hidden motives for their question ("Why put me to the test?"). Whereas He could leave it at that, He accepts the challenge to express Himself on the issue since it gives Him again the opportunity to dissociate Himself from the false messianic hopes of the Jews. By recommending submission to the abhorred Roman tribute, Jesus rejects violent resistance against the occupants and declares Himself unwilling to challenge their rule. He thus disclaims militant political preoccupations as part of His messianic role, which He places in an entirely different sphere by advocating recognition of God's claims ("Render ... to God the things that are God's"). This dissociation of God's will from concern for deliverance from Roman dominion causes all to be "amazed at him." The Pharisees are outraged because of His endorsement of the tax, while the Herodians sulk because of His reminder of obligations to God. They verify at their expense the accuracy of their hypocritical flattery of Jesus, whom they had described as standing on the side of truth without regard for consideration of persons (12:14).

Now the Sadducees try to confute Jesus in public with a favorite argument against the resurrection (12:18–27). Jesus accuses them of being "wrong" (v. 24), of being "quite wrong" (v. 27), and of knowing "neither the scriptures nor the power of God" (v. 24) because of faulty exegesis and prejudice. Here again the evangelist presented Jesus as deliberately accepting confrontations that aggravate the rift between Him and the ethnarchs and that alienate Him further from the Jewish establishment. In this connection, assistance from an unexpected source appears in the person of a seeking scribe (12:28–34). As he and Jesus converse about the first commandment, Jesus brings him to admit that love of God and neighbor is "much more than all whole burnt offerings and sacrifices," thus placing, in true prophetic manner, the spiritual demands of God above the ritual performances of the temple. As Jesus commends this exceptionally discerning scribe with a somewhat reserved, "You are not far from the kingdom of God," one wonders where that leaves the bigoted and antagonistic scribes of the establishment who think they own the kingdom of God. Understandably, "after that no one dared to ask him any question."

But Jesus will not leave the scribes alone until He has made perfectly clear His reasons for dissociating from them. Having shown that He could accept an open-minded scribe, He now explains His distrust of scribes as a class (12:35-44). First, they do not understand their own teaching. On a matter as crucial as the identity of the Messiah, they remain obsessed by physical descent and ignore the more significant dimension of spiritual transcendence, even though it is found in the Scriptures when David called his messianic progeny "Lord" (Ps. 110:1). Implied here is a silent rebuke of the scribes for erroneous, earthly messianic expectations. Second, the scribes are ostentatious in their acts of devotion and eager to receive honors. But they also oppress widows, who, although poor and seemingly insignificant (like the one who drops two copper coins in the temple treasury), can make a greater contribution before God than all the others giving in greater abundance. Characteristically, by way of dramatic contrast and while depicting such antiestablishment occurrences, Mark is careful to add a comment such as, ". . . the great throng heard him gladly" (12:37). But the fact that in the course of this teaching, Jesus has stated that the scribes "will receive the greater condemnation" accentuates further the threatening tension pervading the narrative. The prediction of the temple's destruction (13:2) and the dire forebodings of the Olivet discourse, with its emphasis on the need to "take heed" and "watch" (13:5, 9, 23, 33, 35, 37), mark the transition to the passion with a sense of gloomy apprehension. In this phase of the denouement, Jesus has openly and repeatedly challenged and accused the leaders of the Jews. In the scheme of the Gospel, it is now the leaders' turn to take the initiative.

During the second phase of the transactions between Jesus and the leaders, Mark showed the reaction of the latter as they successfully move against Jesus under the cover of darkness and with recourse to falsehood. Mark also portrayed, however, the noble bearing of Jesus that renders such precautions ridiculous; He has accepted death as part of His messianic destiny. The tragic irony of the situation is that the leaders cause Jesus to die as a pretender political messiah precisely because He has resisted their efforts to make Him a political messiah. They charge Him with the very offense they have incited Him to commit.

As the Passover approaches, the chief priests and scribes seem to waver between two alternate methods of disposing of Jesus (14:1-2). The preferred option is a secret arrest while Jesus moves in and out of Jerusalem during the feast and a private execution (they "were seeking how to arrest him by stealth, and kill him"). The contingency plan calls for a public arrest, trial, and execution, but "not during the feast, lest there be a tumult of the people." The avoidance of a popular uprising seems to constitute a consideration of paramount importance in the manner and timing of Jesus' death. Thus when Judas offers his services to the leaders, they are "glad" because his advance knowledge of the whereabouts of Jesus will facilitate a quiet kidnapping and murder (14:10-11).

Surprisingly Jesus makes Himself vulnerable to exactly this kind of foray by spending the evening in a secluded location, waiting as it were for His captors, so that when they come, they only need to lay hands on Him and seize Him (14:32–50). However, the brief resistance of a sword-wielding follower of Jesus and the successful escape of the disciples (one is almost captured, 14:51–52), renders immediate execution of Jesus hazardous; the multitude might be stirred up by reports of the arrest from the fleeing disciples.[12] Consequently Jesus is taken to the high priest's quarters where the council assembles for an emergency meeting (14:53–65). Now that the arrest of Jesus has become public knowledge, a private execution cannot be carried out for fear of reprisals from the people. Formal charges have to be lodged against Him in order to obtain His death. So the chief priests and the whole council meet the same night in order to expedite the matter before the multitude has time to react. They seek testimony against Him to put Him to death (14:55). Their frantic efforts result in confusion and frustration. But in desperation the high priest rises, faces Jesus, and asks Him point blank, "Are you the Christ, the Son of the Blessed?" In His determination to face the full consequences of His messiahship, Jesus gives an unequivocally self-incriminating answer by claiming for Himself a status infinitely more exalted than that of the petty pseudo-messiah the leaders have tried to make Him. He lays claims to messiahship, to divine sonship, and to the role of glorious fulfiller of history, saying, "I am; and you will see the Son of man seated at the right hand of Power, and coming with the clouds of heaven." Realizing that the audacity of such seemingly preposterous claims will also turn the multitude against Him, the council feels free to prosecute a public indictment. They all condemn Jesus as deserving death (14:64). Then, as if to prove the extravagance of His visionary claims, they treat the self-declared Messiah as a victim completely at their mercy. Making Him an object of contempt, they spit on Him; they cover His face and strike Him, saying, "Prophesy!" And the guards receive Him with blows (14:65).

Since time is still of the essence, the leaders take Jesus to Pilate the very next day after consulting among themselves early in the morning (15:1–15). They lodge against Him the charge of political agitation. They present Him as the aspiring ruler of a restored Jewish kingdom. Taking a careful look at Jesus, Pilate asks Him almost in unbelief, "Are you the King of the Jews?" With reciprocal ambiguity Jesus answers, "You have said so." Realizing that the exchange has been inconclusive, the chief priests resume their accusations (they "accused him of many things"). Invited to answer the charges, Jesus remains silent, and Pilate becomes completely mystified (". . . Jesus made no further answer, so that Pilate

---

12. The evangelist seems to indicate that the intention of the armed band was to kill Jesus on the spot and to silence likewise the three disciples with Him (14:33). When the other disciples appeared also on the scene, as indicated by the sudden presence of the young man (14:51), and fled after having witnessed the arrest, the plan for a private execution was discarded and replaced by that of a public trial.

wondered"). At last, Pilate concludes that Jesus' accusers have unjust motives ("... he perceived that it was out of envy that the chief priests had delivered him up"). He attempts to release Jesus, but the crowd, disappointed at Jesus' seeming powerlessness and instigated by the leaders, turns against Jesus and compels Pilate to free Barabbas, a prisoner arrested for murder and insurrection, and to crucify Jesus. Ironically the Romans release an insurrectionist and condemn to capital punishment for sedition the one who has offended the Jews by refusing to be their national liberator.

As he brought the denouement to a conclusion, the evangelist insisted on two points. In depicting the success of the leaders, he lingered on the unjustified cruelty of Christ's tormentors, which has the effect of suggesting the frightful depths of His humiliation. In the palace of the high priest, Jesus is spat upon, blindfolded and struck in the face, and He is punched by the guards (14:65). In spite of Pilate's efforts, a murderer is preferred to Him during the trial (15:11). Led into the praetorium, in the presence of "the whole battalion," Jesus receives mock homage. He is dressed in a tunic but wears a crown of thorns, is struck with a reed and spat upon again (15:17–19). He is crucified between two robbers (15:28). On the cross He is mercilessly reviled by passers-by, chief priests, scribes, and even the crucified robbers. Finally, as He cries out to God just prior to His death, a bystander, mistakenly thinking He is calling for the eschatological end through the intervention of Elijah, offers Him a drink to prolong His life and make Him suffer further disappointment (15:34–36). For all appearances Jesus is a weak and defenseless victim of His enemies. Miserably nailed to the cross, He struggles as the very symbol of powerlessness, His humiliation is complete.

On the other hand, the noble bearing of Jesus during His torments, His unflinching determination to accomplish His destiny, His private anguish in the face of death, and His composure in public all point to an exalted character and to the inevitable necessity of His death. The passion events framed between the prayer "Not what I will, but what thou will" and the cry "My God, my God, why hast thou forsaken me?" reflect some inscrutable torment tearing at the very being of God on account of men. But once Jesus says, "The hour has come; the Son of man is betrayed into the hands of sinners" (14:41), He goes to meet His fate with assurance and equanimity. When they come to arrest Him at Gethsemane, He is the one in command, reproaching the mob for not coming in broad daylight. His disciples try to resist; He does not. They run away; He stays and gives the signal to march on, saying, "... let the scriptures be fulfilled." In the palace of the high priest, false witnesses exhaust themselves in vain attempts to formulate a consistent accusation. To the high priest who asks Him to present a defense, He responds with silence. He displays the same reserve before Pilate. In both cases He refuses to defend Himself and only speaks to admit to incriminating self-identification as Messiah and King. When beaten, reviled, and tortured, He offers no resistance. When hearing the frightful taunts, tempting Him to come down from the cross and thus prove His divine nature, He resists the temptation in order to fulfill His destiny. And when offered the numbing drink prior to His execution, He refuses, preferring to face His suffering in full consciousness. Indeed the cup He asked in Gethsemane to be removed from Him, He now drinks to the very end.

The crafty ethnarchs, whom Jesus has denounced as usurpers, now gloat in their victory. They think that by killing Him they have proven Him an impostor. The sarcasm of the titulus "The King of the Jews" punctuates the account of the crucifixion with a touch of tragic irony no less than six times (15:2, 9, 12, 18, 26, 32). Thus Jesus dies accused of aspiring to a position that He has strenuously avoided. The triumph of the wily leaders seems complete. They have at last succeeded in forcing the role of messiah-king on Jesus, thus annihilating His claims to a transcendental messiahship. But as Jesus breathes His last, the curtain of the temple is torn in two from top to bottom (15:38). The institution that has stood as a stumbling block between the leaders and Jesus, the very symbol of their self-serving monopoly on the conscience of Israel, is rendered obsolete, ready to be discarded. They and their corrupt establishment and their petty notions of a Jewish king are bypassed and left far behind in the cosmic transaction of the cross. Not a Jew but the centurion "who stood facing him" recognizes the turning of history and exclaims, "Truly this man was a son of God" (15:39). Finally the action of the Gospel that began with an aside announcing Jesus as the Son of God, comes to rest at center stage with the universal ascription of divine sonship to Jesus at the moment of His death. The cross has liberated the Savior of the world from the king of the Jews.

3. *The success of the messianic program.* The other major theme running through the denouement of the Gospel, in addition to those of the disciples' preparation and the leaders' opposition, is the unfolding of the messianic program after the resurrection. In Marcan perspective the work of the disciples after Jesus' resurrection constitutes an integral part of His messianic mission. The strategy for the post-Easter affirmations and activities of the church is defined by Jesus during His earthly ministry between Peter's confession and the passion.[13] This concept of the messianic mission prolongs the denouement of the action beyond the end of the Gospel to the experience of the church, whose suffering and eschatological glory are envisioned and paralleled in Jesus' passion and resurrection. Given the obduracy of the disciples and the vicious opposition of the nation's leaders, the denouement as represented by Mark is an account of catastrophic failure. In spite of their advance preparation, the disciples desert both their Master and their vocation at the critical moment. As for the leaders, when Jesus challenges their misconceptions and aberrant practices, they contrive to put Him to death. What saves the denouement from turning into unrelieved disaster is the evangelist's emphasis in this section of the Gospel on the foreknowledge of Jesus concerning His immediate

13. See pp. 83ff.

fate[14] and especially the course of history beyond His death. Thus He predicts His resurrection, the future labors of His disciples in the midst of hardship, and their subsequent redemption in glory.

During the denouement the disciples are so obsessed with the tragic aspects of Jesus' passion predictions that they miss completely the note of victory accompanying each saying. Jesus refers specifically to His rising from the dead on five different occasions (8:31; 9:9, 31; 10:34; 14:28). Only once do the disciples dwell sufficiently on the subject to question among themselves the significance of "the rising from the dead" (9:10). Unable to reconcile suffering with the role of Messiah, they ignore entirely the possibility of a reversal in the form of resurrection. Their desertion during the crucifixion gives a measure of their incomprehension. Their absence at the burial indicates the despair and the sense of finality with which they view the death of Jesus. On three occasions Jesus gave them a time element, telling them that He would rise from the dead "after three days." On the third day no disciple makes his way to the tomb. Three women do, but to complete the embalming of His body, not to verify the resurrection. They go on the third day accidentally, owing to the exigencies of sabbath restrictions (16:1). Mark emphasized their complete lack of anticipation of anything unusual by reporting their comment, "Who will roll away the stone for us from the door of the tomb?" When they see that the "very large" stone has been moved, they remain so unsuspecting as to enter the tomb. The white-clad messenger who confronts them attempts to reassure them ("Do not be amazed"), as if they should have anticipated this turn of events. He then authenticates his momentous announcement by citing particulars that they can spontaneously verify. "You seek Jesus of Nazareth, who was crucified. . . . he is not here; see the place where they laid him." As the messenger makes his ringing announcement in the familiar words of the resurrection prediction, but in reverse chronological order, "He is risen," it is not recall or comprehension that seizes the women, but terror. And in a scene of unsurpassable dramatic power, Mark brings the Gospel to a close by describing the women fleeing breathlessly from the tomb, rendered speechless with fear.[15]

The Gospel of Mark comes to an end. But not the gospel of Jesus Christ. The latter has a specific beginning (1:1) but no end. The messenger

14. Repeated references in the Scriptures to the foreordination of the Messiah's destiny buttress Jesus' determination to meet His destiny as the accomplishment of God's will. See 9:12–13; 12:10–11; 13:36; 14:49; 15:34.

15. Theodore J. Weeden set forth the fantastic theory that according to Mark, the women remained mute forever after and consequently the disciples were never rehabilitated. *Mark: Traditions in Conflict*, pp. 45–51. It seems very doubtful that Mark would have wanted to imply that the women took it upon themselves to disobey the heavenly order given to them so explicitly in 16:7. To suppose that 16:8b means that the women did not publicize their Easter-morning discovery runs contrary to the indications of the text ("there *you* will see him"). Evidently 8b is intended to dramatize and amplify 8a by describing the flight of the women as they were overcome with aphonic terror.

at the tomb commands the women, ". . . go, tell his disciples and Peter that he is going before you to Galilee; there you will see him, as he told you" (16:7). Before the passion the disciples had promised Jesus that they would stay with Him and never deny Him. Peter had declared that he preferred death to denial, and the other disciples had all concurred (14:31). In the same context Jesus had promised that He would go ahead of the disciples and meet them in Galilee after His resurrection (14:28). The disciples, and Peter in particular, pathetically failed to abide by their resolution, doing precisely what they had pledged never to do. However, once risen, Jesus, according to His promise, is already on His way to Galilee. The angel confirms, ". . . there you will see him, as he told you."[16] His message bespeaks a gracious and undeserved restoration to the status of disciples, a coming of age that eluded them before the passion, a fulfillment of their vocation that has been constantly postponed to this very moment. The Galilee rendezvous also suggests the enlightenment of the many potential disciples who have received a teaching that was to remain veiled until after the passion.[17] Now that the lamp has been removed from under the bushel and placed on a stand, nothing that was hidden has not been made manifest, nothing that was secret has not come to light (4:21–22). Even to those outside, the secret of the kingdom of God can now be revealed so that they may indeed see and perceive, hear and understand, that they should turn again and be forgiven (4:11–12).

Thus the new age inaugurated by the resurrection finds its impetus within Mark's Gospel itself. When Jesus began His ministry, He called the people to make ready for the imminent realization of a long-awaited manifestation of God's transcendence ("The time is fulfilled, and the kingdom of God is at hand; repent, and believe in the gospel," 1:15). Later, in the parables of the kingdom, He elaborated on this new initiative of God in human life and described it as a gradual process unfolding in three successive phases.[18]

The first phase, symbolized in the sowing, fall, and scattering of seed, represents the kingdom embodied in Jesus Christ during His earthly ministry. With His arrival on the scene of human affairs, the kingdom came close at hand (1:15). Those who came to Him expectantly and in faith, like little children, possessed the kingdom of God by virtue of His own

16. It has sometimes been suggested that Mark's Galilee rendezvous is not to be understood as a reference to the postresurrection appearance of Jesus but as a promise of the Parousia. E.g., Weeden, *Mark*, pp. 111–17. This position is invalidated, however, by the fact that Peter is specifically referred to in verse 7 by the messenger: ". . . tell his disciples and Peter that he is going before you to Galilee; there you will see him. . . ." Thus the disciples, Peter, and the women will see Jesus in Galilee. At the time of the writing of the Gospel, the author knew that Peter had died and that the Parousia had obviously not taken place. Consequently Mark could not have understood the statement as a reference to the Parousia since it would have been proven false at the time of writing.

17. See p. 75.

18. See pp. 74–75.

availability ("Let the children come to me . . . for to such belongs the kingdom of God," 10:14). The kingdom of God could be received simply and trustingly, as a child receives (". . . receive the kingdom of God like a child," 10:15). Even a scribe who perceived the need for apprehending spiritual reality directly instead of through the agency of the sacrificial system was declared to be "not far from the kingdom of God." His encounter with Jesus put the kingdom within his reach (12:34). And because Joseph of Arimathea, although a member of the council, was "looking for the kingdom of God," he alone took it upon himself to honor Jesus even at the time of His death, having recognized in Him the very substance of his hope (15:43). According to Mark, with Jesus Christ the kingdom was already present among men. They could become participants in it by putting their faith in Him.

The second phase of the kingdom's progress is pictured in the process of growth also recognizable in the parables. The death and resurrection of Jesus will cause the seed of the kingdom to expand through the agency of the church, since Jesus will remain in close touch with the church. It is probably in this perspective that the transfiguration is best interpreted. According to Mark, apart from its value for the three accompanying disciples, the transfiguration was intended to benefit the new community after the resurrection (". . . he charged them to tell no one what they had seen, until the Son of man should have risen from the dead," 9:9). Then the church was to be told that during His earthly ministry Jesus manifested Himself briefly but convincingly in the glory of His supernatural transcendence. He gave proof of belonging to two worlds simultaneously. In the same manner the church was to believe that after the resurrection the glorified Jesus is actively present in her midst, overseeing the work of the kingdom. Since He belonged to two worlds at once, He was close to them, although invisible. Peter had understandably desired to preserve the experience of the spiritual world's irruption into his own (". . . let us make three booths," 9:5). But this had been as impossible then as it was now. The church was left with the command: "This is my beloved Son; listen to him" (9:7).[19] The kingdom was being realized not through Christ's visible presence but through the disciples' obedience to Him.[20] In this perspective the resurrection marks the dawn of a new phase of God's economy, when the training received by the disciples and prospective disciples prior to the passion becomes effective.[21] In this new age the kingdom of God is manifested in the life of the new community and in the disciples' vocation of service.

19. By approving the authority of Jesus in the presence of Moses and Elijah, the divine voice declared obsolete both Judaism (Moses) and the Baptist's continuing following (Elijah).

20. The statement reported in 9:1 that, along with the command to delay divulgence of the experience (9:9), frames the transfiguration pericope is best interpreted as a prediction of the growth of the church rather than as an eschatological statement.

21. See p. 83.

The third phase of the kingdom corresponds to fruitbearing, to the harvest and to the development of the hospitable, full-grown mustard tree in the parables. It is the eschatological kingdom. Jesus called it also the "life," and He recommended sacrificing hand or foot in order to accede to it rather than going intact but sinful into its opposite, "hell" (9:44–45). Likewise it is preferable to sacrifice an eye and enter the "kingdom of God," rather than to preserve it as inducement to sin and "be thrown into hell" (9:47). The kingdom of God in its present form must be received as a child receives in order to qualify for the kingdom when it comes in such a way as to be entered into (10:15). The kingdom of God is also the privileged destination of those "who can be saved" and from which, except for the grace of God, the rich will be excluded (10:23–27). It is equivalent to that "eternal life" to which the rich young man preferred his possessions (10:17–22). The "elect" will enter this kingdom at the close of the age when human history teeters on the verge of collapse (13:14–22) and the universe disintegrates (13:24–25). Then the Son of man will come in clouds with great power and glory. His angels will gather the elect "from the ends of the earth to the ends of heaven" (13:26–27). But the would-be disciples who have failed to identify with the kingdom in their vocation of service and witness will be rejected when "the Son of man . . . comes in the glory of his Father with the holy angels" (8:38). As for those of the council who decided to put Him to death, they "will see the Son of man seated at the right hand of Power, and coming with the clouds of heaven" (14:62). And in "that day," Christ will drink again a new wine "in the kingdom of God" (14:25).

This dynamic view of the kingdom, which anticipates its expansion in time and space and its increase in visibility and numbers, gives the Gospel a dramatic effect beyond the unfolding of the story itself. The kingdom starts at a specific point in time, shortly before the arrest of John, and outlasts the crumbling of the universe to inaugurate eternity. Taking its abode in one individual as He comes from Nazareth of Galilee to be baptized by John, it sweeps over the world and reaches "to the ends of heaven." The kingdom infiltrates the world of men secretly and enlightens the centuries until its final manifestation becomes radiantly and universally visible. It begins with one, and it closes with the elect "from the four winds, from the ends of the earth." Although the burial of Jesus brings the action of the Gospel to a close, the resurrection sets in motion a new era that finds its definition and impetus within the Gospel but takes place beyond the time span of the Gospel. Thus in the true sense of the word *denouement*, the resurrection brings to a climactic liberation the complication created by the secret of the Messiah whose destiny was to save not by conquest but by suffering.

The foregoing analysis indicates that the Gospel falls naturally into the pattern advocated for Greek tragedy by Aristotle. That such compatibility stems from deliberate design seems undeniable. The classic development of the action, the perfect structural balance, the careful interweaving of motifs, the cohesion of the parts into the whole—all suggest meticulous care in the selection of materials from available sources and fastidious redactional organization. The flawless development of the plot from complication to denouement conforms to Aristotle's requirements for Greek tragedy.

II

Besides the complication-crisis-denouement pattern, Aristotle made two other recommendations concerning the plot of tragedies. The first requires that ideal tragic effect, or what he called the arousing of "pity and fear," be achieved by a combination of three elements: discovery, reversal, and suffering. The other concerns the so-called rule of the three unities. Again, these categories seem to correspond to parallel features in the Gospel of Mark.

Aristotle defined the *discovery* as "a change from ignorance to knowledge," revealing an unknown aspect of relationship between protagonists of a play.[22] He analyzed six types of situations that lead to recognition of identity: (1) discovery by marks, tokens, scars, or inanimate objects; (2) discovery by arbitrary disclosures of identity; (3) discovery through recall of memories; (4) discovery by inference or reasoning; (5) discovery through a mistake; and (6) discovery through the development of the action itself. The last form of discovery was preferred by Aristotle: "The best of all discoveries is that arising from the incidents themselves, when the great surprise comes about through a probable incident."[23] The reasons for his preferring a natural process of recognition to the use of artificial devices or contrived situations are affective and technical. He referred to the greater emotional impact of the tragic discovery when it naturally derives from the action ("love or hate," "good or evil fortune"). But more important, the discovery "form most directly connected with the plot and the action of the piece" contributes to the progress of the play rather than standing in its midst as a contrived addition. "It will also serve to bring about the happy or unhappy ending."[24] As previously cited, Aristotle used two plays by way of illustration.[25] In *Oedipus the King* the tragic identity of the hero is revealed through the interplay of the characters, without "the artifice of signs and necklaces." In the *Iphigenia in Tauris* the heroine's identity is revealed to her brother Orestes in an equally natural manner, "for it was not improbable that she should wish to have a letter taken home." Having stated his preference for discoveries resulting from the action itself, Aristotle said, "Next after them come discoveries through reasoning."[26] He thus manifested a firm dislike of recognition scenes that depend on the production of devices or on artificial stratagems.

22. *On the Art of Poetry*, ed. and trans. Ingram Bywater, 11.47.
23. Ibid., 16.60.
24. Ibid., 11.47.
25. See pp. 54–55.
26. *On the Art of Poetry* 16.60.

The recognition scene of the Gospel meets the specifications suggested in the *Poetics* ("On the Art of Poetry"). Not only does the discovery of Jesus' messianic identity result from prior action, but the dramatic effect of the recognition is heightened by the fact that it is long overdue when it takes place. By word and deed Jesus is presented as attempting to provoke such awareness. When it finally happens, it has a cathartic effect. Although motivated by theological considerations rather than dramatic, Mark's depiction of Jesus' refusal to perform a sign from heaven as proof of His messiahship is faintly reminiscent of Aristotle's aversion to mechanical and contrived means of identification. Moreover, the tilt that occurs in the action from complication to denouement as a direct result of the discovery, indicates that the recognition scene constitutes an integral part of the plot and that it contributes to the progress of the action as Aristotle recommended.

The second element Aristotle considered necessary for a good plot is the *reversal*, also called peripety or recoil. In his own words, "Peripety is the change from one state of things within the play to its opposite of the kind described, and that too in the way we are saying, in the probable or necessary sequence of events." To clarify his point, Aristotle again cited *Oedipus the King* as an example: "Here the opposite state of things is produced by the messenger who, coming to gladden Oedipus and remove his fears as to his mother, reveals the secret of his birth." In the ideal plot, recognition and reversal are joined by a relationship of cause and effect. Thus, "the finest form of discovery is one attended by peripeties [or, reversal], like that which goes with the discovery of Oedipus."[27]

In the Gospel, the recognition of Jesus is immediately followed by a somber prediction of catastrophe. This is the reversal. It is so unexpected that Peter begins to rebuke Jesus. But the newly revealed Messiah protests that it is the will of God for Him. The announcement of this self-imposed fate is the turn of fortune that marks the beginning of the falling action. Ernest W. Burch sensed the interdependence of the recognition and reversal: "In Mark both change of fortune and recognition occur in chapters 8 and 9, namely, the so-called 'confession of Peter' at Caesarea Philippi and the transfiguration scene. These two narratives function mutually to intensify the recognition of Jesus as Messiah, while the 'falling action' toward the denouement reveals the manner in which the action swings upon the massive pivot of the recognition scene."[28]

The acuteness of the sudden reversal is emphasized by Peter's protestations. But the inevitability of the predicted tragedy is expressed by Jesus' identification of His fate with the will of God. This explicit prediction is all the more tragic because the hopes and expectations that the disciples had centered upon Jesus have just been confirmed by the declaration of His messiahship. The natural result of this declaration should be a

27. Ibid., 11.46–47.

28. "Tragic Action in the Second Gospel: A Study of the Narrative of Mark," p. 349.

manifestation of glory and assurance of victory. Instead they receive predictions of shame and apparent defeat. It is a complete reversal.

Aristotle undoubtedly encouraged the juxtaposition of the recognition and the reversal because of its dramatic effect. It is remarkable how in the Gospel the reversal is surrounded by the two phases of the recognition: first, the discovery of Caesarea Philippi; and second, the confirmation on the transfiguration mount. No closer connection could have been made.

Once the reversal takes place, no relief occurs until the resurrection. What seemed, before Peter's confession, a festive circuit through Galilee, suddenly turns into a somber cortege moving toward Jerusalem, which becomes itself the scene of the violent deed.

Finally, the Gospel also contains the third element deemed essential to tragedy by Aristotle, the pathos, variously called the *suffering*, the deed of violence or horror, the tragic incident. He defined it as "an action of a destructive or painful nature, such as murders on the stage, tortures, woundings, and the like."[29] The suffering should be the natural outcome of the reversal.

A critical convention sometimes attributed to Greek tragedians is that deaths and deeds of violence should occur behind the scenes. This idea is certainly not reflected in the *Poetics*. In the above quotation Aristotle specifically mentioned deaths "on the stage," or according to another translation, "before the audience."[30] In any case, if such a rule existed, it does not seem to have affected the tragic poets. Aeschylus did not hesitate to exhibit the bloody corpses of Clytemnestra and Aegisthus in the *Choephoroe*, and this after Orestes holds a dagger over his adulterous mother through an entire scene prior to killing her. Sophocles brought Oedipus back on stage after he has plucked out his own eyes. And Euripides showed Hercules destroying his children in a moment of madness, Alecestis and Hippolytus dying on their couches, Medea standing by the corpses of her children she has just murdered, and Ajax falling upon his sword. As a further refinement in poignancy, Aristotle advised that such deeds be committed within the circle of personae bound by natural ties: "Whenever the tragic deed is done within the family—when murder and the like is done or meditated by brother on brother, by son on father, by mother on son, or son on mother—these are the situations the poet should seek after."[31] Aristotle's canons regarding the deed of violence are not dictated by sadistic inclinations. They relate to his belief that tragedy should imitate life in an exaggerated form, magnified on the stage, in order to convey the poet's message and achieve the intended effect. To be properly tragic the deed of violence must be "in a special sense representative. It must be the kind of act that men are constitutionally liable to commit: an act expressing the fundamental human condition."[32] In

29. *On the Art of Poetry* 11.48.
30. Gilbert Norwood, *Greek Tragedy*, p. 45.
31. *On the Art of Poetry* 14.53.
32. Dorothea Krook, *Elements of Tragedy*, p. 10.

tragedy the most shameful and therefore the most pathetic acts of shame appear to be acts of betrayal or rejection.[33]

These categories are applicable to the passion story, which stands in the Gospel as the counterpart of the deed of violence in tragedy. The account of Jesus' suffering and death is revolting not only because of the physical violence unjustly perpetrated upon a righteous person, but especially because of the unthinkable horror of the situation. It is clear to the reader that Jesus is the Messiah. But the leaders of His own people fail to recognize their deliverer and put Him to death because of His very claim to messiahship. Mercilessly Mark described the full extent of the tragedy. Pilate asks Jesus, "Are you the King of the Jews?"; he asks the crowd, "Do you want me to release for you the King of the Jews?"; and again, "Then what shall I do with the man whom you call the King of the Jews?"; and the horrible answer comes, "Crucify him." Then the soldiers dress Him as a king and salute Him, saying, "Hail, King of the Jews!" On the cross "the inscription of the charge against him" reads "The King of the Jews." And finally the terrible taunt of His torturers lashes at Jesus, agonizing on the cross: "Let the Christ, the King of Israel, come down from the cross. . . ."

The tragic incident of the Gospel occurs among those who in reality are bound by natural ties. It is a story of rejection, betrayal, and regicide. But as Aristotle allowed, the murderer may accomplish his deed "in ignorance of his relationship, and discover that afterwards."[34] The resurrection assures the eventual vindication of Jesus as Messiah, but not until the full fury of human pride has wasted itself against the outpouring of divine mercy.

The last item to be considered with respect to the plot is the rule of the *three unities:* unity of action, unity of time, and unity of place. Attributed to Aristotle during the Renaissance, this literary convention was slavishly observed by the Italian and French tragedians. In France, after much argument, it became the cornerstone of the literary drama. In his versified *Art Poétique* (1674), the neoclassical poet and critic Nicolas Boileau laid down as an absolute rule:

> *Qu'en un lieu, qu'en un jour, un seul fait accompli*
> *Tienne jusqu'à la fin le théâtre rempli.*[35]

This rule, sometimes revered as the "Aristotelian unities" and sometimes mocked as the "weird sisters" of neoclassicism, eventually gave way to the freer conventions of the modern romantic movement.

The rule of the unity of action is unequivocally articulated in the *Poetics.* The story "must represent one action, a complete whole, with its several incidents so closely connected that the transposal or withdrawal of any one of them will disjoin and dislocate the whole. For that which makes no perceptible difference by its presence or absence is no real part

33. Ibid., p. 11.

34. *On the Art of Poetry* 14.54.

35. "A single action occurring in one place and in one day / Should occupy the stage from beginning to end."

of the whole."[36] In other words, the action must be homogeneous, consistent, continuous, and free from elements extraneous to the progress of the plot.

As shown in the above analysis of the complication-denouement pattern of the Gospel, its action is governed by the paradox of the unrecognized presence of the Messiah among His people. The Messiah finds Himself unable to proclaim His messiahship because the nature of His vocation is beyond the understanding of His contemporaries. He is content to demonstrate it for those who have eyes to see and ears to hear. He heals, performs miracles, announces the kingdom, and proclaims the sovereignty of God. But His lasting mission is a spiritual one. Those that surround Him, however, fail to discern it. Their conception of the messiahship, entrenched in nationalistic categories, is entirely opposed to it. Any messianic claimant who does not conform to their expectations is assumed to be an impostor.

Thus the plot of the Gospel resides in the failure of men to recognize in Jesus their spiritual Messiah and the necessity that lays upon Jesus to fulfill His task in spite of their blindness. The efforts of Jesus to discharge fully His duties as the Son of God among men safeguard the unity of the action. The mystery that surrounds Jesus, the amazement of the crowds, the blindness of the disciples, the hostility of the leaders, the explanations of all these troubling elements of the Gospel are found in the dramatic paradox of the unknown Messiah. They also contribute to the development of the action. Each event, each saying of Jesus adds drama and intensity to the plot without diverting interest from the main theme. With every new miracle, new healing, new teaching, new manifestation of authority, the bewilderment of the crowd and the hatred of Jesus' adversaries increase. But the disclosure of Jesus' nature and mission is being prepared for the future. In regard to the revelation of His messiahship, Jesus seems to be constantly winding a time bomb that will explode only after His death, at the resurrection.

Nothing in the Gospel fails to enter into the basic purpose or fit the action. Even what seems completely foreign to the plot contributes to it. A good example is the death of John the Baptist. At first glance the story appears to break the course of the action. But the narration of the death of him who had been so popular with the multitude and yet was put to death by the authorities creates a particular mood in the Gospel when one considers the favor Jesus is winning with the crowds as described in the context.[37] The dramatic effect adds to the intensity and progress of the action. Moreover, the mention of the fact that the disciples of John "came and took his body, and laid it in a tomb" may be a portent of what will happen to the one he announced (6:14–29).

Mark composed the Gospel with the intent of safeguarding unity of action. His selection of material makes this point clear. The absence of

36. *On the Art of Poetry* 8.42.

37. The mission of the twelve disciples (6:7–12) and the feeding of the five thousand (6:31–44).

birth and infancy narratives at the beginning of the Gospel and the omission of appearance stories at the end have raised much speculation. The Gospel begins *in media res*, initiating a plot. It terminates when the plot is at its logical end. Any additional material at the beginning or end would be superfluous and even damaging to the unity of action that characterizes the story.[38] Aristotle's rule seems to have been respected by Mark.

The great tragic writers of the seventeenth century thought that the rule of unity of time and place was as binding upon Greek drama as that of unity of action. They were wrong. Aristotle said little about unity of time and nothing at all about unity of place. Greek tragedy generally respected both unities, however, although no explicit rule enforced them. They were more or less self-imposed by the nature of the plays. Unity of time and place were related to stage presentation. The technical problem of changing scenery and the constant presence on stage of the chorus made it hardly possible to move the play from one place to another. Moreover, the exacting demand of likelihood required that the action presented not exceed disproportionately the lapse of time on stage. Aristotle only made the dispassionate comment that the tragedy "endeavors to keep as far as possible within a single circuit of the sun, or something near that." [39]

Most Greek tragedies attempt to respect the unity of time but none too strenuously. The concept is treated with a greal deal of freedom in the plays of Aeschylus and Euripides. But generally speaking, in Greek and Latin drama the time element does not call attention to itself. Very often separate incidents are telescoped to conceal intervals of time.

The element of time is almost completely disregarded by Mark. Throughout the narrative he omitted all indications of time (periods and delays) except for two that have special significance: the six days between Peter's confession at Caesarea Philippi and the transfiguration, and the three days between Jesus' death and His resurrection. There seems to be deliberate intent to give no indication of length of time. The constant use of simple connectives between sections, such as "and," "now," "immediately," "soon after," and "in those days," constitute telling evidence of Mark's reluctance to mention any lapses of time. In fact, the ministry seems to consist of an impressive sequence of dramatic incidents, relentlessly pressing upon each other without any pause between. The word εὐθύς ("immediately") is found over forty times in the gospel; "its repetition makes the life of Christ seem to pass before us in a rush."[40] It is perfectly plausible that this procedure results from the author's concern to give a chronologically unbroken narrative, the action of which occupies a relatively limited stretch of time. Thus he preserved the unity of time. What is lost in information is gained in dramatic effect. Apparently Mark deemed it more important to transmit a swift-moving and lively account of Jesus' ministry than a conscientious timetable of exact chronology. This method was also consistent with conventional drama-writing.

38. See pp. 134ff.

39. *On the Art of Poetry* 5.34.

40. James A. Kleist, *The Gospel of Saint Mark*, p. 162.

The same held for unity of place as for unity of time in Greek tragedy; it was not formally enforced but generally respected. For instance, in Euripides' *Electra* the whole action takes place in front of a hut on a bleak mountain side, with the river Ruachers in the distance; and in Sophocles' *Antigone*, in front of the royal palace in Thebes. In some plays, however, this limitation is cast aside and more freedom taken. In the *Choephoroe* Aeschylus presented many locations at the same time on the same stage. But more generally the action occurs in a neutral place, a very vaguely defined and conventional location.

It would seem impossible to preserve unity of place in the narration of an itinerant ministry. Mark had Jesus say, "Let us go on to the next towns, that I may preach there also; for that is why I came out." (1:38). But in spite of this difficulty, the Gospel is geographically very simple. The stage is set in Galilee, around the lake area, and it remains there a good part of the time. The action ends there *in absentia* (16:7). Jesus appears as a familiar figure in the cities of Capernaum, Beth-saida, the little towns surrounding the lake, and the regions on the border of Galilee such as Tyre, Sidon, the Decapolis, and the district of Dalmanutha. Most references to displacements are shrouded with vagueness. We know that Jesus goes from one side of the sea to the other, that He is beside the sea or in some lonely place. But Mark gave no attention to precise indications of places. [41] The stage scenery remains the same. Jesus also ministers to people who are not inhabitants of Galilee. But instead of having Jesus go to them, Mark described them coming to Jesus. He thus preserved unity of place. He said that when "Jesus withdrew with his disciples to the sea, . . . a great multitude from Galilee followed; also from Judea and Jerusalem and Idumea and from beyond the Jordan and from about Tyre and Sidon a great multitude . . . came to him" (3:7–8).

The Gospel has only one main change of scenery. It comes as Jesus decides to go down to Judea, where His ministry will find its dramatic climax. The reader-spectator follows Jesus on this sad journey, "on the road going up to Jerusalem," passing through Jericho, Bethphage, and Bethany, and finally to the great city that first acclaims but finally kills the Messiah. As Jesus moves away from the safe and familiar shores of the lake, the forecasts of His tragic fate become more explicit; the danger increases until He is "delivered to the Gentiles" in the hostile Jewish capital city far away from His native and familiar Galilee. But the Gospel ends on the comforting promise of a reunion in Galilee. Thus Mark described a ministry that has breadth and proportion but that does not unnecessarily call attention to details of locality. In a subtle and delicate manner he managed to preserve a reasonable degree of unity of place.

41. "Mark is vague about many geographical details (cf. 5:1; 7:31; 10:1; 11:1), and it is well-nigh impossible to discover any motive for introducing them." Eduard Schweizer, *The Good News According to Mark*, p. 171.

Chapter 5

Other Dramatic Features

I

According to Aristotle the second constituent component of tragedy is character (ethos), since in importance it stands next to the plot.[1] The question as to whether Aristotle intended character to be exhibited by one central figure or whether he intended it to derive from the agon, the action borne out of crisis, constitutes one of the continuing controversies in classical criticism. Against an impressive array of contrary opinion, it has been advanced that Aristotle never entertained the concept of a central figure as a tragic hero and that this invention was imposed on the *Poetics* ("On the Art of Poetry").[2]

It is correct that the *Poetics* contains no specific discussion on the place or role of the tragic hero as the locus of dramatic intensity. But the proponents of an Aristotelian tragic hero point to the several passages in the *Poetics* where Aristotle's specifications presuppose one dominant figure.[3] As the titles of several fifth-century plays indicate, the action of most tragedies revolves around one personage, perhaps the lingering legacy of the original one-actor show. In Mark's time the fashion was to build tragedies around a clearly delineated central figure, as attested by several of Seneca's works. Through the influence of Seneca's tragedies, the tragic hero attained a position of inexpugnable dominance in the theater of the Renaissance.[4]

The comparison of the hero of Greek or Latin tragedy with the Jesus of the Gospel would constitute a futile school exercise rather than a serious demonstration since their portrayals are independent in origin, form, intent, and setting. Should the rapprochement suggest affinities, however, the case for the Gospel-writer's use of elements from the tragedy genre would be further substantiated.

Aristotle's identification of the distinctive marks of the main characters in antique tragedy constitutes a succinct and representative analysis

---

1. *On the Art of Poetry*, ed. and trans. Ingram Bywater, 6.38. As noted previously, Aristotle's enumeration is followed in this study for reasons of convenience, not because of oracular veneration.

2. John Jones, *On Aristotle and Greek Tragedy*, pp. 13–21.

3. Some of these passages are discussed below.

4. The very titles of Jean Racine's tragedies suggest the importance of the hero: *Alexandre, Andromaque, Britannicus, Bérénice, Bajazet, Mithridate, Iphigénie*, and *Phèdre*.

of what we will continue to call, for the sake of convenience, the hero.[5]
Aristotle's first requirement for the depiction of character probably reflects the custom of the day in the selection of subjects: tragic heroes
should be "of the number of those in the enjoyment of great reputation
and prosperity."[6] In accord with this precept, most Attic tragedies draw
their subjects from the Trojan cycle and from the saga of the house of
Laius in the Theban line. The justification for this preference of characters
of exalted station lies in Aristotle's definition of tragedy as "an imitation
of personages better than the ordinary man."[7] Hence the appeal to characters of noble birth and from royal families. And in the eventuality that the
chosen subject does not naturally measure up to these norms, Aristotle
advised recourse to "artistic" embellishment in character portrayal: "We in
our way should follow the example of good portrait-painters, who reproduce the distinctive features of a man, and at the same time, without
losing the likeness, make him handsomer than he is."[8]

Aristotle epitomized this likeness in four points: tragic heroes must
have goodness, propriety (or appropriateness), verisimilitude (or reality),
and self-consistency.[9] The hero will possess goodness if "what a personage
says or does reveals a certain moral purpose; and a good element of character, if the purpose so revealed is good." In other words, the hero must be
endowed with moral motivation so as to opt for the right choices as
dictated by duty. He must also have propriety; he must be true to type. If
the role calls for manly valor or eloquence, the character must be a male.
It is not "appropriate in a female character to be manly, or clever." Beside
the culturally conditioned display of male chauvinism, Aristotle was warning against incongruous characterization that befits comedy better than
tragedy. Third, the characters must be true to life; they must be made
"like the reality." They must feel, love, suffer, and act in a convincing
manner. Otherwise the spectator is unable to identify with the hero and
remains unaffected, which runs at cross-purposes with the cathartic function of tragedy. Finally, characters should be consistent, that is, true to
their own nature, throughout the play. The hero should have unity. And in
case the play requires a character whose dominant trait is inconsistency,
Aristotle recommended that "he should still be consistently inconsistent."

The observance of such conventions contributed to a mode of hero-
portrayal distinctive of ancient tragedy. By necessity it reduced the elements of characterization to the minimum required by the action. The
resulting economy of style and the dignified descriptive spareness add to
the hero's stature by discouraging familiarity. He is seen in silhouette
rather than in minute detail. He is flesh and blood and suffers like all

5. It should be remembered that Aristotle's preference for the works of
Sophocles affected his analysis of the hero.

6. *On the Art of Poetry* 13.50.

7. Ibid., 13.57.

8. Ibid., 15.57.

9. Ibid., 15.55–56.

mortals. But even in dire extremity he is surrounded with an aura of mystery and grandeur that keeps common mortals at a distance. When threatened or afflicted, the hero's aristocratic origins and noble deportment provide an ultimate recourse in the face of engulfing despair. Dorothea Krook defined the intended function of the tragic hero as being "representative of all humanity in embodying some fundamental persistent aspect of man's nature; in meeting his representative situation with the recognizable equipment of a human being." But she recognized also that the hero's tragic role, as over against his human identification, requires that he not be representative in the sense of being an ordinary, undistinguished person. "What he represents is the furthest of human possibility, not its middle or middlemost reaches; what he exhibits is the heights and depths of human experience, the extremes of suffering and knowledge, not their common average pitch and level." And she concluded, "Thus, paradoxically, the hero in tragedy is representative of all humanity, by being exceedingly unlike humanity."[10]

It has already been stated that Mark did not intend to write a Greek tragedy. His was the task of putting together a new form of literary composition that would promote the unique impact of a dynamic and effervescent religious experience. That in so doing, the availability of a compatible literary precedent in the rich heritage of his cultural milieu should have suggested itself to him is understandable, especially in view of the points of correspondence between Jesus in the Gospel and the hero in Greek tragedy. Points of the foregoing description of the tragic hero could equally apply to Jesus in the Gospel; He occupies the central place and the action is entirely dependent upon Him. In addition to being presented as the "Son of David," the scion of a royal family, Jesus possesses additional and exclusive titles of nobility, being introduced from the very beginning as the "Son of God" and being thus designated on the cross. Mortals can identify with Him since He, like the tragic hero, is presented in the fullness of humanity. He moves in a threatening world fraught with contingencies. He is surrounded by unscrupulous and hypocritical fault-finders, boastful but cowardly followers, importunate and fickle crowds, derelicts ravaged in body and devastated in spirit. He Himself is sensitive to the pressure of circumstances. He grieves in empathy and in anger. He is overtaken by emotions and fatigue. He recoils from His tragic destiny and screams in anguish in the presence of death. But He is also "better than the ordinary man," as required of the tragic hero, not only because of His unique relation to God, not only because of His good, benevolent, and compassionate deeds, not only because of the integrity and incisiveness of His teaching, but especially because of His unshakable determination to meet His dire fate and thus accomplish the will of God. Except for the connotations of vindictiveness, Bernard Knox's sketch of Sophocles' main protagonist applies also to Him who dominates the Gospel: "Immovable once his decision is taken, deaf to appeals and persuasion, to reproof and threat, unterrified by physical violence, even by the ultimate violence of death

10. *Elements of Tragedy*, pp. 36–37.

itself, more stubborn as his isolation increases until he has no one to speak
to but the unfeeling landscape, bitter at the disrespect and the mockery
the world levels at what it regards as failure, the hero prays for revenge
and curses his enemies as he welcomes the death that is the predictable
end of his intransigence."[11]

Thus, to some extent, the tragic hero is responsible for the vicissi-
tudes that befall him. His heroic resolve reduces his options to those that
entail suffering. This propensity for catastrophe is described by Aristotle
as hamartia. Since Aristotle repudiated the notion that, in tragedy, misfortune comes about through "vice and depravity,"[12] the term *hamartia* is
obviously devoid of connotations of moral deficiency. Aristotle required
that the hero be brought low "by some error of judgment."[13] This trait or
ideal of the hero need not be reprehensible. It may even consist of a moral
bent or quality that is turned into a liability for the hero by an exceptional
set of circumstances. Such, for instance, is Antigone's loyalty to her family
and attachment to religious traditions, which force her to seek her
brother's burial at the risk of her own life. The fact that the hamartia is
not necessarily a moral flaw has been widely recognized. John Jones stated
that "nearly all professional Aristotelians have felt obliged, in the face of
related passages in the *Nicomachean Ethics* and the *Rhetoric*, to take this
word to mean error of judgment and to exclude any strong implications of
moral fault or shortcoming."[14]

This presence within the heroic character of a driving determination
akin to obsession, often the result of predestination, also suggests some
correspondence with the figure of Christ. Both in tragedy and in the
Gospel, the fateful determination of the hero forces tragic confrontations
with his environment. G. Wilson Knight recognized both the similarity and
the discontinuity between the tragic hero and Jesus: "Generally in drama
the tragic hero, though conceived on a grander scale than his community,
can be said to fail partly at least through some fault. Here the protagonist
is in every way more perfect than his world, the usual tragic relation being
to this extent reversed. Jesus's life distils the quintessence of human
reality: his story presents an absolute, finished and complete life in

11. *The Heroic Temper*, p. 44. Striking parallels between tragedy and the
Gospel may be drawn on the basis of Knox's detailed analysis of the
Sophoclean hero's attitude and character. Pp. 10–42.

12. *On the Art of Poetry* 13.50.

13. Ibid.

14. *Greek Tragedy*, p. 75. Northrop Frye stated that "the great majority
of tragic heroes possess *hybris*, a proud, passionate, obsessed or soaring
mind which brings about a morally intelligible downfall." *Anatomy of
Criticism*, p. 210. Oscar Mandel saw Jesus as part of this majority: "Jesus
appears little different from other prophets of the time who died as a
result of dangerous experiments involving their kinship with God—of
hybris, in short." He adduced Jesus' sayings about the temple (John 2:19;
Matt. 26:61), the twelve legions of angels (Matt. 26:53), and the Son of
man coming in glory (Matt. 26:64), as well as Jesus' cry of dereliction on
the cross, as proof that Jesus' boastful confidence led Him to a despairing
realization of God's abandonment. *Definition of Tragedy*, p. 114.

harmony with a supreme ethic; that is, with the innermost principle of life itself. It has accordingly a purpose and a direction which makes it clash with its environment; it is a life-force in a death-world."[15]

In Greek tragedy the theme of vicarious sacrifice provides a recurring rationale for the hero's determination to fulfill his destiny, even at the cost of suffering and death. In this respect tragedy kept faith with its origin as ritual accompaniment of a religious sacrifice, perpetuating the ancient practice of offering a scapegoat, the pharmakos, as a substitute for human sacrifice. The theme of vicarious suffering occurs in varying degrees in the works of the Attic poets. Aeschylus's Oresteia is based on a chain of events resulting from the sacrifice of Iphigenia at Aulis. The first play of this trilogy, the *Agamemnon*, recounts the vengence of Iphigenia's mother for her daughter's sacrifice. The second, the *Choephoroe*, describes the resulting need for expiation, as Iphigenia's brother, Orestes, puts to death his mother for the murder of his father. In the *Eumenides* Orestes himself barely escapes being put to death by the Furies as a punishment for matricide. The original sacrifice releases a train of expiatory deaths. In Sophocles' *Oedipus the King*, the population of Thebes is delivered from the pestilence that threatens it with extinction only when Oedipus, who is innocent of willful wrongdoing, is visited with retribution and departs from the city. In his own *Oedipus*, Seneca emphasized even more sharply the vicarious nature of the hero's suffering. As he leaves the city, the stricken Oedipus announces its deliverance. The play closes with his declaration,

> *With me in my exile do I bear*
> *All pestilential humors of the land.*

In Albert Cook's words, "one figure suffers extraordinarily in ways for which the gods are responsible, and [the] play dwells on the mystery of that responsibility."[16] With Euripides human sacrifice becomes even more explicit, taking the form of voluntary self-immolation in the cases of Macaria in the *Heracleidae* and Menoecus in the *Phoenissae*.

If Mark was acquainted with Greek drama, or at least with its Latin replica, he could hardly have failed to observe the frequent recurrence of a tragic character destined to suffer vicariously. As in many tragedies, the central figure of the Gospel fulfills a sacrificial role. In view of His foreknowledge of His own suffering and death, Jesus' refusal to escape His destiny, His aggressive challenge of the religious leaders and temple authorities, His self-incriminating answers to the high priest and to Pilate, His defenseless acceptance of violence against Himself—all point to deliberate self-sacrifice illumined by the declaration that He had come "to give his life as a ransom for many." Thus, to a narrator in search of a literary setting for the composition of a Gospel, the treatment of the hero in Greek tragedy would have presented sufficient points of correspondence to suggest itself as a valid precedent for depicting the hero of the Christian

15. *The Christian Renaissance* (New York: Norton, 1962), p. 149.

16. *"Oedipus Rex": A Mirror for Greek Drama*, p. 120.

faith. The French classicist Georges Méautis found the resemblances between the hero of Greek tragedy and the Christ of the Gospel so striking
that he considered the first to be a prophetic prefiguration of the latter,
arising out of *"l'imagination créatrice des Grecs."*[17]

Third in importance, stated Aristotle, is "the element of thought" or
intellectual content (dianoia) of the play.[18] In addition to being the
depiction of action as reflected in the plot, and of character as displayed in
the personae of the play (and more pointedly in the hero), a tragedy
should be the vehicle for the transmission of ideas. Ancient tragedy was
conceived not simply as a form of entertainment but also as a means of
expressing the haunting questions of man, of voicing his deep aspirations
and providing tentative answers to the dilemmas of existence. This intellectual side of tragedy is conveyed by "the power of saying whatever can be
said, or what is appropriate to the occasion." More specifically, the intellectual element appears first in the ideas expressed by the characters when
they interact in discussion or debate. In Aristotle's words it "is shown in
all they say when proving or disproving some particular point." It is also
apparent in every utterance "enunciating some universal proposition," that
is, when characters expound on topics that together constitute the message
of the play. The didactic approach, which was already an accepted element
of Greek tragedy, almost became the *raison d'être* of Roman tragedy as
reflected in the heavily rhetorical expositions of Stoic philosophy in
Seneca's plays.[19]

Although Mark may have been motivated by a complex of multiple
purposes in composing the Gospel, it is evident that the transmission of
instruction from and about Jesus was a preponderant concern. It has often
been observed that the ministry of Jesus as teacher is emphasized more in
Mark than it is in the other three Gospels.[20] Mark applied the term *teacher*
to Him a dozen times, while describing His spoken ministry as "teaching"
in preference to "preaching." In an insightful section of his work, Robert
P. Meye found that the didactic motif permeates the very structure of the
Gospel. He concluded, "One of the most remarkable and most prominent
aspects of the mystery of the kingdom of God as Mark portrays it in the
Gospel is surely that the Messiah chooses to reveal himself to a small
company of disciples and that it is from them that the gospel is to go forth
into the world." This gospel "is none other than the word which the
Twelve received as an esoteric and Messianic *didache.*"[21] In this relation

17. *Sophocles: Essai sur le héros tragique*, p. 243.

18. *On the Art of Poetry* 6.38.

19. Cicero seems to have attributed a pedagogical function to the presentation of tragedy: "Moral exhortations in plays are intended not for the
benefit of fictitious characters (to whom they are apparently addressed)
but for our edification and that of our children." Quoted in F. Warren
Wright, *Cicero and the Theater*, p. 95.

20. See p. 72.

21. *Jesus and the Twelve: Discipleship and Revelation in Mark's Gospel*,
p. 136.

Mark's Gospel fulfilled a function similar to that of tragedy's "intellectual element," which explained and expounded on contemporary experiences of belief in terms of their traditional origin.

In his analysis of the components of tragedy, Aristotle considered the next most important of the four essential constituents to be "diction."[22] Although he developed at length (chaps. 20–22) the choice of words, figures of speech, and grammatical minutiae, his essential recommendation is this: "The perfection of diction is for it to be at once clear and not mean."[23] He recommended a style worthy of the seriousness and dignity of tragedy but not so convoluted and ornamented as to become unintelligible. Aristotle knew that most tragedies were written in verse. Yet he insisted that the expression of thoughts and sentiments through the means of language be "practically the same thing with verse as with prose."[24] The style of most Greek tragedies is characterized by elevated forms of expression befitting their distinction. But in spite of Aristotle's exhortation, nobility of form was rarely sacrificed for clarity of expression, except perhaps in the case of Euripides. It certainly was not in the case of Aeschylus. The language of Latin drama bears the mark of self-conscious striving after declamatory effect. Heavily weighted with high-sounding, rhetorical grandiloquence, it was better suited for displaying oratorical prowess than for depicting action or expressing genuine sentiment. Both Greek tragedy and Seneca's works, however, hold this in common: they were intended for oral interpretation rather than silent reading.

Although the fashioned style of classical Greek tragedy and the prosaic, unpretentious, and colloquial koine of the Gospel cannot be compared, the Gospel, like tragedy, seems to have been intended for oral presentation. Some traits of Mark's style and syntax produce an effect of actuation similar to the animated reality of dramatic performances.

The frequent use of the historic present is notable in Mark's Gospel. It appears there 151 times, versus 78 in Matthew and only 10 in Luke. The impression of vividness and directness that the present tense gives is even conserved in instances of indirect narration, when Mark gave the speaker's words actuality by using the present (2:1) or the perfect (15:44, 47; 16:4). Other times, in the past tense Mark used the imperfect rather than the aorist. He thus brought the events somewhat closer to the reader in a descriptive tense.

One may wonder whether the constant use of the auxiliary verb ἤρξατο ("began") and the familiar adverb εὐθύς ("immediately") was not intended to give an impression of immediacy. The verb is found in Mark twenty-six times, versus only six in Matthew and two in Luke.

The words spoken by Jesus and others in the course of teaching and debates are reported in direct discourse, as though written to be repeated by an actor in the same circumstances. Moreover, the dialogues of the

22. *On the Art of Poetry* 6.39.

23. Ibid., 22.75.

24. Ibid., 6.39.

Gospel follow the stichomythic form used in tragedy. Dialogues in Greek plays often are swiftly exchanged reflections, short repartees that take a fraction of a line or two. Such brief snatches of dialogues are numerous in the Gospel: Jesus' conversations with Legion, the Syrophoenician woman, the father of the epileptic boy, the rich young man, Bartimaeus, etc. It is interesting that the close relationship between a dialogue and the recognition scene in a Greek tragedy like the *Electra* is almost duplicated in the Gospel. In Sophocles' *Electra* the dialogue between the chorus, Electra, and Orestes skillfully prepares for the discovery of the personages' real identities. In the Gospel a dialogue between Jesus and the disciples concerning popular opinion introduces the recognition by Peter.

Mary E. Lyman remarked that Mark used direct discourse in instances where it is "merely a way of bringing a scene more clearly or more impressively before us."[25] Such are some of the commands uttered by Jesus, which sharply intensify dramatic situations: "Be silent, and come out of him!"; "I will; be clean"; "I say to you, rise, take up your pallet and go home"; "Little girl, I say to you, arise"; "Be opened"; "Peace! Be still!" For an even more realistic effect the phrase is sometimes pronounced in Aramaic, but its translation always follows, being an element of the narrative so as not to attract attention: *"Tali tha cumi"*; *"Ephphatha!"*; *"Eloi, Eloi, lama sabachthani?"* Mark's use of Aramaic expressions and occasional Latin terms also has antecedents in Greek tragedy. Aristotle stated that "a certain admixture of unfamiliar terms in necessary. These, the strange word, the metaphor, the ornamental equivalent, etc. . . . will save the language from seeming mean and prosaic."[26]

The emphatic tone of the teacher is reproduced in the Gospel by the use of the double negative and repetitions. The construction οὐ μή is found eight times in the sayings. The manner of Jesus' sayings generally harmonizes with the role He is fulfilling. When performing miracles, He commands with authority; when teaching, He adopts the style of the rabbi. The style of the utterances is closely adapted to the action.

Since Greek drama was intended primarily for performing on stage rather than reading, all the necessary descriptions, narrations, expositions, and feelings were spoken by either the chorus or the actors. This constituted the ῥήσεις, a series of tirades that, when added up, compose a sizable proportion of the play. Because of its nature, the Gospel is free from the tyranny of the tirade. What necessitated a rather formal speech in tragedy could enter directly into the body of the Gospel narration. But the style of this narration offers striking singularities. It is at the same time very plain and very vivid. All the descriptions, all the indications of movement and sentiment are stamped with these two paradoxical characteristics of extreme simplicity and elaborate realism. The narration part of the Gospel has both the dryness of stage directions and the power to create an atmosphere. It can almost bore the reader by its laconism or captivate him through its emotional intensity.

25. *The Christian Epic*, p. 86.
26. *On the Art of Poetry* 22.75.

Several scholars have noticed these antithetical characteristics of the Gospel's style. References to the "idiosyncracies" of Mark are a commonplace. Others have merely seen the plain, artless, and hasty aspect of the Gospel, and as James A. Kleist complained, "We have had it dinned into our ears that St. Mark is dry, and matter-of-fact, and rugged, and uncouth, and pleonastic."[27] Still others have been sensitive to the subtleties, the realism, and the life of the narrative, so that Allan Menzies could say, "... the chief characteristic style of the Gospel is its vividness."[28]

Even the superficial reader of the Gospel of Mark can easily discern in it the recurrence of many disturbing elements that cannot be said to have literary value. On the contrary, those irregular features of syntax and style characterize Mark's language as a very popular and colloquial brand of Greek. Vincent Taylor said that it has "striking affinities with the spoken language of everyday life as it is revealed to us in the papyri and the inscriptions."[29] A brief listing of some peculiarities of the Gospel may establish the theory that Mark composed in writing a Gospel intended to be read aloud.

The Marcan sentence structure is characterized by:

1. *Parataxis.* This consists of the mere ranging of sentences one after the other with no other connection than καί ("and") when the use of subordinate clauses would be expected. Taylor affirmed that this is one of the most noticeable characteristics of Mark's Gospel. The best explanation for this phenomenon is that paratactic expression is one element that distinguished oral discourse from written composition. The unsophisticated ear is far less sensitive to parataxis than the erudite reader's eye. If most of the Gospel was originally a transcript from oral sources, it is understandable that it contains this type of sentence structure. If the Gospel was destined for public reading rather than private study, it is even more understandable. Kleist said that "sometimes parataxis is due to conditions extraneous to the mind. Perhaps foremost among these is the power to express the relation of thought to thought by other means than the spoken word. Gestures, tricks, and looks have expressional value, and many reveal one soul to another more intimately than bare words can do."[30] Parataxis could be an original feature of apostolic preaching that was kept in the Gospel to reproduce for the listeners the reality of oral delivery.

2. *Asyndeta.* These are the abrupt omission of a connective between two coordinated sentences. It occurs thirty-seven times in the Gospel. This too is a device used in emotional or deliberately impressive narration or discourse. A classic example is found in 14:19. "Jesus said, 'Truly, I say to you, one of you will betray me, one who is eating with me.' They began to be sorrowful." The unusual omission of a connective between the words of

27. *The Gospel of Saint Mark*, p. 115.

28. *The Earliest Gospel*, p. 33.

29. *The Gospel According to Mark*, p. 52.

30. *The Gospel of Saint Mark*, p. 13.

Jesus and the following sentence produces the same effect as silence in a conversation when a delicate point has been touched upon.

3. *Anacolutha.* These can be defined as a break or lack of sequence in the structure of a sentence. This is hardly tolerable in a written document, but it occurs constantly in everyday speech. Some thirteen instances of anacolutha can be found in the Gospel of Mark. Not all of these instances consist of confused sentence structure. Some, by reproducing the effect of oral narration, suggest very well the sequence of thought in life while they "illustrate the popular character of Mark's Greek and . . . are due to the rapidity of the movement of thought and action."[31]

4. *Pleonasms.* At first it appears amazing that in a composition giving the impression of such rapidity, there should be any pleonasms. It seems that at times, from fear of losing space and time, Mark omitted proper connectives or wrote phrases that lack correspondence. Then at points he engaged in pleonasms, copious redundancies, and repetitions. The best explanation for this paradox is that Mark was reproducing popular language in spoken style. Thus, what appears to be a tautology is in spoken narration a device to stress a point, create a particular mood, or give more breadth to a saying.

5. *Parenthesis.* This is the periodic structure that identifies the unpolished style of swiftly spoken language. Mark interjected parenthetical phrases as sudden remarks prompted by the thought sequence. Some nineteen parentheses are found in the Gospel. Closely connected with the parenthesis is the process of delayed description. Sometimes while narrating, Mark suddenly disclosed a detail that should have come before, if at all. For instance, the age of Jairus's daughter is disclosed only after the statement that she walked. The description of the Gerasene demoniac is kept until he is said to have appeared before Jesus. We are told that Jesus had ordered Legion to come out only after learning the demoniac's answer to His command. It is only when the woman with the flow of blood has touched Jesus' garments that her reason for doing so is disclosed. Such a practice would be inappropriate in an orderly literary account. In the Gospel it suggests a narrator who faces people raising questions. The delayed descriptions seem to be the answers. They usually follow, not in logical sequence, but as appendices. The added information is an afterthought, given after the significant event has been described.

6. *Peculiarities of syntax.* These too point in the direction of a spoken Gospel. The use of different tenses for verbs in the same sentence is excusable in spontaneous discourse but not in a literary work—unless it serves a purpose. To say that the double negative is transmitted from the Aramaic origin of the sayings is not enough. It should be added that a colloquial form of speech has been kept in the written composition. A peculiar fondness for the sound of such lengthened words may explain the presence of the seven or eight diminutives that appear in the Gospel. For instance, in 14:47 the use of the form ὠτάριον for "ear" does not imply that the servant of the high priest has a small ear. The diminutive is

31. Taylor, *The Gospel According to Mark,* p. 50.

probably used here because of its phonetic value.[32] These peculiarites of the Gospel of Mark can be explained by the clue that they furnish: the Gospel was written down as it was heard, and it was written not for the eye but for the ear.

Another aspect of Mark's style requires consideration. In contrast to the rather homely features just enumerated, it is enhanced by delightful refinements and subtle artistic touches. The Gospel abounds in picturesque details and lifelike suggestions: an expressive gesture or impressive look caught by Mark's pen, or a mood described by a relevant verb, or details of setting given in passing. But the striking thing is that these features do not seem to result from strenuous efforts to produce a work of high literary quality; they appear suddenly and almost naturally, brought in by the narration itself. They are details that could almost be guessed. They seem to be brought into consciousness from a general background of many more motions and feelings. They reveal the art not of a story writer but of a narrator, a person who is interested primarily in recounting the most important facts, but who, in the course of his discourse, can stress a point with a motion, a silence, or an expressive look. It appears that these effects, proper to oral delivery, are deliberately integrated in the Gospel so that they can be renewed with each public reading.

Long lists of descriptive details have often been compiled to show this finer aspect of the Gospel's style,[33] but their particular character has not always been noticed. The indications of gesture, tone, and feeling are unusually vivid because they have a graphic quality. The narration seems to consist of a series of tableaux; the decor and surroundings are soberly suggested; the motions are described with one typical, almost theatrical gesture; the moods are reproduced by meaningful exclamations and conventional reflections. The ensemble results in a narration that is a spectacle of lifelike realism. Seven times Mark described Jesus looking around Him. Sometimes that look is charged with anger, sometimes with sorrow, sometimes with surprise. Twice the look penetrates right to the heart. Would it be possible to recite the passages describing the look of Jesus to an attentive audience without expressing its particular mood? Jesus is often said to take the hand of the sick as He heals them. Could these passages have been read to Roman Christians without at least a gesture of the hand expressing authority and sympathy at the same time?

The desperate scream of the unclean spirit of the man in the synagogue cannot be rendered in a sweet, mellow voice, especially when the narrative says that "he cried out." And Jesus' answer can be read only with a low, authoritative, and determined voice: ". . . Jesus rebuked him,

32. According to C. H. Turner: "The fondness for diminutives grows with the growth of the language. They are absent from Homer; they begin to abound in Aristophanes and the later comedians; in the first century after Christ it must have been a conscious literary archaism to avoid them." "Marcan Usage: Notes, Critical and Exegetical, on the Second Gospel," 29:352.

33. Taylor, *The Gospel According to Mark,* pp. 135–39; Lyman, *The Christian Epic,* pp. 80–90.

saying, 'Be silent, and come out of him!' " The subsequent expression of round-eyed, fearful amazement is perfectly suggested by the whispery, febrile questioning: "What is this? A new teaching! With authority he commands even the unclean spirits, and they obey him."

Jesus' refusal to perform a sign from heaven cannot be rendered properly without the same weary sigh with which He met the request. As Jesus "left" the Pharisees after refusing their request, it seems that His final comment should be said over the shoulder, with eyes averted: "Why does this generation seek a sign? Truly, I say to you, no sign shall be given to this generation."

The cry of Bartimaeus, ". . . Son of David, have mercy on me!" suggests its imploring tone. The annoyance of those hearing the plaintive voice is beautifully rendered by the harsh mention that "many rebuked him, telling him to be silent." But as they hear Jesus call the blind man, the nuisance by the side of the road suddenly becomes the center of attention. Helping hands reach down, and men say, "Take heart; rise, he is calling you." And the surging expectancy of Bartimaeus can be expressed by a rapid motion of the shoulders as he casts his mantle and springs up to rush to Jesus.

When the scene is laid before the cross, Mark described the passers-by railing Jesus as "wagging their heads, saying, 'Aha!' " And the sneering tone of the chief priests and the scribes mocking him cannot be avoided: "He saved others, he cannot save himself."

The preceding instances taken at random illustrate the vividness and realism that the Gospel can have through meaningful recitation. A sensitive reader can bring out its pathos by merely living the story as Mark wrote it, by impersonating the characters and almost mimicking their actions. This would have been particularly easy in the first church of Rome, with its culturally conditioned fondness for the spectacular and the emotional, and with its enthusiasm in the freshness of the Christian experience.

If the idea that Mark originally wrote the Gospel to be read aloud to Christian audiences appears too fantastic, one must remember that in the first century written documents were not so common as to be privately owned. They had to be shared, and the best medium of sharing was public reading, just as in the synagogue. Kleist pointed out that "according to ancient standards the art of words requires warm, emotional reading for its full effect."[34] To substantiate his point he referred to remarks made by Augustine following the explanation of a Biblical text: "A sincere reader is not so much instructed when he carefully analyzes [the text] as he is set on fire when he recites it with glowing feeling."[35] Augustine's observation indicates that a person reading privately was expected to read aloud. Actually the custom of reading silently was apparently unknown in antiquity. Even when no audience was present, the words were articulated vocally while being read visually. The Ethiopian eunuch traveling in a

34. *Memoirs of Saint Peter,* pp. 39–40.

35. *Christian Instruction,* trans. John J. Garigan (New York: Fathers of the Church, 1947), 4.7.21.

chariot on the Gaza road was presumably reading the Scripture to no one but himself; Philip, coming up to him, heard the passage read with sufficient clarity to identify it as a text from the prophecy of Isaiah (Acts 8:26–28). In a revealing passage of the *Confessions*, Augustine related as an unusual practice Ambrose's habit of reading silently by letting his eyes move along the manuscript while making no sound with his voice.[36]

Until the writing of the first written sources, the only medium for circulating the story of Jesus was the spoken word. The first written documents may have been nothing more than *aide-mémoires* devised to preserve in a fixed form the stories that were propagated orally. If the bulk of the Gospel consists of an assemblage of written transcripts of oral tradition, it is not inconceivable that features characteristic of oral communication have been conserved in its final form. Thus, in regard to its origins, it may be permissible to describe the Gospel as the "spoken Gospel." Should this be the case, the definition could also extend to its transcripted form. If the Gospel is a transcript *of* oral discourse, it is ipso facto a transcript *for* oral discourse. It was written down as it was heard, to be heard again. The Gospel was written not to be read silently but to be heard publicly.

This point furnishes a clue to many of the peculiarities, the incongruities and stylistic paradoxes, that have been surveyed above. If these be considered faults, they are imputable to the spontaneity and freedom of the spoken word. The shocking constructions, the capricious thought sequences, the seemingly extraneous details, the euphonious words, the startling confusion of pronouns and tenses—all betray Mark's intent to deliver the Gospel with the vividness, expressiveness, and persuasive power of verbal interpretation. This definition of Mark as the spoken Gospel brings it a step closer to tragedy. Both were written for oral delivery.

Aristotle described the two remaining elements of tragedy—melody and spectacle—as "the pleasurable accessories of tragedy."[37] They obviously are irrelevant to the Gospel. Their absence in the Gospel, however, does not invalidate the theory that Mark used models drawn from tragedy since both melody and spectacle eventually deserted ancient tragedy itself.

Of the two, Aristotle considered melody more important. Melody in the form of lyrics, singing, and dance provided by the chorus was present in tragedy because of its origin as a choral dithyramb. The evolution of dramatic action that resulted from adding actors to the chorus caused the role of the latter to decrease gradually. Common people had formerly been represented on stage by the chorus, and the chorus had interpreted for the audience the emotive dimensions of the play. Once common people entered the stage of tragedy as its main personae, especially in the works of Euripides, the chorus was no longer needed. The increased sophistication of plays eventually robbed the chorus of other functions, such as setting the identity of new characters; providing interlocutors to avoid lengthy soliloquies; marking the passage of time or transitions between sections of

36. 6.3.

37. *On the Art of Poetry* 6.39.

the play; and bringing life and color to the stage that originally was occupied by male actors only, lumbering around like self-propelled Easter Island statues, precariously perched on elevated buskins, their facial expressions hidden behind conventional character-type masks.

Hence the eventual demise of the chorus. Although in the plays of Aeschylus the chorus is integrated into the play as one of the actors, in most of Euripides' tragedies it does no more than provide lyric interludes. Less than a century later Aristotle objected to the apparently widespread practice of dispensing with the chorus. He deplored the fact that "with the later poets, the songs in a play of theirs have no more to do with the plot than that of any other tragedy." The role of the chorus had apparently been reduced to "singing . . . intercalary pieces." With disguised sarcasm Aristotle objected to the incongruity of a chorus extraneous to the action: "What real difference is there between singing such intercalary pieces, and attempting to fit in a speech, or even a whole act, from one play into another?"[38] Judging from the status of the chorus in Latin tragedy, Aristotle had fought a losing battle. There the chorus appears, when it appears at all, as an incongruous convention. In the works of Seneca the chorus provides a sort of *entre-acte* extraneous to the action of the play. It is little more than an excuse for Seneca to expound on topics of his own choosing that have no relation to the play. Moribund in the last stages of ancient tragedy, melody disappeared entirely in Latin and neoclassical tragedy to reenter the dramatic stage in operatic compositions of the seventeenth century.

Aristotle's assignment of last position to the element of spectacle, or stage-presentation, is astounding. Theatrical performances would seem to pertain to the very essence of dramatic expression. And yet a note of disparagement can be detected in Aristotle's evaluation of the importance of stage presentation. He stated that "spectacle, though an attraction, is the least artistic of all the parts, and has least to do with the art of poetry. . . . The getting-up of the spectacle is more a matter for the costumier than the poet."[39] For Aristotle, if the vitality of a tragedy is not felt when read, neither will it be felt when performed. In fact, "the tragic effect is quite possible without a public performance and actors."[40] The tragedy should be composed in such a manner that "even without seeing the things take place, he who simply hears the account of them shall be filled with horror and pity at the incidents; which is just the effect that the mere recital of the story of *Oedipus* would have on one. To produce this same effect by means of the spectacle is less artistic, and requires extraneous aid."[41] Aristotle could never have suspected that some day his prescriptions would find literal fulfillment in unstageable Latin tragedies written in the Greek manner, thus creating a precedent for the Gospel of Mark, in which the tragic form proved to be the harbinger of that immortal drama that had once taken place on the scene of history.

38. Ibid., 18.66.   40. Ibid.
39. Ibid., 6.39.   41. Ibid., 14.52.

II

Besides the categories thus delineated by Aristotle, several other dramatic features distinctive of Greek and Latin tragedies seem to be present in the Gospel. They are, in the order in which they will be briefly surveyed below, the prologue, irony, foreshadowing, forensic debates, hyporcheme, final oracles, messengers, the deus ex machina, and the ending.

1. As a rule, ancient tragedies begin with a *prologue* devised to provide the background information necessary to make the plot intelligible to the audience and to set in motion the action of the play. This introduction is either dramatic or expository. In earlier plays and especially in those of Sophocles, the prologue is dramatic, usually consisting of a scene in which some supernatural being—a god or a ghost—or the characters of the play reveal what has taken place prior to the beginning of the action. They make known identities that will remain hidden to the protagonists, or they predict what is about to take place in the play. In the prologue of Aeschylus's *Prometheus Bound*, divine emissaries of Zeus accuse the hero of stealing fire and giving it to humans, and they begin prosecuting his punishment. The *Ajax* of Sophocles begins with the goddess Athena explaining the madness of Ajax just prior to his entrance on stage. In Euripides' *Hippolytus* the goddess Aphrodite, spurned by the hero, discloses the terrible plan she has devised in revenge. In later tragedies the prologue generally consists of a monologue by one of the characters or by a deity who explains the reason for the play. The very first word of the Gospel (ἀρχή, "beginning") is also used in the *Poetics* to define the essential function of the prologue. For Aristotle the arche (beginning) is something that requires neither explanation nor apology. It is a happening, an event to be accepted as presented. But it is also something begun that is essentially brought to a conclusion: "A beginning [ἀρχή] is that which is not itself necessarily after anything else, and which has naturally something else after it."[42]

It is not entirely unthinkable that the authors of the second and fourth Gospels used the consecrated term ἀρχή at the very start of their compositions to establish a dramatic intensity and signal the beginning of a formal prologue.[43] Mark's prologue—whether limited to the first verse or extended to include the account of the Baptist's heraldic ministry, or that of Jesus' baptism, or that of His desert temptation—fulfills functions similar to those of prologues in Greek tragedies. Concisely but powerfully, it gives the action its original impetus. It makes the unique identity of Jesus known to the reader in a universal frame of reference by the author himself (1:1), in the context of Judaic expectations by the prophets (1:2–3), in its historical setting by John the Baptist (1:4–8), and in its theological significance by the divine voice (1:11). The ambiguities sur-

42. Ibid., 7.40.

43. See Walter E. Bundy, "Dogma and Drama in the Gospel of Mark," p. 70.

rounding the revelation of Jesus' identity are also disclosed by the paradoxical event of His baptism.[44] And finally, the grapplings of Jesus with
Satan in the desert provide a hint of the confrontation between Jesus and
the forces of evil that provides the mainspring of the Gospel's action.

2. Ancient tragedians made frequent use of *dramatic irony* to emphasize the cruelties of fate and arouse the emotions of their audiences.
Although irony can take many different forms, it usually depends on the
characters of the play being ignorant of significant knowledge that is available to the spectator-reader. Joseph T. Shipley defined it as "a device
whereby ironic incongruity is introduced in the very structure of the plot,
by having the spectators aware of elements in the situation of which one
or more of the characters involved are ignorant."[45] The hero of Sophocles'
Oedipus the King provides the classic example of an ironic situation as he
stubbornly pursues an investigation that will result in his own doom while
the audience, taken into the confidence of the dramatist, can only watch
Oedipus's self-inflicted destruction in powerless apprehension. Similar and
other forms of irony abound in practically every ancient tragedy.

The Gospel can be described as a drama of mistaken identity.[46] It is
pervaded with ironic intensity from beginning to end. The themes of the
Son of God moving incognito amidst humanity, of the Messiah rejected by
His own people, of the interplay between befuddled disciples, wondering
multitudes, hostile relatives, murderous enemies, and screaming demons,
of a messianic destiny requiring suffering and ransom, of the ignominious
execution under the ascription of royalty, and of the final reversal from
abject annihilation to triumphant vindication—all combine to render the
emotional pitch of the Gospel almost unbearable. The dramatic irony that
permeates the very structure of the Gospel finds its highest expression in
the ethnarchs' resolve to destroy Jesus in order to shatter His messianic
pretensions, which, when carried out, in fact accomplishes His messianic
destiny.

Irony is also found in the dialogue and in the scene-by-scene development of the Gospel. The irony here alternates between three common
forms. First, the irony expressed in subtle sarcasm or in almost imperceptible touches of humor, of which some instances follow:

"... he taught them as one who had authority, and not as the
scribes."

---

44. "The Jordan vision is also dramatic in its technique. Into the prosaic
scene depicted in verse 9 it introduces, with startling suddenness, the un-
seen forces actually operative in the destinies of the actors on the stage of
history. It gives the reader a glimpse behind the scenes. He is allowed to
see what the action itself does not disclose until later. It is a sort of
dramatic aside which, at the very beginning, lets the reader in on the secret
of the hero's true nature and identity. It is 'an epiphany; the heavenly
status of Jesus is for a moment visible.' " Ibid., pp. 74–75.

45. *Dictionary of World Literary Terms*, p. 165.

46. "As a literary work, Mark has a kinship with 'disguise' dramas in
which the writer and the audience share information which key characters
lack." Samuel Sandmel, "Prolegomena to a Commentary on Mark,"
p. 299.

Jesus tells the cleansed leper, " 'See that you *say nothing to any one. . . .*' But he went out and *began to talk freely* . . . and to *spread the news.* "

As Jesus heals the *dumb* and *deaf* man, he charges onlookers "to *tell no one*; but the more he charged them, the more zealously they *proclaimed* it."

In Capernaum the *whole city* gathers together about the door.

The Gerasenes come and see "the demoniac sitting there, clothed and in his right mind . . . and they were *afraid.*"

The disciples and Jesus are mobbed by a great crowd so that they do not have leisure *to eat.* So Jesus looks for a lonely place, but He finds another throng and *feeds* five thousand.

The fellow-citizens of Jesus exclaim, "What mighty works are wrought by his hands!" And they *take offense at Him.*

The disciples say to Jesus, "Send *them* away . . . to . . . buy themselves something to eat." But He answers them, "*You* give them something to eat."

Jesus asks the disciples, " 'What were you discussing on the way?' But they were silent; for on the way they had discussed with one another who was the greatest."

Jesus tells Bartimaeus, " 'Go *your* way. . . .' And immediately he [Bartimaeus] followed *him* [Jesus] on the way.

". . . a young man followed him, with nothing but a linen cloth about his body; and they seized him, but he left the linen cloth and ran away *naked.* "

The disciples question "what the rising from the dead meant."

The second form of nondramatic irony in the Gospel derives from the use of esoteric language or from utterances that have a meaning intelligible to the audience and select characters but not to the main protagonists. In this category falls much of the teaching of Jesus, delivered in seemingly cryptic sayings and parables that are intended to keep its meaning veiled until after the resurrection. To the reader who knows that the kingdom is being ushered in by Jesus Himself, the meaning of the parables of the kingdom is clear. But irony results when not even the disciples understand them. Like those outside, they see but do not perceive; they hear but do not understand. It is also ironic when Jesus speaks of Himself in the third person and uses the ambiguous title "Son of man." Again, the reader knows that Jesus is referring to Himself, but this identification does not become clear to the personae of the Gospel until the momentous confrontation with the high priest when Jesus affirms, "I am [the Christ, the Son of the Blessed]; and you will see the Son of man seated at the right hand of Power. . . ."

A third form of irony is that which occurs when the reverse of an expected course of action takes place, or when an effect of paradox or contrast is produced. The cross and the empty tomb constitute the supreme irony, but a number of other instances are also found in the Gospel. A few examples follow:

". . . a voice came from heaven, 'Thou art my beloved Son; with thee I am well pleased.' The Spirit immediately drove him out into the wilderness."

". . . he was with the wild beasts; and the angels ministered to him."

The Gerasenes begin "*to beg* Jesus *to depart* from their neighborhood. . . . the man who had been possessed with demons *begged* him that he might be *with him.*"

Jesus tells him to go home and tell *his friends* how much the *Lord* has done for him. He leaves and proclaims *in the Decapolis* how much *Jesus* has done for him.

Those bringing children to Jesus are rebuked by the disciples. Jesus rebukes the disciples and takes the children in His arms.

To the heavenly rapture of the transfiguration succeeds the depressing sight of the epileptic boy.

Jesus, seeing the rich young ruler, loves him; the ruler's countenance falls and he goes away sorrowful.

Many rebuked Bartimaeus, telling him to be silent; Jesus stops and says, "Call him."

A woman anoints Jesus with ointment worth three hundred denarii while Judas betrays him for money.

Peter says vehemently, "If I must die with you, I will not deny you." Later he invokes a curse on himself and swears, "I do not know this man of whom you speak."

False witnesses fail to bring up a charge against Jesus, but He seals His own doom with one sentence.

When the centurion sees that He has breathed His last, he says, "Truly this man was a Son of God."

The women bring spices with which to embalm Him. They are told, "He has risen. He is not here. . . ."

" '. . . go, tell his disciples and Peter. . . . they went out and fled from the tomb . . . and they said nothing to any one. . . .'"

Whether fortuitous or intentional, the presence of irony in the Gospel, of both the dramatic and the nonliterary kinds, can hardly be denied. The ironic tension inherent in the structure of the plot and the touches of irony skillfully woven into the narration suggest a work of intuitive if not deliberate artistry. In this respect the thoughtful opinion of Morton Enslin seems to be verified: "The longer I study the Gospel of Mark, the more dissatisfied I find myself with the conventional representation of this gospel as a loosely put together catena of ancient traditions. On every page, on the contrary, it appears to reveal the definite, deliberate, and conscious craftsmanship of the author—and despite adverse judgment easily expressed through the years, it is no mean craftsmanship either."[47]

47. "The Artistry of Mark," p. 399. J. C. Kamerbeek's description of irony in *Oedipus the King* applies to the Gospel as well: "The dramatic irony directly deriving from the presuppositions of the play is the element *par excellence* which lends to its dramatic structure its incomparable

3. *Foreshadowing* is another device that was familiar to ancient tragedians. Its function is to create suspense through allusions, veiled predictions, and portentous actions interspersed within the play and pointing to its tragic outcome. Such intimations of disaster, ranging from discreet innuendos to explicit forewarnings, can be made by secondary protagonists in the play, by the onlooking chorus, by the future victims of disaster themselves, and even by the supernatural beings that populate many ancient tragedies. Sophocles used foreshadowing in almost all of his plays. It is also found in the works of the other authors, as well as in their Latin replicas. The fifty daughters of Danaus, because of whom war threatens between Argos and Egypt in Aeschylus's *Suppliants*, move throughout the play under the cloud of their predicted suicide. In his *Seven Against Thebes* the death of the defender of the sixth gate at the hand of the attacker, his own brother, is predicted by a seer. This fulfills the warning to their father that he would die childless. The brothers slay each other while Thebes triumphs. In Euripides' *Alcestis* the heroine accepts sacrificial death in the place of her husband, who is really none other than Apollo sentenced to live in human form by irate Zeus. But as death approaches, there are also hints of her resurrection. Thus predicted through the play, her resurrection finally takes place and after three days she is restored to her surprised husband. Richard G. Moulton described foreshadowing as "oracular action, that is, a train of events including an oracle and its fulfillment, and in which destiny is seen working gradually out of mystery into clearness. It is one of the most common and most powerful dramatic motives."[48]

Several motifs run through the Gospel to form together an element of foreshadowing comparable to that of Greek tragedy. They consist of originally veiled references that become increasingly specific as events converge towards the passion. These motifs are, for example, the arrest and death of John and related sayings of Jesus, the decision of the ethnarchs to destroy Jesus and the ensuing efforts to ensnare Him, the introduction of Judas early in the Gospel as the betrayer and his scheming activity, the three post–Caesarea Philippi predictions and accompanying statements like the cup and baptism sayings, the burial saying at the Bethany anointing, the ransom saying, the fate of the son in the parable of the wicked tenants.[49] The thematic arrangement and the progression of this foreshadowing suggest that it is there by design and not simply the fortuitous result of random enumeration. Something of Mark's method is apparent in his use of the word παραδίδωμι and derivatives. The word is first used at the beginning of Jesus' ministry to describe John's arrest (1:14). From then on the word is repeated through the Gospel like an ominous leitmotif. It is used by Mark to describe Judas as the *betrayer* (3:19), by Jesus to predict the *delivering* of the Son of man into the hands of men in

---

unity." *The Plays of Sophocles: Commentaries;* Part 4: *The Oedipus Tyrannus*, p. 25.

48. *The Literary Study of the Bible*, p. 103.

49. See pp. 66ff. and 80ff.

general (9:33) and Gentiles in particular (10:33), and by Mark to describe Judas going to the priests to *betray* Jesus (14:10) and seeking an opportunity to *betray* Him (14:11). During the Last Supper Jesus denounces the presence of a *betrayer* among the twelve (14:8) and invokes a malediction upon him who will *betray* the Son of man (14:21). In the garden Jesus announces the imminence of the *betrayal* (14:41), and, pointing to Judas, says, "See, the *betrayer*" (14:42). By using this one word, Mark linked together the foreshadowing motifs of John the Baptist, Judas, and the ethnarchs' plot with the Son of man predictions, and he caused them to converge toward the climax of the passion. But Mark did not abandon the term he had thus invested with dramatic power. He drew its full potential by using it to describe the realization of that which it foreshadowed. The fateful moment arrives when Judas *betrays* Jesus to the chief priests, scribes, and elders (14:44). In turn, they *deliver* Him up to Pilate (15:1, 10), who *delivers* Him to the soldiers for execution (15:15). This chain-reaction of betrayals extends beyond the ministry of Jesus to the life-situation of the early church as Jesus predicts that His followers will be *betrayed* to councils and synagogues (13:9), *delivered up* for trial (13:11), *delivered up* to death by blood relatives (13:12) into the hands of governors and kings, presumably Jews betraying Christians to Gentile authorities, following a pattern identical to the betrayal of Jesus.[50] Whether informed or not by the techniques of Greek tragedy, it seems that foreshadowing is skillfully used in the Gospel of Mark to create dramatic suspense.

4. Mark's predilection for scenes of confrontation between Jesus and His opponents has often been noticed, but rarely has attention been drawn to its dramatic effect. And yet the close succession of tense *debates* at the outset of Jesus' ministry sets the action in motion as they cause the discomfitted Pharisees to conspire against Him. Further confrontations scattered through the narrative illustrate the uncompromising counter-cultural attitude of Jesus vis-à-vis the Jewish establishment.[51]

Such debates have precedent both in Greek and Latin tragedies, being in phenomenal abundance in the latter. The works of Seneca have sometimes been considered mere pretexts for scenes of "forensic debates," in which dozens of lines of argumentative rhetoric are dispensed in sticho-mythic repartees. To modern literary tastes they are tedious and stilted exercises in pedantry, but if abundance is a measure of their popularity,

50. I Corinthians 11:23b seems to indicate that this word had acquired a stereotyped meaning in reference to the death of Jesus. It is found in the same context in Acts 3:13, where it stands as a prelude for a development similar to the Marcan scheme of Jewish betrayal of Jesus and His followers to Gentile authorities. Believers and apostles are delivered up, by Jews, for imprisonment (8:3; 12:4), to Gentiles (21:11), to a centurion (27:1), and to the Romans (28:17).

51. Debates over the right to forgive sins (2:6–11), association with outcasts (2:15–17), fasting (2:18–20), the sabbath (2:23–28), ritual purification (7:1–8), divorce (10:2–9), authority (11:27–32), tribute to Caesar (12:13–17), resurrection (12:18–27).

they must have delighted first-century readers.[52] Rarely present in Sophocles, such debates appear regularly in the tragedies of Euripides. Thus Medea and her estranged husband, Jason, engage in a sharp verbal duel of mutual accusation in the second episode of the *Medea*. In *Hippolytus* the young hero, taken to task by his father after discovering his wife's suicide over her incestuous frustrations, engages in a somewhat incongruous debate on the merits of chastity, humility, and honesty. The debate in *Heracles* takes a more passionate turn. Amphitryon argues with the tyrant Lycus for the lives of Heracles' family, who in his absence have taken refuge at the altar of Zeus. And in the *Suppliants* the conflict over the burial of heroes is set aside while Theseus, king of Athens, engages in a long debate with a representative of rival Thebes over the relative merits of democracy and tyranny. Obviously the debates of the Gospel are different in content and form from those of tragedy. But even if no relation exists between the practice of including debates in Greek and Latin tragedies and Mark's inclusion of about ten debate scenes, the dramatic qualities of these scenes must be recognized. They not only expound Christian doctrine, but they also enhance the stature of Jesus as He stands up to His detractors. By confuting them, He causes the action to move forward and the tension to increase as the protagonists entrench themselves more firmly in their respective positions.

5. The *hyporcheme* was a well-known dramatic convention practiced especially by Sophocles. It consisted of a joyful scene that involves the chorus and sometimes other characters; takes the form of a dance, procession, or lyrics expressing confidence and happiness; and occurs just before the catastrophic climax of the play. The hyporcheme emphasizes, by way of contrast, the crushing impact of the tragic incident. It is a sudden outburst of joy, more or less ecstatic, not destined to be realized.

When he learns that the one who he thinks is his father (but who is not) has died in Corinth, Oedipus exults; this makes it impossible for him to fulfill the prophecy that he will commit patricide. The chorus echoes his joyful mood by singing the praises of Mount Cithaeron, where Oedipus was exposed and protected as an infant. Moments later, disaster strikes; a herdsman enters and, forced by Oedipus, reveals the latter's identity as the murderer of his father and the husband of his mother. In *Antigone*, when Creon finally decides to grant burial to Polyneices and to release Antigone in order to save Haemon, her lover, and his son from death, the chorus, sensing that events will take a happier turn, sings a hymn of deliverance and praises the god Bacchus for his assistance. No sooner have they finished than a messenger arrives and announces the suicide of Antigone, which is followed by the suicide of Haemon and then that of his own mother, Creon's wife. Ajax, whose death has been foreshadowed from the

52. Stichomythic exchanges appear in all of Seneca's tragedies, especially in the *Agamemnon*. Here they alternate with unusually long tirades, the longest being the speech of Eurybates, messenger of Agamemnon, which goes on uninterrupted for no less than 160 lines. A remarkable rapid-fire exchange is also found in the *Octavia*, where Seneca recommended moderation in the use of power to his imperial pupil, Nero.

opening scenes of the *Ajax*, suddenly seems to relent from his hubristic ways. The chorus bursts out in a song of joy, exulting over the seeming repentence of the hero and the prevention of disaster. In the next scene the suicide of Ajax is reported. These examples illustrate the pattern of the hyporcheme. Disaster threatens. Due to misunderstanding, a happy turn of events is expected and a joyful demonstration takes place. Fate remains imperturbable, however, and catastrophes occur as foreordained.

As the final phase of Jesus' ministry progresses, the emotional intensity of the narrative reaches its highest point in the silent procession of Jesus leading the reticent disciples to Jerusalem. Mark commented that the disciples who followed Jesus are amazed (presumably at His somber determination and daring) and afraid (probably of the predictable outcome of the journey). Mark emphasized the pathos of the scene by showing Jesus telling the disciples what is to happen to Him in details He has not yet disclosed—He will be condemned to death, delivered to the Gentiles, mocked, spit upon, scourged, and killed (10:32–34). But as the group draws near to Jerusalem, it is met by a joyful demonstration comparable to a modern ticker-tape parade. People spread clothes on the ground. Some go before and others follow Jesus, waving branches and shouting hosannas and praises to God (11:1–10).[53] But this outburst of joy suddenly gives place to dark forebodings as the ethnarchs move against Jesus in response to His intervention in the temple (11:18), thus initiating the tragic events of the passion. The contrasting mood of the "triumphal entry" with the events surrounding it, the exuberance and acclamations of the chorus-like crowd welcoming Jesus are reminiscent of the hyporcheme. The effect of anguish and of relentless tragedy that follows conveys the same emotional impact as the hyporcheme of tragedy.

6. The question of the relevance of the "little apocalypse" (Mark 13) has often been raised. This section has commonly been considered an independent, apocalyptic cento inserted somewhat arbitrarily in the narrative to correct eschatological conceptions contrary to the redactor's views. The theory of the dramatic structure of the Gospel, however, makes allowance for chapter 13 as an integral part of the composition and as a contribution to the progress of the action. Again, Greek and Latin tragedy offer a parallel that justifies the place and suggests the intent of the Marcan apocalypse.

The dramatic device called *final oracles* appears in tragedies in which the hero, on the verge of disaster, utters, through supernatural insight or out of sheer desperation, oracles announcing the doom of his adversaries. These oracles "have the effect of giving a back-turn of fate at the last moment."[54] Thus Aeschylus's Prometheus, nailed to the mountain and about to be thrown into the abyss, prophesies his future restoration through deliverance by Hercules, who will ironically be a future progeny

53. Although intelligible in context, Mark did not explain the sudden outburst of popular acclaim. John related it to the resurrection of Lazarus (12:17–18). See p. 87.

54. Moulton, *Literary Study*, p. 192.

of Zeus, and foretells his enemy's downfall when Zeus will be hurled from his throne. Because of his refusal to compromise with wrong, Prometheus accepts his sacrifice. But he envisages future victory and the defeat of adverse forces. Although vindictive, his utterances are not devoid of noble exaltation. His oracle ends with the warning,

> *So, in his crashing fall shall Zeus discover*
> *How different are rule and slavery.*

In Euripides' *Hecuba*, King Polymestor of Thrace, physically blinded by Hecuba and her Trojan friends and about to be banished to a desert island, levels oracles at both Hecuba, who is offered the unhappy prospect of being transformed into a bitch and drowned in the sea, and at Agamemnon, who, more nobly, is promised death at the hand of his wrathful wife, Clytemnestra. Seneca's dying Hercules in *Hercules on Oeta* remembers that an oracle has been pronounced against him:

> *By the hand of one whom thou hast slain, some day,*
> *Victorious Hercules, shalt thou be laid low. . . .*

While he suffers the fulfillment of the prophecy, he in turn shouts imprecations and announces the collapse of the universe:

> *O Jupiter,*
> *My death throughout the kingdom of the sky*
> *Shall shake thy sovereignty.*

The classic example of imprecatory oracles is provided by Cassandra, whose name has become synonymous with prophets of doom. She appears prominently in Aeschylus's *Agamemnon*, in Euripides' *Trojan Women*, and in Seneca's *Agamemnon*.

It has sometimes been observed that the little apocalypse of Mark serves a purpose similar to that of the final oracles in ancient tragedy.[55] It is introduced by a blunt prediction of the destruction of the temple (v. 2), which the disciples mistakenly interpret in apocalyptic terms (v. 4). The development that follows, predicts the destruction of Jerusalem and dissociates Christian eschatological expectations from the destiny of Israel. Jesus tells the four "core" disciples (v. 3—hence, the binding character of the contents of the apocalypse for the author's contemporary reader) that the Jewish nation which is rejecting Him will receive appropriate retribution and that history will move on toward the Parousia independently of Israel's fate. These themes are developed in four sections and a conclusion.

The first section (vv. 5–8) is a warning not to mistake imminent wars (probably the Jewish civil war and the ensuing Roman repression) as the end and not to follow siren-voices (probably those of Judaizing Christian leaders) that so interpret them (v. 5). Such wars are to be given a significance similar to that of natural catastrophes like earthquakes and famines,

---

55. C. H. Dodd believed that its purpose is to assure the reader "that the story of suffering and defeat to which it is the immediate prelude has for its other side that eternal weight of glory which Christ attained through his passion." *The Apostolic Preaching and Its Developments*, p. 79.

of which there will be many more ("this is but the beginning") before the end comes.

The second section (vv. 9–13) is an admonition not to eschew fratricidal Jewish persecution by consenting to Judaizing compromises but to turn such persecutions into a springboard for witness among the Gentiles and an opportunity for universal outreach.[56]

The third section (vv. 14–23) is a prediction of the desecration of the temple and of an unprecedented (v. 19) devastation of Jerusalem. It also contains a dual warning: the first is directed against the belief that the Parousia will be concomitant with the collapse of Israel (v. 21), a belief that false leaders will exploit (v. 22); the second is in the form of an advance notice (v. 23) so that Christians, instead of clinging to the doomed nation of Israel in aberrant eschatological hopes, will dissociate themselves from Judaism and realize their own identity (vv. 15–16).

The fourth section (vv. 24–27) distinguishes "that tribulation," meaning the destruction of Israel, from "those days" of the Parousia, which will have a cosmic frame of reference (vv. 24–25) and will therefore transcend narrow Jewish apocalyptic categories and affect the "elect" from among all of mankind (v. 27).

The conclusion of the passage (vv. 28–37) answers the "when?" of verse 4 from a twofold perspective. First, the final phase of history, that preceding the Parousia, has already begun, and the demise of Israel is a sign of the acceleration of history towards the end (vv. 29–30). Second, although the Parousia-end may well be imminent, the time of its occurrence remains unpredictable (vv. 32–33). In any case it is not to be linked with the fate of Israel. Therefore, disciples should beware of eschatological speculations. They should be active in the Master's work (v. 35) and watchful (vv. 35–36).

Thus understood, the little apocalypse resembles in some ways the final oracles of tragedy. Just prior to His suffering and death at the hands of the Jewish leaders, Jesus predicts the annihilation of the nation they represent and promises His followers inevitable victory of His cause. Such a dismissal of pro-Jewish eschatological speculations is congruent with the essential theme of the Gospel: Jesus' rejection of current Jewish messianic expectations and the substitution of His own universal concept of the Messiah's role. Enslin came to similar conclusions in regard to this chapter of the Gospel: "The eschatological section is seen to be a genuine part of the fundamental problem; it provides the only solution to the tragedy, a veritable deus ex machina. This section may well be wrought from different sayings, some of them already grouped, and put ready-made in Jesus' mouth. But it is no patch on the garment. It stands as the great prophecy of ultimate victory even through disaster, and makes possible the great crescendo to the book: 'Verily I say unto you, This generation shall not pass away, until all these things be accomplished.' Victory and reward, and they are soon to come."[57]

56. See note 50 above.

57. "The Artistry of Mark," p. 375.

7. When the action of a Greek or Latin tragedy included an event beyond theatrical enactment due to its magnitude or gruesomeness, the authors had recourse to two devices to portray it. One is to have the deed occur behind the scenes, often accompanied by cries of suffering in case of death, prior to the visual disclosure of the result through doors flung open. Thus, in the last scene of Aeschylus's *Agamemnon*, the palace doors open to reveal the dead bodies of Agamemnon and Cassandra, who have been killed by the adulterous Clytemnestra. Her turn comes in the *Choephoroe* when the doors open upon the spectacle of her corpse and that of her lover, Aegisthus. In Euripides' *Medea* the cries of children being killed by their mother within the palace are heard by the audience, but their bodies are not displayed. In Seneca's unbenignant version of the same theme, Medea slaughters her boys on stage, delaying long enough between killings to fit in a few tirades, and vindictively brandishes their corpses at her unfaithful husband.

The other technique consists of a verbal report given on stage by the ubiquitous *messenger* of ancient drama, generally a loquacious eye-witness and a secondary character of the play, such as a servant, soldier, herald, errand-boy, or nurse. In Aeschylus's and in Seneca's *Agamemnon*, a herald describes the terrible storm that wrecked the Greek fleet on its way from Troy. In Sophocles' and in Seneca's *Oedipus*, a messenger describes how the hero has inflicted blindness upon himself prior to Oedipus's appearance on stage. Seneca's description of the act requires no less than thirty-five lines of gory, anatomical details. In Euripides' and in Seneca's *Medea*, a messenger rushes in to give a twitch-by-twitch account of the death of King Creon and his daughter through Medea's gift of the magic robe and crown. In a passage probably unsurpassed in atrocity in all classical literature, Seneca portrayed in his *Thyestes* the drunken hero feasting on the flesh of his own children just prior to his vengeful brother's disclosure of how he murdered and elaborately barbecued them for the meal.[58]

Although Mark described the crucifixion in direct narration, the dignity and restraint of the account make it contrast sharply with the lurid excesses of Latin tragedy.[59] By emphasizing the horror of the deed and the stubborn blindness of its perpetrators rather than the physical aspect of Jesus' sufferings, Mark pointed to the deeper significance of the crucifixion. The tragedy lies not in the intensity or the details of the sufferings

58. "I hewed their lifeless bodies limb from limb; / I carved them into bits, and part I seethed / In brazen kettles, part before the fire / On spits I roasted. From their living limbs / I carved the tender flesh, and saw it hiss / And sputter on the slender spit, the while / With my own hand I kept the fire a-blaze (Atreus in act 5). In the play, darkness falls upon the earth while this deed is consummated. In Frank J. Miller, ed. and trans., *The Tragedies of Seneca* (Chicago: University of Chicago, 1907), p. 329.

59. In Euripides' *Hippolytus* a messenger describes to his father the hero's chariot accident. Although fatally wounded, Hippolytus is not dismembered. In Seneca's play a messenger describes, in twenty-five lines of macabre details, his body being scattered in shreds over the countryside.

of Jesus, who thus accomplishes His messianic mandate, but in the harrowing scandal of the "King of the Jews" being overpowered, mocked, and
tortured by His own people. Therefore a direct, sober report of the actions
surrounding the cross rather than a minute description of the crucified
one's torments provides the most effective commentary on the fearful
contradiction of the cross. Thus understood, the description of the crucifixion does not require the mediation of a messenger.

Not so for the resurrection. The spectacle of one dying is a daily
occurrence that can be described and comprehended. But owing to its
uniqueness, the resurrection can be neither described nor comprehended.
It can only be authenticated by an eyewitness and by solid evidence.
Consequently, when the women come to the tomb to finish embalming
the body of Jesus, a messenger is present to testify to what took place
("He has risen"), and as evidence, the doors are flung open. In this case the
stone is rolled away, thus revealing that the tomb is empty (". . . he is not
here; *see* the place where they laid him."). Thus the two devices used in
ancient drama to attest to events that cannot be shown find their counter-
parts in the last scene of the Gospel.

A curious fact should be noted in regard to the resurrection-
messenger. By virtue of the miraculous nature of the resurrection, the
account handed down to Mark certainly contained the tradition reflected
in the other synoptic Gospels that the messenger was angelic. Mark seems
bent, however, on emphasizing the immanent aspect of the messenger,
whereas Matthew and Luke made full allowance for the supernatural
character of the intervention.

For Mark the messenger is a youth;[60] in Matthew he is an angel, and
in Luke, not only one full-grown man but "two men." In Mark the youth
is wearing simply a white tunic; in Matthew the angel is "like lightening
and his raiment white as snow," and in Luke the men are "in dazzling
apparel." In Matthew the angel rolls back the stone and sits upon it victor-
iously. In Luke the two men appear suddenly out of thin air and stand by
the women. But in Mark the women enter the tomb and find the youth
already sitting there, which seems, to say the least, a casual posture for an
angel. The odd precision about the youth's location in the tomb ("on the
right side") is also intended to minimize the connotations of transcendence that are characteristic of an ethereal supernatural presence. It
helps bring the messenger down to earth by localizing him like a flesh-and-
blood being. Whereas Matthew's angel elicits fear (he tells the women, "Do
not be afraid") and the women in Luke are "frightened" and look down at
the ground," in Mark they are simply "amazed" and they stay to hear the
messenger's speech. No immediate reaction of fear is recorded or implied
in Mark. Trembling, astonishment, and aphonic fright seize them only
after the messenger communicates his message to them. Holy terror falls
upon them once they perceive the significance of the vacant tomb and

---

60. Νεανίσκος, the ending of which has diminutive force and which therefore suggests familiar usage, is better translated "youth" or even "young
fellow" than "young man."

once the transcendental dimension of the resurrection begins to make its impact upon them.

Mark's more-human-than-supernatural messenger cannot be attributed to the relative primitiveness of his gospel-tradition since he holds no reservations about angels. He has them minister to Jesus in less auspicious circumstances at the very outset of His ministry. The explanation for this toning down of the messenger's significance in Mark is probably to be found in the concept of the messenger in tragedy, where the messenger is generally a negligible character in a subordinate position. In neither Greek nor Latin dramatic tradition is the messenger a supernatural being. Just as at the beginning of the Gospel John the Baptist aggrandized the person of Jesus by minimizing his own importance, so at the very end the apparent lowliness of the herald of the resurrection exalts the uniqueness and supernatural stature of the risen Christ.

8. The messenger speech that often appeared in the exodos, the closing section of the play, was frequently associated with another device of Greek tragedy called *deus ex machina*, meaning "god from the machine." This designation was derived from the crane-like contraption from which a divine deliverer descended on stage or appeared above it in extremis to resolve desperate situations. Although used by other tragedians, this technique was especially developed by Euripides. Twelve of his eighteen extant plays end with a deus ex machina intervening at the height of the crisis to render justice, predict future reversals, effect reconciliations, and bring the dead back to life. In Sophocles' *Philoctetes* the god Heracles appears from above the stage and outlines for Philoctetes, banished to a desert island off the coast of Lemnos, a course of action that will lead him to victory over Troy and to happiness. While Hippolytus, in Euripides' play of the same name, lay dying on the stage bearing the curse of his father, the goddess Diana appears just before it is too late. She soothes and comforts him and effects a beautiful reconciliation between father and son. In the *Alcestis* Euripides made Heracles, the son of Zeus, appear to restore to life Alcestis, who had given her life for her husband. Roman tragedians who were contemporaries of Horace probably had excessive recourse to the deus ex machina since in his *Ars Poetica* ("On the Art of Poetry") Horace advised that "a *deus ex machina* should not be introduced unless some entanglement develops which requires such a person to unravel it."[61] The predicament of Seneca's Medea certainly met that requirement. Stranded on the palace roof with the bodies of her dead sons and threatened by her husband's vengeful fury, she is taken away through the air by a dragon-drawn chariot.

In the Gospel the bleak but meticulous description of the burial of Jesus has accents of hopeless finality. Joseph asks for "the body of Jesus." Pilate, wondering if Jesus is "already dead," summons the centurion to see if Jesus has already been dead for a while.[62] Having received confirmation,

---

61. *On the Art of Poetry*, ed. and trans. T. S. Dorsch, p. 85.

62. This rendering combines the two readings in 15:44b, which are both well attested, without doing violence to either.

Pilate *grants* the *corpse* (τὸ πτῶμα) to Joseph, who wraps it in a shroud and seals it with a stone in a rock-hewn tomb. The conspicuous absence of the disciples and the presence of Galilean women alone, the compassionate intervention of a stranger in legal procedures, the three women returning to the tomb for the embalmment and their concern for the removal of the stone—all contribute to create an impression of haggard desolation and abandonment. As the mourners wonder, "Who will roll away the stone for us from the door of the tomb?" they discover that it has already been removed. Mark accentuated the wondrous character of the fact by mentioning that the stone "was very large." The miracle becomes evident when the white-robed messenger tells the women of the great happening and announces the victorious march through Galilee. Overcome by the manifest presence of divinity, the women can do only one thing: run.

9. Considered from the viewpoint of dramatic composition, the *conclusion* of the Gospel at 16:8 is not only perfectly appropriate but also a stroke of genius. The Gospel ends even more abruptly than it begins, on a finale of poignant grandeur. The omission of postresurrection appearances is consistent with Mark's method of rigorous selection previously observed. He is an epitomizer. His method is to sketch and reduce rather than embellish. The comparative brevity of Mark cannot be explained merely in terms of the limited amount of sources available to him. The very diversity of the birth narratives, the genealogies, the resurrection appearances in Matthew and Luke attest to the richness of early tradition. But to begin his work, Mark chose to state in one line a powerful combination of the name "Jesus" with six Greek words summarizing what Matthew and Luke took several chapters to recount. The terse announcement of the entrance of the Christ, the Son of God, upon the scene of history suggests grandiose antecedents rendered even more momentous by the mystery surrounding them. Likewise for the temptation pericope, the omission of the elaborate threefold story for the simple statement that Jesus spent forty days in the wilderness in the presence of Satan, wild beasts, and angels conjures up visions of a gigantic epic on the cosmic scale of clashing spiritual powers. Suggestive epitome carries greater evocative power than detailed narration. It also requires more skill.

Similar comments could be made on almost every part of the Gospel. Even the passion story, which occupies one third of Mark's Gospel, reflects his tendency to mention only that which is suggestive and significant. This feature of the Gospel has not gone unnoticed. Of the passion account C. H. Dodd said: "The story is told with extraordinary simplicity and force. There is no dwelling on grim details, and certainly no attempt to work on our feelings, yet no one with a scrap of imagination can read the story without being profoundly moved."[63]

The evocative simplicity of the narrative is even more apparent in its climactic conclusion. The "He has risen" constitutes the consummation that illumines retrospectively the whole Gospel. And yet, as the action of the Gospel unfolds, it anticipates, almost ordains, the resurrection. Conse-

63. *About the Gospels*, p. 4.

quently, once it takes place there is no need for proof or elaboration. Evidences for the resurrection abound sufficiently within the Gospel to make it complete once it is proclaimed at the very end that "He has risen." Of course the detailed narration of appearances is important. But it is the task of a chronicler, and Mark was no mere chronicler. By the sparseness of his style, by the careful balance of descriptive details, and even by his omissions Mark forced the sensitive reader to use his own imagination, to extrapolate and participate in the Gospel by making it come alive in his own mind. Further elaboration on the resurrection in the form of appearance narratives would have been superfluous and even detrimental to Mark's style. According to Enslin, by referring to the appearances in Galilee (14:28; 16:7), Mark "makes perfectly clear that he knows such stories and expects his readers to realize it. Actually his restraint here is very effective. It is always the mark of the later (and often less skillful) hand to make explicit what the earlier master had left implicit. Readers of Homer sense that Helen of Troy was divinely fair despite the fact that the poet does not feel called upon to give her dimensions and color scheme in the manner customary to reports of an American bathing beauty contest."[64] The dramatic power of the Gospel's ending is conveyed as much by what is left unsaid as by what is said regarding the resurrection.[65] This method was not unknown to the ancient tragic poets. Some of their most profound works let the action continue beyond the last scene. In Aeschylus's *Prometheus Bound* the suspense lingers as the uncompromising hero describes in the closing scene the beginning of the storm that threatens to engulf him. In Sophocles' *Oedipus the King* the hero, having chosen the greater punishment of blindness over deliverance by death, slowly departs from Thebes toward an unknown destiny as the play ends. In the closing scene of Euripides' *Phoenissae*, tension persists between Antigone and Creon over the fate of her unburied brother, but the sequel is left untold to produce the kind of afterthought that constitutes one of the marks of an authentic work of art.

Not infrequently, ancient tragedies ended on a departure, even on a hasty exit of the kind described in the last verse of the Gospel. A stage suddenly left vacant by the sometimes precipitate dismissal of the characters seems to have been an acceptable convention for ending tragedies. In Aeschylus's *Choephoroe* Orestes, after wreaking retribution on his murderous mother, is struck by visions that cause him to rush off the stage and

---

64. "The Artistry of Mark," p. 394.

65. Just as appearance stories may have been left out of the Gospel because they would have had an anticlimactic effect in the Marcan composition, other elements of the ministry may have been deliberately omitted for similar reasons. This theory may explain, for instance, the absence in Mark (and through it in Matthew and Luke) of the story of the raising of Lazarus. Even if this tradition was available to Mark, its inclusion would have been detrimental to his purpose since he made the whole Gospel converge on the resurrection. In the raising of Jairus's daughter, Mark reported Jesus' claim that she is not dead but only sleeping. In the Marcan method the resurrection of Jesus has to stand in glorious isolation as the apotheosis of the story.

seek refuge at the shrine of Apollo. In Aeschylus's *Eumenides* the Furies, finally transformed into genial spirits, are led away by the goddess Athena as the play closes. Heracles in Euripides' tragedy of the same name is banished from Thebes at the end of the play so that he departs without being allowed to attend to the burial of his wife and children. In Seneca's *Trojan Women (Troades)* Hecuba and her fellow-captives leave burning Troy behind to board the Greek ships when a messenger urges them to hasten to the shore. The messenger's terse command with which the play ends stands in sharp contrast to his generally prolix performance:

> *Ye captives, haste you to the winding shore;*
> *The sails are spread, and long delay is o'er.*

If Mark was inspired by tragedy in structuring the Gospel, the dramatic effectiveness of graphic action in the form of rapid departures to bring a composition to an expressive end could hardly have escaped his notice. In this case, his intention to end the Gospel with the description of the women fleeing from the explosion of transcendence that met them at the gaping tomb cannot be doubted.

Even proponents of a mutilated ending at 16:8 have sometimes recognized the artistic effect of the present ending of Mark. Wilfred L. Knox admitted that if 16:8 were the original ending, it would constitute a successful "dramatic aposiopesis." But to accept this hypothesis, he said, would be tantamount to recognizing "that by a pure accident [Mark] happened to hit on a conclusion which suits the technique of a highly sophisticated type of modern literature. The odds against such a coincidence . . . seem to me to be so enormous as not to be worth considering."[66] Two objections need to be raised against this view. First, dramatic aposiopesis is as old as literature itself. In the Book of Genesis, when Joseph asks his brothers about his father after having identified himself to them, they are so confounded that they remain speechless (Gen. 45:3). Second, attributing the dramatic device to mere chance is hardly necessary since Mark otherwise displays evidences of deliberate dramatic sophistication.[67] Knox's position typifies an attitude often reflected in commentaries and studies on the Gospel of Mark. Its artistic effects are denoted, but their presence is attributed to fortuitous strokes of primitive talent, or to unwitting combinations of words and ideas, or, worse, to mechanical hazards such as the accidental mutilation of the manuscript at precisely the most appropriate word. In artistic endeavors serendipity is the result of diligence, not chance.

In the voluminous controversy surrounding the ending of Mark, one argument has been made to weigh heavily in favor of the mutilation theory at 16:8. It is the long-standing myth that a book cannot end with the

66. "The Ending of Saint Mark's Gospel," p. 23.

67. In a statement of astonishing candor, Knox revealed his reason for rejecting Marcan artistic involvement: "In any case the supposition [that Mark ended the Gospel with a deliberate dramatic artifice] credits him with a degree of originality which would invalidate the whole method of form-criticism." Ibid.

construction ἐφοβοῦντο γάρ ("for they were afraid"). Thanks to many painstaking efforts, this belief is now being exploded. Numerous precedents have established that sentences and even paragraphs can end with the word γάρ ("for") and that a two-word sentence has to end with γάρ. Such endings have been found in Homer, Plato, the *Poetics*, the Septuagint,[68] the papyri, and notably in the tragedies of Aeschylus, Sophocles, and Euripides.[69] It stands to reason that if the final sentence of a book is a two-word phrase that includes the word γάρ, then the book ends with the word γάρ. This point is cogently made in a brief article by P. W. van der Horst, who after surveying the status of the question in recent research, reported finding a precedent in Plotinus's *Enneads*,[70] confirmed by his editor Porphyry, of a book actually ending with γάρ. He concluded, ". . . the argument that a book cannot end with the word γάρ, is absolutely invalid."[71]

It is hoped that the present study will contribute to the refutation of Enslin's judgment that "Mark lays demands on his readers which they have often been unable to meet."[72] It would be equally unfortunate, however, for one to interpret this study as an attempt to permute the Gospel into a Greek tragedy. The differences between the two forms remain considerable. The Gospel was designed for reading, perhaps public reading, not for stage presentation. It was written in colloquial prose and not in verse as tragedies were. Although large sections of the Gospel consist of dialogue, its style is essentially that of narration and not dramatic dialogue. The rule that no more than three interlocutors address each other on the stage at one time, which was generally respected in tragedies, was not observed in the Gospel. Moreover, although it is common to outline the Gospel in five major sections, it does not fall readily into the rigid five-act pattern of Latin tragedy and even less in the stereotyped format of Greek tragedy.[73] In the last analysis, such formal differences between the Gospel and tragedy may simply reflect the radical difference between the gospel-story

68. One remarkable instance in the Greek Old Testament is found in the very sentence cited above as an instance of aposiopesis parallel to the ending of Mark. The fact that Genesis 45:3 also ends with a two-word sentence (ἐταράχθησαν γάρ) may be due to more than mere coincidence.

69. See R. R. Ottley, "*Ephobounto gar*, Mark 16:8"; and R. H. Lightfoot, *Locality and Doctrine in the Gospels*, pp. 1–48.

70. 5.5, 32.

71. "Can a Book End with *Gar?* A Note on Mark 16:8."

72. "The Artistry of Mark," p. 395.

73. Greek tragedies consisted of: a prologue; the parados, or entrance, of the chorus; a variable number (usually not more than five) of episodes separated by stasima, or choral odes; and the exodos, the final action of the play. In his *On the Art of Poetry* Horace ruled: "If you want your play to be called for and given a second performance, it should not be either shorter or longer than five acts." He also stated, "There should not be more than three *speaking* characters on the stage at the same time" (italics ours). P. 85.

and the subjects of tragedy.[74] When Mark undertook to recount the one ultimate drama of world redemption, his enterprise exploded by necessity the canons of any model, however successfully they had been used to tell lesser, interchangeable stories. The points at which the Gospel differs most from tragedy are precisely those at which the Gospel protects its content from formal infringements that would alter the received tradition and rob it of its uniqueness. By combining reverence for evangelical tradition with appreciation for dramatic expression, without letting the latter dominate the former, Mark was able to reach beyond the categories of Jewish thought and beyond the achievements of Greek genius to proclaim the universal summons of Christianity, "from the ends of the earth to the ends of heaven." Amos Wilder's assessment of the distinctive appeal of the New Testament is especially relevant to the Gospel of Mark: ". . . perhaps the special character of the stories of the New Testament lies in the fact that they are not told for themselves, that they are not only about other people, but that they are always about us. They locate us in the very midst of the great story and plot of all time and space, and therefore relate us to the great dramatist and storyteller, God himself."[75]

74. The Gospel "sets man's whole world astir—whereas the entanglements of fate and passion which Greco-Roman antiquity knows, always directly concern simply the individual, the one person involved in them." Erich Auerbach, *Mimesis*, p. 43.

75. *The Language of the Gospel*, p. 65.

Chapter 6

Conclusion

In addition to results already obtained in this study, recourse to the genre approach for understanding Mark provides insight in two important areas of Gospel criticism. One concerns the problem of defining a suitable methodology for detecting the redaction history of the Gospel; the other, discovering Mark's purpose in writing the Gospel.

Owing to the absence of pre-Marcan documents, the formulation of a methodology adequate for determining the Gospel's redaction history has often eluded New Testament scholars. Robert H. Stein bared the problem when he stated, "Although there has been a great deal of redaktionsgeschichtlich investigation, the question of methodology has frequently been glossed over."[1] As a corrective measure, he proposed that a thorough methodology should include the investigation of the various areas where Mark's editorial activity can be discerned. He defined them as the Marcan seams, insertions, and summaries; the Marcan creation of pericopes and modification of the material; the Marcan selection, omission, and arrangement of the material; the introduction, conclusion, and vocabulary of the Gospel; and finally the christological titles used by Mark. A suggestion could be made to improve on Stein's classification. To avoid investigating each of the itemized areas in isolation from the others and thus run the risk of losing perspective on the Gospel as an entity, the correlating themes from which it derives its unity should be articulated in their specific relation to each category. Once recognized, the dramatic structure of the Gospel provides that integrating, comprehensive perspective that makes possible the delineation of both the distinctive redactic features of each part and the interdependence of the components. An investigation of the redaction history of the Gospel lies beyond the scope of this study. But the foregoing discussion of such areas as the introduction, conclusion, vocabulary, selection and arrangement of material, and use of Christological titles, from the viewpoint of Mark's dramatic scheme, suggests that new and rewarding avenues may be pursued within this perspective.

From indications already accumulated in the present study, it appears that Mark's editorial contribution lies more in the subtle and discriminating emphasis of available traditional themes than in the creation of new motifs, more in the selection and omission of materials at his disposition than in their manipulation and transformation. The dynamics

---

1. "The Proper Methodology for Ascertaining a Markan Redaction History," p. 181.

of the story reveal a development at the same time too spontaneous and too complex to be the product of editorial invention. The harmoniously interlaced motifs of increasing incomprehension and rejection in the first part of the Gospel, culminating in the intricate web of intrigues, met with somber determination by Jesus in the second half, evoke the verisimilitude of the turmoils of life rather than the creative powers of a skilled fiction-writer. The development of the plot reflects such a degree of intricate refinement and throbs with such compelling force that its alleged creation by either one individual or the combined imaginative powers of a community would have constituted an event infinitely more momentous than the location of the life-setting of the gospel tradition in the actual ministry of Jesus.

The very existence of the Gospel, and that of Matthew and Luke after Mark, bears witness to the importance attached to the historical Jesus by the early church. And yet redaction criticism has not been freed from some of the more gratuitous premises shared with form criticism regarding the alleged lack of historical consciousness on the part of the first generation of Christians. The Gospel of Mark is often described as an attempt to "historicize" ethereal beliefs about Jesus created by the early church communities through some mysterious process of spontaneous theological generation. There is no explanation for the faith of early Christians, however, without a consistent frame of reference between Jesus and the early church at every phase of its theological development. To describe the Gospel as an attempt to historicize nebulous religious traditions spawned in the euphoric experience of Christians singularly bereft of historical curiosity, implies that at some point during the first decades of the church, the historical Jesus was deemed dispensable and consequently was discarded. Such a theory is consistent neither with the fact that the Gospels were written nor with their form and content. The very existence of the Gospel of Mark suggests that it was composed in response to a situation receptive to historical data, and that its acceptance, as evidenced in its use by Matthew and Luke, was founded on an identifiable continuum between the faith of its recipients and its content. As a redactor, Mark necessarily transmitted rather than created the story of Jesus. He probably could have taken no more liberties with the material he received and transmitted than he would have allowed the original recipients of his Gospel to take with it. And if Matthew's and Luke's treatment of Mark or of Marcan sources constitutes any evidence, their conservative approach indicates that in contradistinction to contemporary practices, fidelity was a concern and restraint the rule for transmitting gospel traditions. There is no reason to believe that the preserving instinct reflected in the very nature of the Matthean and Lucan Gospel-writing enterprise and in their deferential use of Marcan sources was not also operative in Mark's handling of the material available to him.[2] Nor does the theory of Mark's formal dependence on

2. Although they operate within the cultural framework of higher standards of accuracy, the reporting and editing of modern communications media often fail to exhibit the concern for objectivity discernible in the

drama impugn his integrity as transmitter of the tradition. Since he was obviously not motivated by pretensions to literary achievement, Mark cannot be accused of having deformed the material just for the sake of writing a story in the manner of Greek drama. It was the very nature of the story itself, with its quintessential concentration of all that is tragic about life, which called for the use of tragedy as a suitable armature for its orderly recording and preservation. Mark's use of Greek drama actually enhances the chances for his reliability by demonstrating his concern for an effective presentation, that is, for a presentation acceptable to its intended readers. As aesthetically effective as a dramatized rendition might have been, it probably would not have found acceptance without passing the test of conformity to prevalent information about the historical Jesus. The Gospel bears witness to the existence of such an interest in Mark's community. There is no reason to doubt that a consistent pattern of historical awareness did exist at every stage of the life-setting of the gospel tradition. The postulate according to which such interest disappeared after Easter to revive with the writing of Mark is the first fantasy that needs to be corrected in order to formulate a proper methodology for investigating the redaction history of Mark.

Efforts to determine Mark's purpose in writing the Gospel have produced an ever-swelling spate of theories. Predictably some of those theories are mutually exclusive, so their respective value has to be established by careful investigation. Their mere multiplicity, however, does not necessarily rule out of consideration even the less popular of these proposals. It is quite conceivable that Mark incorporated into the Gospel his response to a number of secondary issues in addition to the main thrust of his work. Such a multi-pronged approach need not be attributed to a deliberate process of painstaking selection of motives and to the laborious incorporation of motifs on the part of the author. It may simply reflect the intensity of his involvement in the ambiguities and complexities of a dynamic and effervescent life-situation. In order to react sensitively to ambient needs when writing the Gospel, Mark could well have served concurrently a number of purposes, some didactic, others apologetic, polemic, doctrinal, evangelistic, ecclesiological, apocalyptic, etc.

The question that arises from this study is: Was Mark's use of elements from Greek tragedy prompted only by the affinity of the Gospel story with the drama genre, or was his recourse to a Graeco-Roman literary model intended to convey a message in itself. The radical nature of

---

synoptic Gospels. Obviously such an opinion is contested by some. Norman Perrin is one: "The nature of the synoptic tradition is such that the burden of proof will be upon the claims to authenticity." *Rediscovering the Teaching of Jesus* (New York: Harper and Row, 1967), p. 39. The opposite opinion was expressed by Archibald M. Hunter: "In this country it is a principle of justice that a man is innocent until proved guilty. So we may regard the works and words attributed to Jesus in the Synoptics as authentic, unless cogent arguments are adduced to show that they are not so." *Introducing New Testament Theology* (Philadelphia: Westminster, 1957), p. 11. To advocate the reversal of investigatory procedures is hardly to set a blazing precedent for unbiased scholarship.

such an unlikely alliance between a religious tradition of Jewish antecedents and a Gentile art form indicate that Mark was not merely bowing
to literary convenience but that his use of tragedy was a deliberate ideological act. Clues pointing to the meaning of this gesture can be found in
some of the emphases within the Gospel and in corresponding inferences
that can be made about the life-situation of the Marcan church community.

Several of the recurring motifs reflected in the development of the
plot (as delineated in chapters 3 and 4) point, on one hand, in the direction of an anti-Judaic-establishment attitude, and, on the other, of its
positive corollary, an affirmation of the universal scope of Jesus' ministry.
By casting the Gospel in a Gentile cultural mold totally foreign to Jewish
religious and literary concerns, Mark powerfully demonstrated that the
story of Jesus explodes the narrow categories popularly ascribed to it and
that it really belongs to all mankind. More effectively than any argumentation, the tragedy-form of the Gospel provided to those outside the faith
as well as to Christians the incontrovertible vindication of its claim to
independence from particularisms, both Jewish and Judaic. In this manner
the Gospel constituted in form and content a defiant manifesto of its
enfranchisement from sectarian implications and a bold declaration of its
universal relevance.

For the non-Christian reader Mark's Gospel clarified several misconceptions. Because of the Jewish origin of their faith and the early
spread of Christianity through synagogue and proselytes, Christians were
often regarded as Jews or as Jewish proselytes in the Roman world. Although this confusion afforded them immunities that Judaism enjoyed as
religio licita, it also presented several disadvantages. In the syncretistic
religious milieu of the first century, Jewish exclusiveness often prompted
repressive measures. When anti-Jewish persecutions took place, Christians
sometimes suffered with the Jews among whom they usually lived.[3] The
fact that Christians were persecuted while the Jews were left unharmed
during the Neronian turmoil (when they were easily lumped together)
seems to point to high-placed advocates for the Jews, if not accusers of the
Christians. In such cases the Christians were undoubtedly pursued as a
seditious, extremist sect spawned by Judaism. Later the long-seething
Zealot revolt in Palestine and its bloody aftermath would bear heavy consequences for Jews in the Roman world, and popular identification of
Christians with Jews would threaten the very life of the church.

Since the Gospel was presumably written at this critical juncture,
one might expect to detect in it an effort to demonstrate the church's

3. "Christians who no longer attended services in the synagogue but who
persisted in living in the Jewish quarter would still be considered Jews by
the civil authorities as well as by the Jewish authorities." Douglas R. Hare,
*The Theme of Jewish Persecution of Christians According to the Gospel of
St. Matthew*, p. 105. "The Jews were regarded as irreconcilable enemies of
the rest of humanity, and this charge, the *odium generis humani*, was to be
passed on to the Christians." W. H. C. Frend, *Martyrdom and Persecution
in the Early Church*, p. 101.

independence vis-à-vis Judaism. As a matter of fact, the Gospel is replete with themes emphasizing Jesus' detachment from Judaism and Jewish opposition to Him. Since they have been surveyed above, a mere enumeration should suffice to establish the fact that one of Mark's objectives was to stress the consummation of the radical dissociation of Christianity from its parent religion.

According to Mark, Jesus begins His ministry not in Jerusalem, as might be expected, but in Galilee. He avoids going to Jerusalem except for His death, preferring to make Galilee and Gentile territories the locus of His redemptive activity. Mark generally used the name *Jerusalem* with negative connotations. Jesus recruits His followers from the ranks of ordinary people, even persons normally objectionable to Jewish officialdom. Jesus foils attempts to politicize His ministry for the benefit of prevalent Messianic expectations by silencing excessive publicity and indiscreet divulgence of His Messiahship, moving away from the scenes of miracles, dismissing and eschewing crowds that gather around Him, and shunning popular acclaim. Jesus denies that the religious authorities of Judaism have any authority over Him and affirms that He has authority over the law and the temple. Twice He physically challenges the corrupt use made of the temple and finally pronounces doom upon it. His only contacts with the synagogue occur in situations where He defies religious leaders in word and deed. Birth narratives that would stress Jesus' identity with the Jews are omitted, and He is described as repudiating hostile blood relatives. When Jesus defines His ministry, He does so in terms of servanthood and vicarious suffering rather than conquest and seditious activity. And when open conflict with Judaic officialdom becomes inevitable, Jesus accepts it in the face of murderous conspiracies. Mark portrayed Jesus as a determined fulfiller of destiny whose rejection of earthly power makes Him fatally vulnerable to the antagonism of Jewish authorities. The answers thus provided by Mark to the question of the relationship between the church and Judaism are of the most forceful kind. He simply let the facts speak for themselves. But in order to invest his proclamation of Christian liberation with still greater persuasive cogency, he couched the narrative in the tragedy form, a medium of literary expression despised by traditional Jews but revered by the Gentile inquirer.

To an outsider to the faith, Mark was intent to show not only the chasm separating Christianity from Judaism but also the universal appeal of Christianity. In the Gospel he pointedly described Jesus ministering to the Gentiles.[4] They come to Him from their countries; He goes to their cities and villages; He heals their sick and their demoniacs; He preaches a gospel and announces a kingdom embracing all men and nations. But the universal appeal of the Gospel ultimately rests in the very nature of its central figure. By virtue of His supernatural uniqueness, He transcends all human categories. He is neither a Jewish messianic folk hero nor his Hellenistic wonder-working counterpart, a Θεῖος ἀνήρ ("God-man"). Jesus does not compete with the deified emperor, whose political mandate He

4. See pp. 90–91.

recognizes as legitimate while subtly dissociating it from connotations of divinity (12:17). Mark presented Him as the Son of God, whose destiny among men incongruously necessitates death. It is precisely when He dies ignominiously on a Roman cross that He is rightly acknowledged as Son of God by the Gentile par excellence, a Roman centurion.[5] And at that very moment, when humanity (represented by the Gentile soldier) gains access to the faith, the temple (representing Judaism) is desecrated through an act of God and becomes obsolete (15:38). In all the literary achievements of mankind, there was one mode of poetic expression dedicated to depicting the inexorability of divine decrees and the fulfillment of destiny. Tragedy was the consecrated medium for contemplating the mysterious outworkings of fate and affirming the ultimate triumph of humane and righteous causes over infaust and unjust forces. By using the form of tragedy to describe the momentous release of God's redemptive concern to all mankind, Mark firmly proclaimed the Gospel's universal relevance.

Finally, it is not inconceivable that Mark intended the form of the Gospel to carry a particular significance for the Christian reader to whom it was primarily addressed. There is evidence that Mark's antipathy for Jerusalem was directed not only at the institutions of Judaism that had remained impervious if not hostile to the Gospel but also at the Jewish segment of the Christian church represented by the disciples. Mark mercilessly depicted the failure of the Twelve to understand Jesus—His teaching, His mission, His death, and His predicted resurrection. They are forever in the dark as to the nature and ministry of Jesus, forever wondering, exclaiming, and questioning. Even at the moment of greatest insight, Peter draws the sharpest rebuke for substituting a human program for God's design (8:33). Often working at cross-purposes with Jesus, they draw reprimands on several occasions. Finally they disappear in a confusion of betrayal, denial, and shameful desertion. Mark's message is clear: the disciples were complete failures during Jesus' ministry. Neither they nor their position can be regarded as sacred. Only the tradition and mission entrusted to them by Jesus are sacred. The disciples' unique claim of distinction and authority resides in the story of which they are eyewitnesses and transmitters. By committing that story to writing, Mark transferred

5. "The zealot revolt in Palestine had created the suspicion that the church in Rome were (sic) worshipping as a world-saviour a Jew who had Zealot sympathies and had been judicially punished as a rebel agitator, while in A.D. 71 the emperor Vespasian was being acclaimed in Rome as a heaven-sent saviour and peace-maker. To relieve the Roman Christians' embarrassment and solve his problems someone (why should it not have been John Mark?) compiled the Markan Gospel and portrayed Jesus, a Jew of Palestine but detached from his environment, prophet and teacher but owing authority only to God, a supernatural personality, exceeding the pagan imperial Saviour, Vespasian, on the power of his personal magnetism and his miraculous powers, proclaiming the obsolesence of the externals of Judaism, crucified through the malicious denunciation of the Jewish authorities, acknowledged by a Gentile as the heaven-sent saviour of mankind." H. C. Snape, "Christian Origins in Rome with Special Reference to Mark's Gospel."

apostolic authority to his Gospel and rendered the function of "apostle" superfluous.

The records of the early church, especially the Book of the Acts of the Apostles and Paul's Epistles, indicate that after Pentecost the Twelve identified themselves with the static, Jerusalem-based, Jewish-oriented form of early Christianity. In contrast to the progressive wing of the church represented by converted Diaspora Jews, proselytes, and Gentiles, the Jerusalemite Christians headed by the disciples favored the observance of the Mosaic law and advocated its imposition on Gentile converts to Christianity. They were influenced by converted Pharisaic legalists and frustrated apocalyptists who, refusing to regard as final the Jews' rejection of Jesus, immersed themselves in Judaizing speculations. For them the new covenant was an adjunct to the old, whereas Gentile-oriented Christians considered the old covenant obsolete because superseded by the new.

The Gospel of Mark and especially the form in which it is laid may constitute a part of the long struggle waged by the Gentile-oriented church to free itself from Judaizing encroachments. This struggle seems to have come into the open first with the conflict that resulted in the establishment of the leadership of the Seven representing the Hellenist segment of the Jerusalem church (Acts 6). This leadership grew into an irresistible movement that eventually eclipsed the Twelve and caused them to disappear completely from the Lucan record after the Jerusalem Council (Acts 15). Among them were men like Stephen, who at the cost of his life called for a formal break with Judaism (Acts 7); men like his Diaspora fellow-believers who took the gospel to the Gentiles and established the first missionary church in Antioch while the Twelve remained huddled in the shadows of the Jerusalem temple (Acts 8:1; 11:19); men like Philip, who, following in Jesus' footsteps, dared to take the gospel to the Samaritans; men like Saul of Tarsus, who became the apostle to the Gentiles while Simon Peter was recovering from his state of shock over the conversion of Cornelius; and men like the author of the Epistle to the Hebrews, who urged Jewish Christians nostalgic for the fading glories of Judaism to consider it defunct and to realize the superiority and finality of the Christian faith (Heb. 8). Mark stands in the same tradition. His Gospel vibrates with the revolutionary temper of the early missionaries to the Gentiles. Their universal vision pervades it. No wonder then that our author would audaciously shatter the monopoly claimed over the gospel message by the Twelve and their Jewish fellow-believers. By casting the story in the form of Greek tragedy, he demonstrated that the sacred story was not the exclusive property of Jewish disciples but belonged to all mankind.

For the believer, the dramatic form of the Gospel was meaningful in one more dimension. The shadows of persecution, the forebodings of rejection and suffering, cast a gloom over the Gospel of Mark. The wild beasts that had stalked Jesus in the desert had become a frightful reality for Christians in the midst of imperial Rome. They were experiencing the full implications of being disciples of Jesus, whose destiny was repeating itself in their own lives. They needed to be reminded of Jesus' words of encouragement, of His exhortations to abnegation, of His promises of vindication. But most of all they needed to be reminded of Him and His example. For Christians living in tragic circumstances, the tragic form of the Gospel was perfectly suited to keep the tragic yet victorious death of their Master vivid in their minds. The function of tragedy, according to Aristotle, is to arouse and purge the emotions of pity and fear. Likewise the Gospel, by depicting the sufferings of Jesus, would free endangered Christians from anxiety for their own lives and would steel them against self-pity and fear of death. The Gospel showed them that in authentic discipleship, their destiny was to follow their Master. And if His fate was duplicated in their lives, the Parousia would be for them what the resurrection had become for Him, the vindication and justification of their sacrifice.

Undoubtedly not all of Mark's original readers were qualified to discern the deeper significance of the form of his Gospel. Matthew and Luke probably did, but different needs and circumstances called for other forms of presentation on their part. John seems to have recognized the dramatic pattern of the Gospel and, in some ways, to have followed suit. Since Mark wrote a Gospel and not a tragedy, he made no self-conscious effort to indicate any dependence on the latter. Consequently such dependence easily passes undetected. This is certainly what Mark wanted. His intention was not to call attention to himself as a writer but to release with powerful conviction the explosive impact of the liberated Gospel.

Ancient tragedy was the highest expression of the genius of man yearning for truth. It epitomized the upreach toward transcendence of minds ridden with myth but forever in quest of ultimate reality. The drama of the Greeks prefigured unconsciously but expectantly the supreme drama of history, the Incarnation. The life of the crucified and risen Son of God brought forth the unique, decisive, and all-encompassing fulfillment. It represented the very essence of tragedy in its highest form. It deserved nothing less than to be laid in the immortal frame fashioned by the masters of old, and better justice could not have been done to tragedy than to crown it with the story conceived in heaven, enacted on the cross, and penned on earth by an obscure disciple called John Mark.

Bibliography

Aristotle. *On the Art of Poetry.* Edited and translated by Ingram Bywater. Oxford: Clarendon, 1967.

_____. *On the Art of Poetry.* Edited and translated by Lane Cooper. New York: Cornell University, 1947.

Arrowsmith, William. "The Criticism of Greek Tragedy." *Tulane Drama Review* 3 (1959): 31–57.

Auerbach, Erich. *Mimesis.* Translated by W. R. Trask. Princeton: Princeton University, 1953.

Bailey, Cyril. *The Mind of Rome.* Oxford: Clarendon, 1926.

Bates, Alfred. *Greek and Roman Drama.* 2 vols. London: Historical, 1906.

Beach, Curtis. *The Gospel of Mark: Its Making and Meaning.* New York: Harper and Row, 1959.

Beardslee, W. A. *Literary Criticism of the New Testament.* Philadelphia: Fortress, 1970.

Blatherwick, David. "The Markan Silhouette." *New Testament Studies* 17 (1970): 184–92.

Bornkamm, Günther; Barth, Gerhard; and Held, H. J. *Tradition and Interpretation in Matthew.* Translated by Percy Scott. Philadelphia: Westminster, 1963.

Bowra, C. M. *Sophoclean Tragedy.* Oxford: Clarendon, 1960.

Brereton, Geoffrey. *Principles of Tragedy.* Miami: University of Miami, 1968.

Briggs, Robert Cook. *Interpreting the Gospels.* Nashville: Abingdon, 1969.

Bundy, Walter E. "Dogma and Drama in the Gospel of Mark." In *New Testament Studies,* edited by Edwin Prince Booth. New York: Abingdon-Cokesbury, 1942.

Burch, Ernest W. "Tragic Action in the Second Gospel: A Study of the Narrative of Mark." *Journal of Religion* 11 (1931): 346–58.

Burkhill, T. A. *Mysterious Revelation.* Ithaca, N.Y.: Cornell University, 1963.

_____. *New Light on the Earliest Gospel.* Ithaca, N.Y.: Cornell University, 1972.

Burkitt, F. C. *The Gospel History and Its Transmission.* Edinburgh: T. and T. Clark, 1906.

Cadbury, Henry J. *The Making of Luke-Acts.* New York: Macmillan, 1927.

Carrington, Philip. *The Primitive Christian Calendar.* Cambridge: Cambridge University, 1952.

Conzelmann, Hans. *The Theology of Saint Luke.* Translated by Geoffrey Buswell. New York: Harper and Row, 1961.

Cook, Albert, ed. *"Oedipus Rex": A Mirror for Greek Drama.* Belmont, Calif.: Wadsworth, 1963.

Cooper, Charles W. *Preface to Drama.* New York: Ronald, 1955.

Copley, Frank O. *Latin Literature.* Ann Arbor: University of Michigan, 1969.

d'Alton, John F. *Horace and His Age.* New York: Russell and Russell, 1962.

de Romilly, Jacqueline. *Time in Greek Tragedy.* Ithaca, N.Y.: Cornell University, 1968.

Dibelius, Martin. *Studies in the Acts of the Apostles.* Edited by Heinrich Greeven. Translated by Mary Ling. London: Scribner, 1956.

Dinter, Paul E. "Redaction Criticism of the Gospel of Mark: A Survey." *The Dunwoodee Review* 10 (1970): 178–97.

Dodd, C. H. *About the Gospels.* Cambridge: Cambridge University, 1950.

————. *The Apostolic Preaching and Its Developments.* New York: Harper, 1949.

————. *New Testament Studies.* Manchester: Manchester University, 1953.

Duckworth, George E., ed. *The Complete Roman Drama.* 2 vols. New York: Random, 1942.

Duff, John Wright. *A Literary History of Rome.* London: Bern, 1953.

Duncan, Robert. "The Problem of Evil: A Comparison of Classical and Biblical Versions." *Christian Scholar's Review* 3 (1973): 24–32.

Dunn, J. D. G. "The Messiah's Secret in Mark." *Tyndale Bulletin* 21 (1970): 92–117.

Else, Gerald F. *The Origin and Early Form of Greek Tragedy.* Cambridge: Harvard University, 1965.

Enslin, Morton. "The Artistry of Mark." *Journal of Biblical Literature* 66 (1947): 385–99.

Evans, J. A. S. "*Aeneid* 2 and the Art of the Theater." *Classical Journal* 58 (1963): 255–58.

Farmer, William R. *The Synoptic Problem.* New York: Macmillan, 1964.

Farrer, Austin M. *A Study in St. Mark.* New York: Oxford University, 1952.

Fränkel, Herman. *Ovid.* Berkeley: University of California, 1969.

Frend, W. H. C. *Martyrdom and Persecution in the Early Church.* Garden City, N.Y.: Anchor, 1967.

Friedländer, Ludwig. *Roman Life and Manners,* vol. 2. Translated by J. H. Freese and L. A. Magnus. London: Routledge, 1904.

Frye, Northrop. *Anatomy of Criticism.* Princeton: Princeton University, 1957.

————. *Tables of Identity.* Studies in Poetic Mythology. New York: Harcourt, Brace, and Wild, 1963.

Gassner, John. *Masters of the Drama.* New York: Dover, 1945.

Gilbert, A. H. "The Aristotelian Catharsis." *Philosophical Review* 35 (1926): 301–14.

Grant, Frederick C. *The Earliest Gospel.* New York: Abingdon-Cokesbury, 1943.

Guy, Harold A. *The Origin of the Gospel of Mark.* London: Hodder and Stoughton, 1954.

Hadas, Moses. *A History of Greek Literature.* New York: Columbia University, 1950.

_____. *A History of Latin Literature.* New York: Columbia University, 1952.

Haigh, Arthur E. *The Tragic Drama of the Greeks.* Oxford: Clarendon, 1925.

Hamilton, Edith. *The Greek Way.* New York: Norton, 1930.

Hare, Douglas R. *The Theme of Jewish Persecution of Christians According to the Gospel of St. Matthew.* Cambridge: Cambridge University, 1967.

Harsh, Philip W. *A Handbook of Classical Drama.* Stanford, Calif.: Stanford University, 1944.

Hathorn, Richmond Y. *Tragedy, Myth, and Mystery.* Bloomington: Indiana University, 1962.

Hiebert, D. Edmond. *Mark: A Portrait of the Servant.* Chicago: Moody, 1974.

Horace. *On the Art of Poetry.* In *Classical Literary Criticism,* edited and translated by T. S. Dorsch. Baltimore: Penguin, 1965.

Horst, P. W. van der. "Can a Book End with *Gar?* A Note on Mark 16:8." *The Journal of Theological Studies* 23 (1972): 121–24.

Johnson, Sherman E. *A Commentary on the Gospel According to St. Mark.* New York: Harper, 1961.

Jones, John. *On Aristotle and Greek Tragedy.* London: Chatto and Windus, 1962.

Kähler, Martin. *The So-Called Historical Jesus and the Historical, Biblical Christ.* Edited and translated by C. E. Braaten. Philadelphia: Fortress, 1969.

Kamerbeek, J. C. *The Plays of Sophocles: Commentaries.* Part 4: *The Oedipus Tyrannus.* Leiden: Brill, 1967.

Kee, Howard Clark. *Community of the New Age: Studies in Mark's Gospel.* Philadelphia: Westminster, 1977.

Kitto, H. D. F. *Form and Meaning in Drama.* London: Methuen, 1960.

_____. *Greek Tragedy.* London: Methuen, 1961.

Kleist, James A. *Memoirs of Saint Peter.* Milwaukee: Bruce, 1932.

_____. *The Gospel of Saint Mark.* Milwaukee: Bruce, 1936.

Knigge, Heinz-Dieter. "The Meaning of Mark." *Interpretation* 22 (1968): 53–70.

Knight, G. Wilson. *The Christian Renaissance.* New York: Norton, 1962.

Knox, Bernard. *The Heroic Temper.* Berkeley: University of California, 1964.

Knox, Wilfred L. "The Ending of Saint Mark's Gospel." *The Harvard Theological Review* 35 (1942): 13–23.

_____. *The Sources of the Synoptic Gospels.* Cambridge: Cambridge University, 1953.

Krook, Dorothea. *Elements of Tragedy.* New Haven: Yale University, 1969.

Lamb, Sidney. *Tragedy.* Toronto: CBC, 1965.

Lane, William L. *Commentary on the Gospel of Mark.* New International Commentary on the New Testament. Grand Rapids: Eerdmans, 1974.

Lesky, Albin. *Greek Tragedy.* New York: Barnes and Noble, 1967.

Lieberman, Saul. *Greek in Jewish Palestine.* New York: Jewish Theological Seminary of America, 1942.

Lightfoot, R. H. *Locality and Doctrine in the Gospels.* London: Hodder and Stoughton, 1938.

Lucas, Frank L. *Tragedy: Serious Drama in Relation to Aristotle's "Poetics."* Rev. ed. New York: Macmillan, 1958.

Lyman, Mary E. *The Christian Epic.* New York: Scribner, 1936.

Mandel, Oscar. *Definition of Tragedy.* New York: New York University, 1961.

Marrou, H. I. *A History of Education in Antiquity.* Translated by George Lamb. New York: Sheed and Ward, 1956.

Martin, Ralph P. *Mark: Evangelist and Theologian.* London: Paternoster, 1972.

Marxsen, Willi. *Introduction to the New Testament.* Translated by Geoffrey Buswell. Philadelphia: Portiers, 1968.

Matera, Frank J. "Interpreting Mark: Some Recent Theories of Redaction Criticism." *Louvain Studies* 2 (1968): 113–31.

Méautis, Georges. *Sophocles: Essai sur le héros tragique.* Paris: Michel, 1957.

Mendell, Clarence W. *Our Seneca.* Hamden, Conn.: Archon, 1968.

Menzies, Allan. *The Earliest Gospel.* London: Macmillan, 1901.

Meye, Robert P. *Jesus and the Twelve: Discipleship and Revelation in Mark's Gospel.* Grand Rapids: Eerdmans, 1968.

Moule, C. F. D. *The Birth of the New Testament.* New York: Harper and Row, 1962.

Moulton, Richard G. *The Literary Study of the Bible.* Boston: Heath, 1899.

Myers, Henry A. *Tragedy.* Ithaca, N.Y.: Cornell University, 1956.

Neill, Stephen. *The Interpretation of the New Testament.* London: Oxford University, 1964.

Nicoll, Allardyce. *The Theory of Drama.* New York: Bloom, 1966.

Nietzsche, Friedrich. *The Birth of Tragedy.* Translated by William A. Haussman. 2nd ed. Edinburgh: Foulis, 1910.

Norwood, Gilbert. *Greek Tragedy.* London: Methuen, 1920.

Oates, Whitney J. *The Complete Greek Drama.* 2 vols. New York: Random, 1938.

Ottley, R. R. "*Ephobounto gar,* Mark 16:8." *The Journal of Theological Studies* 27 (1926): 407–9.

Perrin, Norman. "The Literary *Gattung* Gospel." *Expository Times* 82 (1970): 4–7.

————. *Rediscovering the Teaching of Jesus.* New York: Harper and Row, 1967.

Quesnell, Quentin. *The Mind of Mark: Interpretation and Method Through the Exegesis of Mark 6:52.* Analecta Biblica, no. 38. Rome: Pontifical Biblical Institute, 1969.

Riddle, Donald W. *The Gospels: Their Origin and Growth.* Chicago: University of Chicago, 1939.

_____. "The Martyr Motif in the Gospel According to Mark." *Journal of Religion* 4 (1924): 397–410.

Rose, Herbert J. *A Handbook of Greek Literature.* London: Methuen, 1948.

_____. *A Handbook of Latin Literature.* New York: Dutton, 1960.

Saintsbury, George E. B. *A History of Criticism and Literary Taste in Europe.* 3 vols. Edinburgh: Blackwood, 1934–1935.

Sandmel, Samuel. "Prolegomena to a Commentary on Mark." *Journal of Bible and Religion* 31 (1963): 294–300.

Schille, Gottfried. *"Bemerkungen zur Formgeschichte des Evangeliums."* *New Testament Studies* 4 (1957): 1–24; 5 (1958): 1–11.

Schmidt, Carl L. *Der Rahmen der Geschichte Jesu.* Berlin, 1919.

Schweizer, Eduard. *The Good News According to Mark.* Translated by D. H. Madvig. Richmond: John Knox, 1970.

Scott, Nathan A., ed. *The Tragic Vision and the Christian Faith.* New York: Association, 1957.

Sellar, William Y. *The Roman Poets of the Augustan Age.* Oxford: Clarendon, 1891.

Seneca. *Seneca: His Tenne Tragedies.* Edited and translated by Thomas Newton. 2 vols. New York: AMS, 1967.

_____. *Four Tragedies and "Octavia."* Translated by E. F. Watling. Baltimore: Penguin, 1966.

Sewall, Richard B. *The Vision of Tragedy.* New Haven: Yale University, 1959.

Shipley, Joseph T., ed. *Dictionary of World Literary Terms.* Boston: The Writer, 1970.

Snape, H. C. "Christian Origins in Rome with Special Reference to Mark's Gospel." *The Modern Churchman* 13 (1970): 230–44.

Stein, Robert H. "The Proper Methodology for Ascertaining a Markan Redaction History." *Novum Testamentum* 13 (1971): 181–98.

Streeter, B. H. *The Four Gospels: A Study of Origins.* London: Macmillan, 1936.

Taylor, Vincent. *The Gospel According to Mark.* London: Macmillan, 1959.

Trocmé, Etienne. *La formation de l'Evangile selon Marc.* Paris: Presses Universitaires de France, 1963.

Turner, C. H. "Marcan Usage: Notes, Critical and Exegetical, on the Second Gospel." *Journal of Theological Studies* 25 (1924): 377–86; 26 (1925): 12–20, 145–56, 225–40, 337–46; 27 (1926): 58–62; 28 (1927): 9–30, 349–62; 29 (1928): 275–89, 346–61.

Vielhauer, Philip. *"Erwägungen zur Christologie des Markus Evangeliums."* In *Zeit und Geschichte: Dankesgabe an Rudolf Bultmann zum 80*, edited by Erich Dinkler. Tübingen: Mohr, 1964.

Votaw, C. W. "The Gospels and Contemporary Biographies." *American Journal of Theology* 14 (1915): 45–73, 217–49.

Ward, Adolphus W. *A History of English Dramatic Literature on the Death of Queen Anne.* 3 vols. New York: Octagon, 1966.

Weeden, Theodore J. *Mark: Traditions in Conflict.* Philadelphia: Fortress, 1971.

Wilder, Amos. *The Language of the Gospel.* New York: Harper and Row, 1964.

Wright, F. Warren. *Cicero and the Theater.* Smith College Classical Studies, no. 11. Northampton: Smith College, 1931.

General Index

Scripture Index